GW01339297

ANATOMY AND PHYSIOLOGY OF YOGIC PRACTICES

MEDICINE AND SPIRITUALITY SERIES

The primary goal of the series is to explore and study the relationship between spirituality and health in a concise and readable format. It will seek to integrate spirituality into medicine on a scientific basis. It will shed new light on major contemporary issues in this fascinating area of research. It'll bridge the chasm between health and well-being on the one side and religion and spirituality on the other. It'll provide a comprehensive review of the research on the interface between medicine and spirituality. It'll also endeavour to go beyond research by offering clear, concise and helpful recommendations on how to address spiritual and health issues and how to utilize the expertise of all professionals to provide the best and most compassionate care possible.

The series is aimed at general readers with interest in health-spirituality interaction. The different volumes in it will be informative, objective, meaningful, relevant and interesting to them.

- Anatomy and Physiology of Yogic Practices: Understanding of the Yogic Concepts and Physiological Mechanism of the Yogic Practices–Dr. M.M. Gore
- Making Health Care Whole: Integrating Spirituality Into Patient Care–Cristina M. Puchalski & Betty Ferrell
- Healing Our Hormones Healing Our Lives: Solutions to Common Hormonal Conditions–Linda Crockett

General Editor
Dr. V.K. Nigam, M.S., Laparoscopic Surgeon

Editorial Board
Dr. J.K. Sharma, M.D., Diabetes/Cardiology
Dr. A.S. Puri, M.D., Gastroenterology
Dr. M.M. Gore, Ph.D., Ayurveda/Naturopathy
Dr. N.A. Gaur, Ph.D., Spirituality
Dr. K.S. Charak, M.S., F.R.C.S./Surgery

MEDICINE AND SPIRITUALITY SERIES

ANATOMY AND PHYSIOLOGY OF YOGIC PRACTICES

Understanding of the Yogic Concepts and
Physiological Mechanism of the Yogic Practices

Dr. Makarand Madhukar Gore
Ph.D.

New Age Books

MEDICINE AND SPIRITUALITY SERIES
ANATOMY AND PHYSIOLOGY OF YOGIC PRACTICES

ISBN: 978-81-7822-390-2 (Series)
ISBN: 978-81-7822-391-9

Reprint: Delhi, **2014**
Fifth revised edition: Delhi, 2012
Fourth revised and enlarged edition: Delhi, 2008, 2010

© 2005 Author

All rights reserved. No part of this publication may be reproduced or transmitted in any form or by any means, electronic or mechanical, including photocopying, recording, or by any information storage and retrieval system, without permission in writing from the publishers.

Library of Congress Cataloging-in-Publication Data
Gore, Markarand Madhukar
ISBN 978-81-7822-391-9 (hbk. : alk. paper)—
Includes bibliography, appendix, index
Yoga/Heath/Selfhelp

Published by
NEW AGE BOOKS
A-44 Naraina Industrial Area, Phase-I
New Delhi (India)-110 028
E-mail: nab@newagebooksindia.com
Website: www.newagebooksindia.com

Printed and published by
RP Jain for New Age Books
A-44, Naraina Industrial Area
Phase-I, New Delhi-110 028. India

Dedicated to and in the memory of
Swami Kuvalayananda

(1883–1966)

A great pioneer of scientific research in yoga and the founder and director of Kaivalyadhama

Contents

Message from the President of India   ix
Foreword   xi
Preface   xiii
Introduction   xv

PART ONE
BASIC ANATOMY AND PHYSIOLOGY

1. The Human Body — 3
2. The Digestive System — 11
3. The Circulatory System — 17
4. The Respiratory System — 25
5. The Muscular System — 37
6. The Nervous System — 53
7. The Endocrine System — 71
8. The Skeletal System — 79
9. The Excretory System — 85
10. Homeostasis — 87
11. Posture — 89

PART TWO
ANATOMY AND PHYSIOLOGY OF YOGIC PRACTICES

1. Asana — 97
2. Mudra, Bandha and Kriyas — 137
3. Pranayama — 163
4. The Science of Aum — 209

Bibliography — 217
Appendix — 219
Index — 229

Message from the President of India

A.P.J. Abdul Kalam

Rashtrapati Bhavan
New Delhi - 110004

November 3, 2003

Dear Dr. Gore,

Thank you for your letter sending therewith a copy of your book *"Anatomy and Physiology of Yogic Practices"*. Particularly I liked page 90 of the book.

My best wishes.

Yours sincerely,

(A P J Abdul Kalam)

Dr M M Gore,
Research Officer,
Scientific Research Deptt.,
At & PO: Kaivalyadhama
Lonavla-410 403
Distt Pune (MS)

(Since this is the new edition, please see the page no. 181 instead of page no. 90)

Foreword

*Keep the mind and body in perfect condition,
these are the requisites to achieve the desired goals.*
                                                    Rig Veda

More than two thousand years ago Patanjali, who is considered the father of yoga, compiled 195 Sutras which still serve as guidelines for using yoga in daily life to attain health and gain freedom from diseases. Yoga also helps to achieve spiritual, mental and physical health and is the main reason why it has now become an international phenomenon. American cardiologist Dean Ornish, for example, who is the discoverer of the reversibility of atherosclerosis has proved that even severely blocked arteries can be opened without surgery with regular meditation, yoga, diet and aerobic exercises.

The fact is, today's competitive world with people striving for material success is producing enormous levels of anxiety and stress leading to hypertension, cardiovascular problems and diabetes which, in turn, increases anxiety and stress even more, forming a vicious circle. Typically, we try to tackle this problem with just medicines without taking its root causes into consideration. Yoga, on the other hand, acts both on physiological and psychic levels bringing physical and mental equilibrium, thus calming both mind and body. It is now almost universally accepted that regular practice of yoga has long lasting therapeutic value and prevents such conditions.

Critical, however, to the basis of understanding yoga is possessing sound knowledge of anatomy (structure) and physiology (function) of the human body which then promotes an understanding of the philosophy of yoga as an established and scientific way to achieve health. The human body is a very complex configuration of muscles, bones, nerves, vessels and other organs and a clear knowledge of these can further help us to identify health problems and diseases. Most importantly, anatomy and physiology explains that all systems of the body function together to work as a cohesive, holistic and healthy unit.

The *Anatomy and Physiology of Yogic Practices* is a very well written book for students of Yoga as well as those studying alternative medicine because it is penned in a clear and lucid language so that the average person can also learn about the structure of the human body in relation to yogic practices. Moreover, it is to the point and does not describe unnecessary details of body function and organisation which may not be required by a student of yoga. Yet, in spite of this, the author has explained certain aspects of physiology in detail such as respiratory physiology that is relevant to pranayama along with physiology of the nervous system in relation to asanas.

The *Anatomy and Physiology of Yogic Practices* also deals with using yoga as therapy. The techniques of various yogic practices are described in detail to enable the reader to easily learn these procedures - especially pranayam.

I am impressed by Dr Makarand Madhukar Gore who has been a teacher of yoga for 10 years, due to his books' contents and the way it is expounded. I recommend his book to students of alternative medicine and yoga and also to the general public as regular practice of yoga calms and quietens the mind and body which is a much needed quality in today's world.

I also feel privileged to write the Foreword for this book which is sure to help yoga students since not many books have been written on this particular aspect of the topic and students and learners of yoga must be feeling the vacuum. In fact I see this book becoming part of a curriculum in various institutes that inculcate yogic practices.

Dr. Vinod Kumar Nigam, M.S.
Laparoscopic Surgeon
Apollo Clinic, Max Hospital

Preface

I am very happy to present the fourth edition of this book, which is revised thoroughly in every sense. All the editions were very much appreciated by the readers through their letters and personal communication. Additional chapters on *Sitkari, Shitali, Bhastrika* and *Suryabhedan pranayama*, based on the recent scientific research, special chapter on the science of Aum and the complete modification of the whole text are the main features of this edition. The book is also available in Italian, German, Hindi and Marathi. The book is a National Award winner. Hon. President Dr. A.P.J. Abdul Kalam, a great scientist, has appreciated the book in his letter (November 23, 2003) addressed to me. He liked the chapter on deep breathing and *pranayama* the most. I thank him for his appreciation.

I express my gratitude to Dr. M.L. Gharote, ex-principal, G.S. College of Yoga and Cultural Synthesis, who guided and encouraged me to write the book. I am deeply indebted to my institution, Kaivalyadhama, which has been the main source of my knowledge and understanding of yoga. I sincerely thank Dr. Dhananjay Gunde (orthopaedic surgeon), a renowned yoga therapist, for writing the foreword for the second edition.

The blessings of my mother Dr. Vimla Gore are always with me. I thank my wife Bharati for publishing the third edition of this book. I am sure, the readers would welcome this edition too.

Gudhipadwa,
April 9, 2005

Dr. M.M. Gore

Introduction

Yoga is a traditional and cultural science of India. Apart from yoga, India has contributed other sciences like *Sanskrit grammar, mathematics, kamashashtra,* and *ayurveda* to the humankind. Ayurveda includes yoga as a part of an ideal lifestyle and maintenance of health (*swastha vritta*). Lord Shrikrishna has explained various faculties of yoga in Bhagwad Geeta. Yoga is further explored in the great treatise, *Dnyaneshwari* written by Saint Dnyaneshwar. Yoga literally means 'union' or 'to join', i.e., union with the divine consciousness. *Hatha yoga, ashtang yoga, bhakti yoga, mantra yoga, dnyan yoga, karma yoga, raj yoga* appear like different types of yoga due to their different methods and techniques but the main objective of all of them is liberation, salvation or to attain *samadhi,* the highest state of *chitta* (consciousness) by controlling its *vrittis* (tendencies, desires) arising in it, out of attachment with the materialistic world, so as to merge into the divine principle (absolute consciousness). Yoga is one of the six great philosophies of India. It is an experiential science.

YOGA AND LIFESTYLE

Yoga is a part of the Indian lifestyle. Real comfort lies in good health. Disease-free condition and contentment at the level of mind are essential components of happiness. Those who practise yoga as daily ritual would experience great deal of peace of mind and joy. Such people always think in positive way and lead a very happy life. Yoga has got the potential to bring prosperity and happiness to anybody from any profession. Since yoga brings about suitable changes in the behavioral pattern and the attitude of a person, the personal relationship at home and in the society are also improved. This is the reason why western countries are now following Indian lifestyle which includes yoga. They have understood that yoga is a 'means' to manage stress and to lead a healthy and happy life.

YOGA AS A THERAPY

'Stress' is an outcome of the modern lifestyle. It is produced out of dissatisfaction, frustration and dejection when there is negative interaction between the self-projection and the adverse internal as well as the external environmental conditions. At present, the human existence is challenged by the stress disorders or the psychosomatic diseases such as hypertension, hyperacidity, insomnia, heart diseases, diabetes, asthma, etc. Although the system of yoga is not developed for the purpose of treatment, it has been observed through the applied research that the regular practice of yoga not only controls these diseases but also promotes and maintains the healthy condition of body and mind and prevents the disease process. Yoga is not an alternative to any conventional therapy but it definitely supports the healing process. Today, the popularity of yoga is mostly because of its therapeutic value. Yoga has a potential to tranquilize and balance the mind, which is the key in the management of stress disorders.

HATHA YOGA

Kriyas, asanas, pranayamas, bandha, mudra, and *nadanusandhan* are to be practiced in this sequence. All these practices are from *hatha yoga. Hathapradipika, Gherand Samhita, Vshishtha Samhita, Hatharatnavali* are important ancient *hathayogic* texts. Practice of *hatha yoga* promotes health and prepares an individual for spiritual aspects of yoga like awakening of the *kundalini, dhyan* and *samadhi*. It works on two principles, i.e., *Ha* (Sun) and *Tha* (Moon) and brings about the balance in between the two. *Hatha yoga* is aware of the fact that,

हठं विना राजयोगो राजयोगं विना हठः ।
न सिध्यति ततो युग्ममानिष्पत्तेः समभ्यसेत् ॥
—*Hathapradipika* II:76

Introduction

Meaning: without the practice of *hatha yoga*, the practice of *Raj yoga* will not be successful and without *raj yoga* no perfection is attained in *hatha yoga*. Hence one should practice both simultaneously.

ASHTANG YOGA

यमनियमासन प्राणायाम प्रत्याहार धारणाध्यान
समाधयोंऽष्टावड्गानि ।

—*Patanjali Yoga Sutra* 2:2a

Yama, niyama, asana, pranayama, pratyahar, dharana, dhyan and *samadhi* are eight parts of *ashtang yoga* of Yogi Patanjali. He describes the whole yoga in total 195 aphorisms, divided into four parts. He defines yoga as *chittavritti nirodhah* (चित्तवृत्ति निरोध:) and then writes remaining aphorisms to explain how to achieve it. He considers yoga as a discipline. Unless yoga is practiced regularly, sincerely and in a most disciplined manner, one can not reap its benefits. First four steps are known as *bahirang yoga* (external part of yoga) and the rest four steps form the *antarang yoga* (internal part of yoga) or the *raj yoga*. Patanjali does not mention the names of *asanas* or *pranayamas* but elucidates the fathoms of the human psychology and recommends prophylactic measures to promote and maintain the physical and mental health.

Ahimsa (non-violence), *satya* (truthfulness), *asteya* (non-stealing), *brahmacharya* (abstinence), and *aparigrah* (non-possessiveness) are five *yamas* or the vows of self-restraint (the don'ts) that are meant for one's virtuous attitude towards the society. Purification of self is necessary before proceeding to yoga practices or simultaneously, to reap the full benefits of yoga. Such purification is achieved by observing these rules (commandments) of Patanjali. This would improve values and provide the moral foundation for the *yogasadhana*.

Shauch (purity, cleanliness), *santosh* (contentment), *tapa* (austerity), *swadhyay* (self-study) and *Ishwar pranidhana* (surrender to God) are the five *niyamas* (observances) of the yogic discipline that lay the foundation of the yogic attitude. The sincere observance of these ten vows (*mahavratas*) would help us to progress faster on the spiritual path since they increase the purity of our mind.

WHO SHOULD PRACTICE YOGA?

Hatha yoga says that all young, old or too old, patients, weak persons can learn and practice yoga. That means anybody can practice yoga after the age of seven. There is no restriction of caste, creed, religion, cult or country. It is open for all. The only rule is that it should be practiced daily as a routine and be a part of your lifestyle. The basic lessons in yoga should be learnt, in the beginning, from an expert yoga teacher. Remember, yoga teacher, yoga therapist and a yoga instructor are three different persons.

TIME, PLACE AND DIRECTION

The best time to practice yoga is at sunrise. The practice after bathing yields better results as the circulation of the body increases after bath. While practicing one should preferably face the east and the place should have good ventilation. It should be free from mosquitoes and foul odors. The atmospheric conditions should be suitable. Too cold or warm weather should be avoided.

The *sadhak* should practice yoga in a relaxed manner, with deep faith (श्रद्धा *shraddha*) and devotion (भक्ति *bhakti*). He should pay attention to different sensations arising during the practice and analyze them on the basis of the scientific information provided in this book. It will help him to progress on the spiritual path.

SCIENTIFIC RESEARCH ON YOGA

The scientific nature of yoga was first revealed when Swami Kuvalayananda conducted most fundamental scientific experiments in yoga in 1924. He established Kaivalyadhama Institute for scientific research on yoga. These research findings removed various misconceptions about yoga and the mystical

Introduction

sheath lying over it in those days. He and Dr. S.L.Vinekar then described the principles of yoga therapy in terms of anatomy and physiology. Based on this, the subject 'anatomy and physiology of yogic practices' was further developed by Dr. M.V. Bhole. The subject of anatomy and physiology of yogic practices is a mandatory subject for diploma courses in yoga in all the yoga institutions. It helps to understand the mechanism of yogic practices and their appropriate application for the patient or a spiritual aspirant or the normal individual. However, there was no book available on it till 1984.

The first part of the book deals with only that part of the basic anatomy and physiology, which is important in understanding the mechanism of yoga practices. This time a special note, in the form of tips 'from yoga point of view', has been added so as to understand various concepts and aphorisms of yoga clearly.

The second part of the book describes the traditional technique of *asanas, pranayamas, bandhas, mudras, kriyas* (cleansing practices), their possible mechanism, effects and the research findings about these yogic practices so that the insight as well as the interest of a student would increase.

This book would help the reader:

1. To learn the basic structure and various functions of the body.
2. To understand the yogic concepts, the correct technique and the mechanism of the yogic practices as well as their physiological effects on the human body.
3. To know whether we can modify the techniques of these yoga practices with the help of the scientific information about them, for better application.
4. To understand the principles of yogic therapy, its application, contra-indication and limitations.
5. To know the scientific aspect of the *Aum* chanting.

PART ONE

BASIC ANATOMY AND PHYSIOLOGY

One

The Human Body

Anatomy and physiology are biological sciences. Anatomy is the science of structure of a living organism. It studies the form and structure of the body and its various parts like bones, muscles, nerves etc. It provides us with the knowledge regarding the construction of our body. How is our body built-up? What is it made-up of? How are the various organs arranged? Such questions can be answered through the science of anatomy.

Physiology is the science of functions of the body. It explains the working of the different parts, systems and various processes going on continuously inside our body. How do the organs work? How do the muscles, heart, brain, etc., function and for what do they work? How do they coordinate with each other? How are they controlled? We can find answers to these questions with the help of this branch of science.

Both these sciences are deeply connected with each other. We study them separately for the sake of our understanding. In the present book we are going to study the fundamentals of these two sciences together.

The human body consists of three distinct parts, namely head, trunk and the extremities. The hands are upper extremities and the legs are lower extremities. Trunk is differentiated into the chest (thoracic) part and the abdominal part (Fig. 1). These two parts are separated internally (Fig. 2) by a muscular curtain called the *diaphragm*. The human body is well organized for its different vital functions. Such functional organization of the organs in the body, is known as a system. For example, the digestive system for the function of digestion, the respiratory system for the function of exchange of gases between the organism and the atmosphere, etc. These systems are interdependent on each other. The total function of the body depends on the integration of these systems.

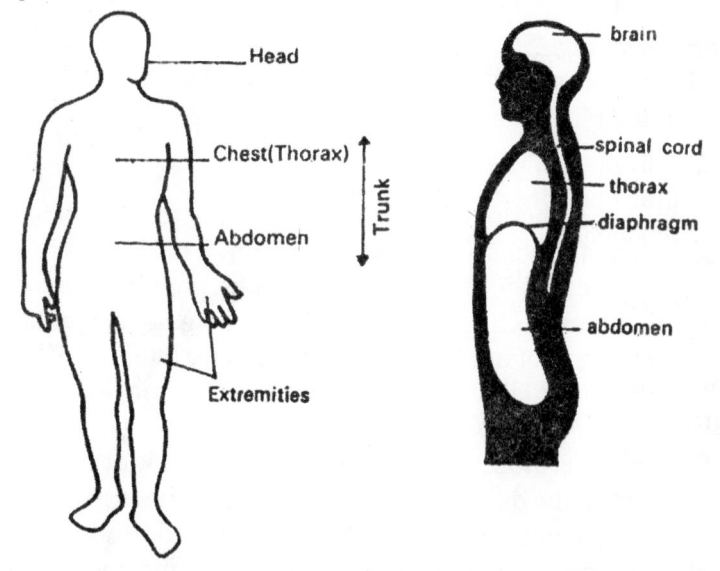

Fig. 1: Human Body

Fig. 2: Internal Divisions of Human Body

A system is constructed of some parts which are grouped together for a specific function. These parts work together in perfect coordination. For example, mouth, teeth, stomach, liver, intestine, pancreas and colon work together as digestive system to provide nutrition to the body. Every organ is composed of four specific tissues. These tissues are organized in various proportions and patterns. Tissues are made up of a group of specialized cells.

For example, muscular tissue is composed of the muscle fibers, which are nothing but the modified cells specialized for contraction and production of the force. Nerve tissue is made of nerve fibers, which are the modified cells to conduct the nerve impulses.

THE CELL

Each and every part of our body is composed of tiny microscopic units called the 'cell'. Cell is the structural and functional unit of the body. Cells have different shapes and sizes according to their nature of work. For example, muscle (cells) fibers are spindle shaped for contraction; glandular cells are cubical in form, specialized for secretion.

Every cell is covered and well protected by a very thin wall called the *plasma membrane*. A cell is composed of:

1. A living stuff called *Cytoplasm* (Fig. 3), a colloid substance that contains many microscopic structures called *cell organelles*.
2. A highly specialized structure in the center of the cell called *nucleus*, which controls all the cellular activities.

Thus the cell can absorb the nourishment, transport the oxygen, expel the waste material, respond to different situations, grow and reproduce the cell of its own kind, just like an organism.

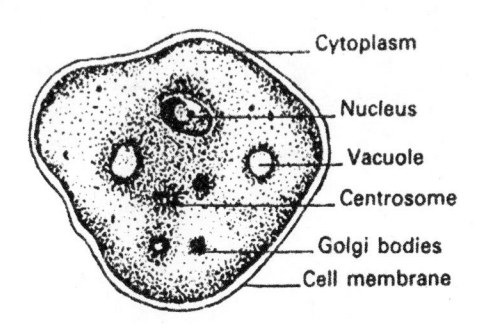

Fig. 3: The Animal Cell

THE TISSUES

Cells are highly organized units but they do not function in isolation. They work together in a group of similar cells forming a tissue. Every tissue has its specialized function to perform. Tissues of our body are classified into four principal types according to their structure and function. These are, (1) epithelial tissue, (2) connective tissue, (3) muscular tissue and (4) nervous tissue.

1. Epithelial tissue

It covers the body surface and forms the glands. It forms external layer of the skin, (Fig. 4) internal lining (the mucous membrane) of the buccal cavity and the hollow organs. The gastrointestinal tract is lined with the epithelial tissues. Main functions of this tissue are secretion, protection, absorption and excretion. Glandular epithelium of various glands discharge special secretions, e.g., hormones from endocrine glands, digestive juices from gastric glands in the stomach. Ciliated epithelium of the respiratory tract protects the tract by expelling the dust particles coming in along with the inhaled air. Intestinal epithelium absorbs the digested food material in the intestine.

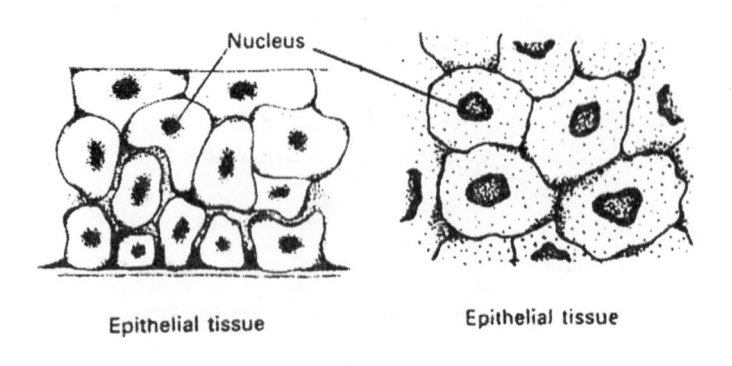

Fig. 4: The Epithelial Tissue

2. Connective tissue

It includes the blood cells, loose and dense (fiber) connective tissue, adipose tissue, lymph, cartilages and bones. Major functions of connective tissue are to connect, anchor and support the other tissues of the body and to form structural framework of the body. Other examples of connective tissue are, rigid cartilages of the joints, pinna of ear, nose, epiglottis, etc. Connective tissue (Fig. 5) contains considerable extra-cellular material between the cells. Subcutaneous layer of skin contains adipose tissue, which stores fat for the body. Connective tissue binds the parts together. This is the most abundant tissue in the body.

Fibrous tissue   Adipose (fat) tissue

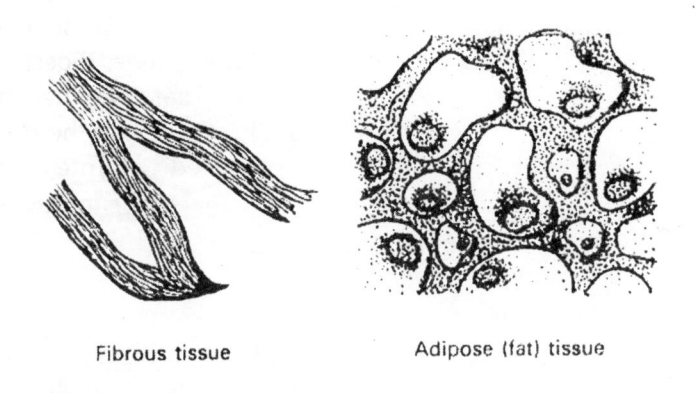

Fig. 5: The Connective Tissue

3. Muscular tissue

It is responsible for the movements of the body and parts. This is because of its characteristic function of contraction. Mainly three types of muscle fibers (Fig. 6) are constructed from this tissue.
1. cardiac muscle, forming the walls of the heart,
2. smooth muscles of internal parts like intestine, and
3. striated muscles or skeletal muscles like biceps.

It is attached with the bones with the help of tendons.

Movement is an essential body function, which results from the contraction and relaxation of muscles. Other functions of this tissue are, the maintenance of posture and heat production. Muscle is composed of special elongated cells or fibers.

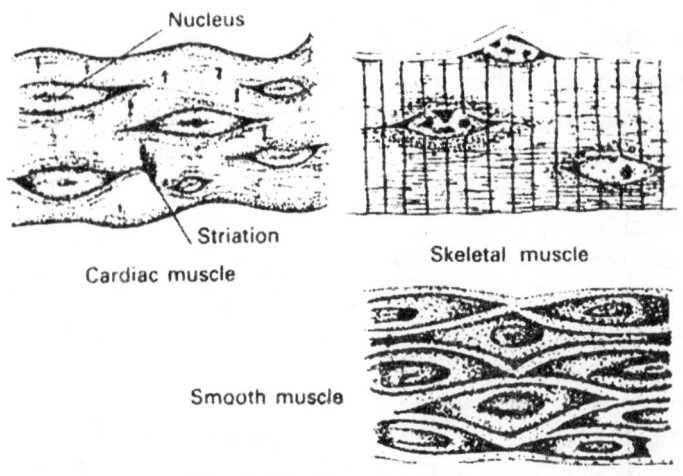

Fig. 6: The Muscular Tissue

4. Nervous tissue

It constructs the whole nervous system. It initiates and transmits nerve impulses that coordinate the body activities. It establishes the relationship between the body and its surrounding environment. The main properties of this tissue are excitability and conductivity. Nervous tissue responds to various stimuli. Nervous tissue (Fig. 7) is composed of nerve cells and their processes. These processes form the nerve fibers. Such unit of nervous tissue is known as *neuron*. They construct the nerves in the body.

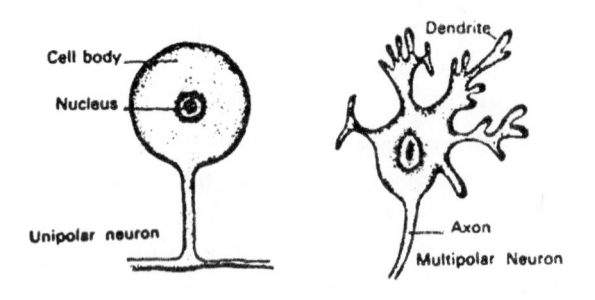

Fig. 7: The Nervous Tissue

ORGANS

Different kinds of tissues join together to form a higher level of organization called the organ. The shape and size of organs can be recognized. Each organ has a complex structure and it performs a specific function for the body. For example, the stomach is composed of smooth muscles, glandular epithelial tissue, blood vessels, and nervous tissue and performs the function of digestion. Outer layer of the stomach is made-up of connective tissue and epithelium that protects the stomach and reduces the friction when the stomach moves and rubs against other organs. The muscle tissue layers of the stomach contract to mix the food and pass it on to the intestine. The inner layer of epithelium produces mucous, acid and enzymes. Other examples of organs are liver, heart, brain, lungs, uterus (in women), urinary bladder, etc.

SYSTEMS

A system is an association of parts that have a common function. There are eleven main systems viz., skeletal system, muscular system, digestive system, respiratory system, nervous system, circulatory system, urinary system, endocrine system, reproductive system, integument system (skin) and immune system. Although we study these systems separately, all of them coordinate with each other and are interdependent on each other in such a way that there exists no line of separation in respect of their structure and function. Some organs even belong to more than one system. For example, liver is a part of the digestive as well as the excretory system.

These systems help the organisms to exchange molecules across their body surface between the internal and external environments. For example, respiratory system exchanges oxygen and carbon dioxide between the air and the blood. All these systems together constitute the body of a living organism.

Now we shall study in detail the anatomy and physiology of some of the important systems and their relevance to the yoga practices.

Two

The Digestive System

It is also known as alimentary or gastrointestinal system. It provides nourishment to all the body cells from the external environment. Food intake; its digestion, absorption and assimilation; water balance; elimination of residue, waste products and poisonous substances are the main functions of this system. The system includes gastrointestinal tract (alimentary canal), salivary glands and portions of liver and pancreas. The alimentary canal is a continuous tube. It consists of mouth (buccal cavity), throat (pharynx), esophagus, stomach, small intestine, large intestine (colon), rectum and anal canal, ending in the anus (Fig. 8).

The oral cavity (mouth) is made-up of a small outer portion (vestibule) between the teeth and the lips and the inner major part between the teeth and the tongue. Roof of the mouth consists of a hard and soft palate. Soft palate helps in swallowing, sucking, blowing and producing sound. The uvula hangs down from the soft palate.

The tongue is a muscular organ. It helps in chewing, swallowing, speaking and tasting. Pharynx is a muscular tube, which leads to esophagus and ends into the stomach. Digestive glands are situated in the wall of the stomach. They secret juices, containing enzymes, which break down the food particles into simple soluble substances. Carbohydrates (sugar, starch), proteins and fats are three important nutrients of our food. They are digested due to chemical actions of enzymes. This digested food is easily absorbed through inner wall of the small intestine into the blood capillaries. Pancreas and liver also help in digestion by supplying the pancreatic juice and bile respectively. The absorbed food particles are carried to the liver and then into the general circulation. The longitudinal and circular muscles of the alimentary wall contract alternately and produce wave like periodic movements of the tract. This involuntary muscular movement is known as *peristalsis*. Peristaltic movements are controlled by medulla oblongata (refer page 58). This peristaltic movement pushes the food forward along the tract during the process of digestion.

The stomach opens into the duodenum, which further leads to small intestine. The small intestine is about 5 meters long. It joins large intestine (colon), which is about 1.5 meters long and has got three distinct parts, viz., ascending, transverse and descending colon. Last parts of the large intestine are known as rectum and anal canal, which open to the external environment through anus. The colon contents are greatly influenced during *uddiyan, nauli* and *basti kriyas*.

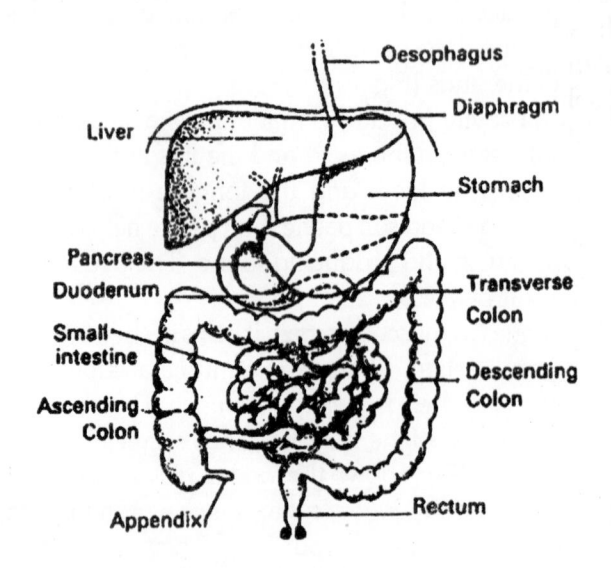

Fig. 8: The Alimentary System

Most of the digested food is absorbed in the small intestine. The large intestine absorbs mainly sodium along with the large quantities of water. This makes the fecal material dry. In turn, potassium is transported from blood capillaries into the lumen of the large intestine to keep feces moisturized. Repeated enemas or diarrhea may lead to serious loss of potassium in the body and therefore one may experience weakness in the muscles. The large intestine also absorbs some of the products synthesized by the bacteria. For example, small amounts of vitamins, which are synthesized by bacteria in the large intestine, are absorbed by the large intestine itself.

Undigested, unwanted and toxic residues of food are passed on to the rectum and then eliminated through the anus during the process of defecation. This evacuation of the bowel is assisted by a deep inspiration followed by closure of the glottis and contraction of the abdominal and chest muscles, causing a marked increase in intrathoracic pressure. There is a sudden rise in the blood pressure. This is followed by a fall in the blood pressure due to decreased venous return (returning blood) to the heart.

Internal and external anal sphincters guard anus. The internal anal sphincter is made-up of smooth muscle. The external anal sphincter is a skeletal muscle, which can be controlled voluntarily.

The smooth muscles of the digestive parts are involuntary muscles, which are not working under our will. Major autonomic nerve of the gastrointestinal tract (GIT) is the vagus nerve, which sends branches to the stomach, small intestine and upper portion of large intestine. This nerve is composed of efferent parasympathetic fibers and many afferent fibers (conveying information to the nervous system) from receptors and nerve plexuses in the GIT wall. Sympathetic nerve fibers are also supplied to the GIT. In short, the activity of smooth muscles and exocrine (digestive) glands are controlled by the autonomic nervous system and the internal nerve plexus as well as the hormones secreted by GIT itself. Gastrointestinal receptors initiate reflexes and the information is conveyed to the central nervous system (CNS). Short reflexes bring about self-regulation in the tract. Strong reflexes, however, bring CNS into action and our attention is drawn. For example, the sight of food initiates reflex, which involves CNS and one thinks about the food items and their selection. Complex behavioral changes due to emotions and moods can influence the GIT through CNS and the appetite may be increased or reduced.

Sometimes we become aware of a few sensations like pressure, pain, temperature, or burning in the abdominal region. This is mainly due to various visceroreceptors situated along the GIT. When they are stimulated because of stretching, pressure or the chemical action, the strong sensory impulses are sent to the CNS and our attention is drawn. Hunger and appetite are such sensations coming from the stomach. The appetite center lies in the lateral hypothalamus (refer page 57), which on stimulation can increase the food intake. The medial hypothalamus contains satiety center, which on stimulation inhibits the food intake.

The entire digestive and other parts are properly held and protected by means of very strong muscles that form the wall of the belly. This abdominal wall prevents displacement of the stomach, intestine or any other organ in the abdomen. The abdominal wall also provides mechanical support to the abdominal viscera as it contains strong rectus abdominus muscles. This helps to maintain the tone of the involuntary muscles of the abdominal organs.

From yoga point of view

1. Once the liquid food material enters the stomach, it will be digested and later on absorbed in the small intestine within half an hour. Solid food (e.g., lunch) will take 2–2.5 hours for main digestion and 4–6 hours for complete absorption. That is why yoga practices should be done either in the morning or in the evening with an empty stomach.
2. The central nervous system has no direct control on the digestive function but the appetite and satiety centers lie in the hypothalamus. Our emotional balance and behavior are also controlled by the hypothalamic centers. It has been found that even the muscular tone of the smooth muscles of

the visceral parts is affected due to our emotional status (e.g., anger, hatred and irritation). Thus our digestion is affected due to our thinking style, tense and unsatisfied mind and the negative approach. This causes indigestion, acidity, and gastric troubles. If the digestive function is disturbed, our health is also affected. It is therefore advisable to maintain mental peace and balance all the time, with the positive approach, contentment and happiness, which can also be achieved through yoga.
3. Almost all the *asanas* as well as *kriyas* influence stomach, colon, urinary bladder and the liver.
4. *Dhauti* is mainly related to esophagus and stomach while *Basti* is concerned with the anus, rectum and the colon.
5. The external sphincters of the anus are contracted and relaxed alternately in *Ashwini mudra*.

Three

The Circulatory System

The circulatory system includes the heart, blood vessels and the blood. It transports the nutrients and oxygen to the tissues and removes carbon dioxide and other waste products of metabolism from the tissues. For this purpose the blood is continuously circulated in the body by rhythmic pumping action of the heart and through a complex network of the blood vessels. The blood acts as a vehicle that carries the products of digestion from the alimentary canal and the oxygen from the lungs to the tissues. While returning to the heart, the blood brings the toxic substances or the waste products back to the heart. The kidneys, lungs and the skin eliminate these substances when the blood circulate through them. The blood thus communicates with all the systems and organs, regulates the water level and the temperature of the body.

THE HEART

The heart is situated in the chest cavity between the two lungs. It is covered by fibrous sac known as *pericardium*. Two-third part of the heart lies on the left side. The human heart is divided longitudinally into right and left halves, each consisting of two chambers, an upper one; the atrium or auricle; and the lower one, the ventricle. The atrium and the ventricle of the same side are connected with each other through atrioventricular valve. These valves permit the blood to flow from atrium to ventricle but not in the reverse direction. The heart muscle receives its blood supply via arterial branches, i.e., right and left coronary arteries arising from the aorta. The heart is an involuntary muscle. It is also known as cardiac muscle, which initiates its own contraction and controls it quite independently. It contracts and relaxes for average 70 times in a minute in a healthy adult. A phase of contraction is called *systole* while the relaxation phase of the heart muscle is known as *diastole*. Systole is the time of action to propel the blood into the respective blood vessels whereas diastole is the time of rest. The primary controlling center of cardiac function is in the *medulla oblongata*. This center also regulates blood pressure. The heart is supplied with the sympathetic and parasympathetic branches of autonomic nervous system (ANS) that accelerates the heart or slows it down respectively. Thus the hypothalamus can influence the blood pressure, as it is also the center for emotions like pain, anger, and body temperature.

BLOOD PRESSURE

Certain pressure is always exerted on the walls of the arteries as the blood flows through them during systolic and diastolic phases of cardiac function. The pressure is highest during contraction of the heart and lowest when the heart is relaxing. Hence it is known as systolic and diastolic blood pressure respectively. An average blood pressure for a normal healthy adult is 120 mmHg (systolic) and 80 mmHg (diastolic). Age, sex, time of the day, posture, exercise, emotions, lack of oxygen and changes in the metabolism are some of the factors, which can influence the heart rate as well as the blood pressure.

CONTROL OF BLOOD PRESSURE

The carotid arteries in the upper neck region are divided into external and internal carotid arteries. At this bifurcation, wall of the artery is thinner, containing large number of nerve endings. This small portion of the artery is called the **carotid sinus**. These nerve endings are highly sensitive to stretch. Stretching of the wall of the artery is related to the pressure within the artery and hence the carotid sinus serves as a pressure receptor (baroreceptor). These nerve endings are connected with the cardiac center in the medulla oblongata by

The Circulatory System

glossopharyngeal (IXth cranial) nerve (Fig. 9). Aortic arch also possesses similar kind of nerve endings, which constitutes second important arterial baroreceptor. The afferent fibers from these receptors travel through the vagus (Xth cranial) nerve. An increase in the arterial pressure stimulates the carotid sinus and baroreceptors at the aortic arch. These impulses reach to the medulla oblongata through afferent nerves. The cardiac centers inhibit sympathetic activity and increase parasympathetic activity, which causes slowing down of the heart and dilation of the arteriols. As a result, the cardiac output is reduced and blood pressure returns to the normal level.

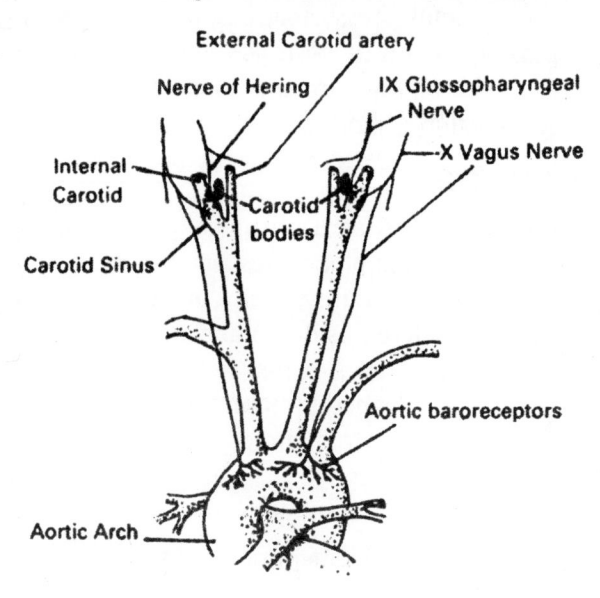

Fig. 9: The Carotid Sinus and Aortic Baroreceptors

EFFECT OF EXERCISES

An increased muscular activity during exercise requires increased blood supply for the oxygen and nutrients such as glucose. Waste products such as carbon dioxide, lactic acid, water and heat are to be removed rapidly from the muscles. Naturally the cardiac output is increased from 5 liter per minute to 35 liter per minute (as in a trained athlete). The skeletal muscle arterioles are dilated due to sympathetic influence. The peripheral resistance is decreased and heart rate is increased. This is mainly because the sympathetic activity is greatly increased than the parasympathetic activity during exercise.

The venous return to the heart is also simultaneously increased during the exercise. The respiratory rate is increased in coordination with the increased blood circulation. Veinules and arterioles are constricted and the contraction of heart muscle becomes more forceful. The systolic blood pressure is increased while the diastolic blood pressure is relatively constant. After the exercise, the blood pressure and the heart rate are reduced to normal level within a short time.

HYPERTENSION

Hypertension is defined as a chronically increased arterial pressure. That means the blood pressure remains elevated on the higher level. If the pressure remains increased beyond 140/90 mmHg, it is considered as hypertension.

Diastolic blood pressure is a real index of hypertension. If the hypertension is prolonged for many days the result may be fatal, like cardiac arrest, brain stroke (rupture of the cerebral blood vessel) or kidney damage.

The cause of hypertension may be,

1. excessive secretion of epinephrine due to tumors in adrenal medulla,
2. malfunctioning of kidneys due to decreased blood supply.

It is then known as *renal hypertension,* since kidneys are involved in it. When the cause of hypertension is not known, as it happens in most of the cases, it is known as *essential hypertension.* Excessive sodium ingestion or retention in the body is an important factor in essential hypertension and hence salt intake is strictly reduced in such cases. Obese persons, smokers, persons having constant mental or emotional tension,

The Circulatory System

persons constantly undergoing some kind of stress or the other, are prone to develop essential hypertension. Obese persons must reduce the weight sincerely through proper regulation of diet and appropriate exercises. Relaxation shows a positive effect in reducing the hypertension. Relaxation induces parasympathetic tone, which dilates the arterioles, decreases heart rate and reduces the blood pressure. Many drugs also achieve this temporarily. Yogic relaxation has been found most effective in controlling essential hypertension, particularly when the cause is emotional or psychological tensions and stress.

BLOOD CIRCULATION

Each drop of blood travels twice, i.e., once through the *pulmonary circulation* and then through the *systemic circulation* in the body. During the systemic circulation, pure (oxygenated) blood is pumped out forcefully from the left ventricle into aorta. It is carried then to all the body parts (parts and tissues). Arteries divide into smaller branches. The smallest branches are called *arterioles*. These further branch into still fine and thin vessels, called *capillaries*. Capillaries unite again to form bigger vessels, called *venules*. The waste material such as carbon dioxide, is picked up from the tissues and conducted through these venules into still bigger vessels, called veins. Such different veins from various parts unite to form larger veins. Thus the inferior vena cava collects impure (deoxygenated) blood from the lower portion of the body and the superior vena cava brings the impure blood from the upper half of the body and empty their blood into right atrium of the heart. Right atrium pushes this blood to the right ventricle. From here the pulmonary circulation starts. The right ventricle forces out this impure blood through the *pulmonary artery* into the lungs. Within the lungs, the capillaries of the arteries are in contact with the alveoli. Their walls are very thin, which lie side-by-side. During inhalation, the oxygen is easily absorbed from the alveoli into these capillaries in exchange of carbon dioxide. Capillaries reunite to form venules and finally the veins. With the next push, this oxygenated blood travels from lungs to the left auricle through *pulmonary veins* and finally reaches down to the left ventricle. Thus pulmonary veins bring oxygenated blood from the lungs to the heart, to be pumped again for the systemic circulation. It will be interesting to know that the brain requires 20 percent of the total circulating blood.

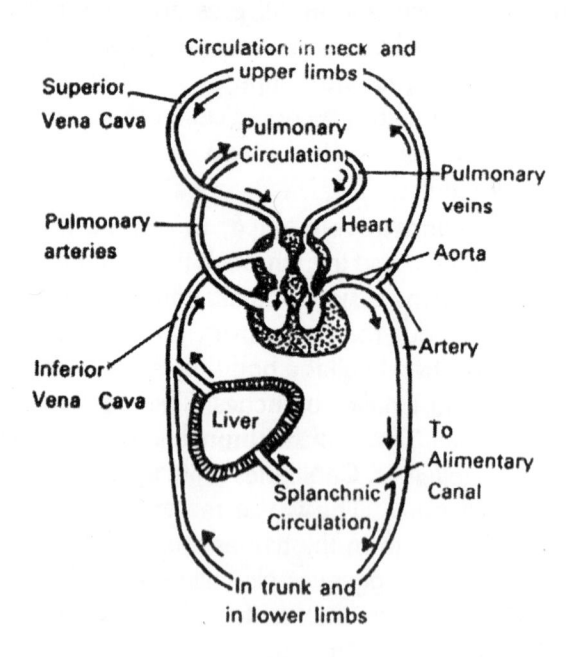

Fig. 10: The Blood Circulation

THE BLOOD

The average total quantity of blood which is constantly circulated in a healthy adult human body is approximately 5 liters. Blood is composed of two parts (1) Blood cells (45 percent) and (2) Plasma, i.e., liquid part (55 percent).
Blood cells are of three types:
 (i) Red blood cells (RBC) or Erythrocytes,
 (ii) White blood cells (WBC) or Leucocytes,
 (iii) Blood platelets or Thrombocytes.

1. Red Blood Cells (RBC)

Each cubic mm of blood contains approximately 5 million erythrocytes. Each RBC is a biconcave disc. It is thicker at the edge than in the center. It contains iron combined with protein, *hemoglobin;* that can bind with oxygen very quickly. It also contains an enzyme called *carbonic anhydrase,* which facilitates the transportation of carbon dioxide. Average life of an erythrocyte is about 120 days. Destruction of RBC is done in liver, spleen, bone marrow and lymph nodes. Hemoglobin is converted into bilirubin that is released into the blood. The liver cells pick up this substance from blood and add it to the bile. New erythrocytes are produced in red bone marrow. Thus RBCs help in exchange of oxygen and carbon dioxide between the atmosphere and the body.

2. White Blood Cells (WBC)

One cubic mm of blood contains about 7000 WBCs. They are of various shapes and size. Neutrophils (50–70 percent) and eosinophils (0.1 percent) form one group of WBC while monocytes (2–8 percent) and lymphocytes (20–40 percent) constitute another group of leucocytes. The primary function of WBCs is protection. They destroy harmful bacteria and foreign organic particles. This defense mechanism is related with our immunity system that works against infectious disease.

3. Blood Platelets

In each cubic mm of blood there are about 2,50,000 blood platelets. These are colorless and are smaller than RBCs. Blood platelets do not contain nucleus. Plasma contains protein, known as *fibrinogen.* They are irregular in shape. They help in the process of blood clotting. This is known as *blood coagulation.* In case of injury when blood comes in contact with the air, the blood platelets are destroyed and thrombokinase enzyme is released. *Thrombokinase* converts inactive *thrombogen* into an active *thrombin.* In the presence of thrombin, the fibrinogen (plasma protein) is converted into a dense substance, *fibrin.* Filaments of fibrin get intertwined and thus a clot is formed at the site of injury within a few minutes. This prevents further bleeding or loss of blood.

Plasma is viscous proteinous fluid. It consists of 90 percent water and 10 percent organic and inorganic substances and the antibodies. Antibodies play a protective role against various bacteria, virus, toxins and other microscopic organisms.

Plasma proteins are classified into three broad groups, albumins, globulins and fibrinogen. Serum is formed when fibrinogen is converted to fibrin during the process of blood coagulation (clotting).

From yoga point of view

1. Many *asanas* e.g., *Shirshasana, Sarvangasana, Viparita karni, Halasana, Mayurasana,* few *pranayamas* like *Ujjayi* and *Bhastrika pranayama* as well as *uddiyan, nauli, Jalandhar bandha* specially influence the blood circulation. That is why you must learn them from an expert so that you can practice them safely as per your capacity and need, without taxing the circulatory system.
2. Those who are suffering from high blood pressure should not practice above mentioned *asanas, pranayamas* and *kriyas*.
3. The heart rate and the blood pressure should not increase too much while doing *asana* or *pranayama*.
4. It has been observed that the workload on the cardiac function during *Padmasana* and *Vajrasana* is even less than that of sitting on a chair.
5. When the body and mind are properly relaxed and mental peace is experienced, the muscle tone is reduced. The blood vessels are also relaxed which are otherwise constricted due to tension. The heart rate is reduced. Blood pressure comes to the normal level. This is possible by regular practice of *Shavasana*.
6. It has been observed that the peripheral blood circulation is reduced and the circulation at a particular body part (e.g., the endocrine glands, the facial muscles) is purposely enhanced to supply blood to the specific tissue. That is why the yoga practitioner always looks fresh and energetic and has brightness on his face.

Four

The Respiratory System

An organism requires not only nutrients but also oxygen. In the process of metabolism, tissues continuously consume oxygen and produce carbon dioxide. As we know, carbon dioxide is a toxic gas and should be thrown out of the body. For this purpose there must be a continuous process for exchange of these gases between the organism and the environment.

Respiration is the process by which oxygen is absorbed in the blood, food material is metabolized with oxygen and carbon dioxide and the end-product of this oxidation is eliminated from the body. The transportation of the gases takes place through the circulating blood. The exchange of gases between blood and tissue is known as *internal respiration* and the exchange of gases between the blood and the environment (in lungs) is known as *external respiration*.

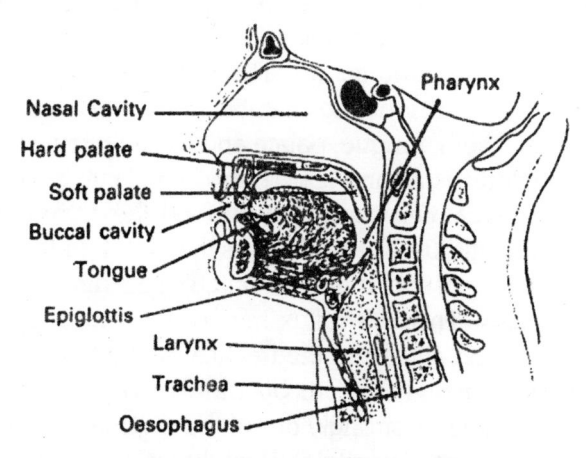

Fig. 11: The Upper Respiratory Tract

Respiratory parts may be divided into two parts:
1. The air passage through which the air flows during the respiration.
2. The respiratory surface, i.e., alveoli in the lungs where the gases are exchanged between the atmospheric air and the blood.

We can breathe through the nose as well as the mouth but the normal route is the nose. The respiratory passage starts from the two nostrils. Nostrils lead to right and left nasal cavities that open into the *pharynx*. This is the upper part of our throat. Buccal cavity or the mouth also opens into the pharynx. Thus, it is a common passage for both, food and air. The *larynx* or the voice box is a short passage that connects the pharynx with trachea. Larynx also acts as a protective sphincter to prevent solids and liquids from entering into the bronchi and lungs. Its major function is production of the sound. The mucous membrane of the larynx is arranged into two pairs of vocal folds or cords. Skeletal muscles of the larynx are attached to the vocal cords. The glottis or the opening of the larynx can be narrowed and the air is directed towards the vocal cords during the expiration. The vocal cords vibrate and produce sound. The pitch of the sound can be controlled voluntarily by changing the tension or relaxation of the vocal cords and the glottis. This is why during the quiet breathing, the air moves in and out without producing any sound. The mouth, pharynx and the nasal cavity act as resonating chambers and improve the quality of the voice. Teeth, tongue, palate and lips help to form words.

The epiglottis is a long leaf shaped cartilage, covering the top of the larynx. When we swallow the food, the larynx is elevated and the epiglottis just like a lid closes the glottis. In this way the larynx is closed off and the food or liquids are directed towards the esophagus. This is a reflex mechanism and therefore no food particle can enter into the trachea. If anything other than the air reaches up to the larynx by mistake, a cough reflex helps to expel the material strongly out of the respiratory tract.

The trachea or the windpipe is a tubular air passage starting from the larynx. At the length of about 12 centimeters, it splits up into right and left branches called *bronchi*. Trachea lies anterior to the esophagus. The wall of the trachea is composed of smooth muscles; elastic connective tissue and C-shaped horizontal rings of cartilage placed one above the other on the anterior side. That is why, when we swallow food, the esophagus is expanded and the trachea is pushed only from the posterior side. The anterior side of the tracheal wall, on the other hand, gets a rigid support due to these cartilaginous rings. Thus, the trachea cannot collapse inward or the air passage is never obstructed mechanically.

Bronchi also contain such C-shaped rings of cartilage. Bronchi open up into the lungs on right and left sides and divide several times like branches of a tree. The smallest division is *bronchiole*. This is the end of the conducting portion and starting of the respiratory portion. Now the air way ends into air sacs called *alveoli*. Numerous alveoli together look like clusters of grapes. Alveoli are in close contact with the microscopic blood capillaries. Walls of the blood capillaries and the alveoli lie side-by-side. These walls are so thin that carbon dioxide and oxygen easily pass through the partition.

Lungs are made up of a spongy substance. Left lung is divided into two lobes and, right lung is divided into three lobes. Two thin membranes cover the lungs. The outer membrane, which is attached to the wall of the thoracic cavity, is called *parietal pleura*. The inner membrane, which encloses lungs is called *visceral pleura*. A lubricating fluid between the two membranes prevents friction of the membranes with each other when the lungs expand or reduce to normal during inhalation and exhalation. Thus, lungs are well protected in a cage made up of ribs and a diaphragm.

INSPIRATION

In normal quiet breathing, inspiration starts with the contraction of the external intercostal (between the ribs) muscles and diaphragm in order to increase the dimensions of the thoracic cage in all the directions. Ribs and sternum bone move upward and outward, diaphragm descends and therefore the lungs are expanded to fill the thoracic cavity. Now as the lungs expand the pressure inside the lungs is lowered. It is less than the atmospheric pressure, i.e., 760 mmHg and in order to make it equal to the atmospheric pressure, air rushes from the atmosphere into the lungs. The volume of air flowing in and out of the alveoli is directly proportional to the pressure gradient between the alveoli and the atmosphere and inversely proportional to the resistance to the airflow offered by the airways. For example, in deeper breath the increased expansion of thoracic cage (chest) and greater drop in intra-alveolar pressure increases the flow of air into the lungs.

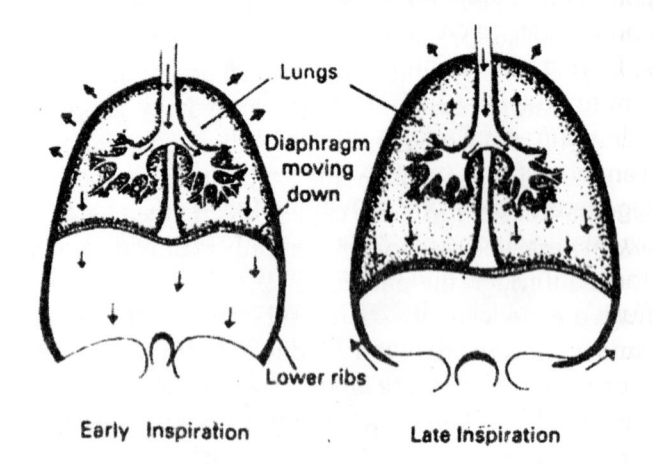

Fig. 12: The Act of Inspiration

Normally the airway offers negligible resistance to the airflow, as the diameter is adequately large. But in certain diseases like asthma, which is characterized by severe bronchiolar (smooth muscle) contraction, the obstruction in the airway further increases further due to excess bronchial secretion. This increased resistance prevents airflow partially or completely. Airway diameter and the resistance may be altered by physical, nervous or chemical factors. Nervous regulation of airway is through the autonomic nervous system (ANS). Sympathetic

The Respiratory System

branch causes relaxation of the smooth muscles of the airway and decreases the resistance while parasympathetic nerves brings about smooth muscle contraction and thus increases the airway resistance. Epinephrine (a hormone from adrenal gland) brings about airway dilation. This is the reason why epinephrine is administered to the asthmatic patient suffering from airway constriction during the attack. Histamine and few other chemicals also cause bronchiolar constriction and increase the airway resistance during an allergic attack. Smooth muscles of the bronchioles are highly sensitive to carbon dioxide concentration around them. This is important for maintaining ventilation and blood supply in the lungs in a right proportion. Pulmonary arteries carry deoxygenated (venous) blood to the lungs. During inspiration the partial pressure of oxygen (pO_2) is 105 mmHg while pO_2 of deoxygenated blood, flowing through the pulmonary capillaries is only 40 mmHg. As a result of this difference in pO_2, oxygen diffuses from the alveoli into deoxygenated blood of the pulmonary capillaries and pO_2 of this oxygenated blood becomes 105 mmHg. Oxygen combines with the hemoglobin and forms Oxyhemoglobin. While oxygen is diffusing from alveoli into the deoxygenated blood in the capillaries, carbon dioxide also diffuses from deoxygenated blood of the capillaries into alveoli since the pCO_2 of alveoli is 40 mmHg, while pCO_2 in deoxygenated blood is 45 mmHg. Thus, oxygen and carbon dioxide are exchanged across the thin wall of alveoli and blood capillaries. Now this oxygenated blood is carried through pulmonary veins to the left atrium for systemic blood circulation.

EXPIRATION

Breathing-out process or expiration is a passive process since there is no muscular contraction in it. Expiration begins when the external intercostals muscles relax, the ribs move downward and the diaphragm ascends. The diameter of the thorax is decreased and thus the lungs are pressed. The pressure in the lungs at this moment is greater than the atmospheric pressure. The stretched lungs tend to recoil and assume their original size. The air is thus forced out of the lungs during the expiration or exhalation. Both inhalation and exhalation together constitute the act of respiration. The rate of respiration in a normal healthy adult is about 14–20 breaths per minute. The rate of respiration depends on the metabolic rate of the body. During sleep the rate of breathing is minimum. The depth and number of breaths per minute are adjusted as per the body's demand for the oxygen and the production of Carbon dioxide. In asthma patients, the expiration becomes difficult as the diameter of the trachea reduces (due to constriction) during the attack.

Composition of the Inspired and Expired Air

Air	Oxygen %	Carbon dioxide %	Nitrogen & other gases %
Inspired air	20.13	0.04	79.03
Expired air	16.3	4.0	79.7

LUNG VOLUMES AND CAPACITIES

During quiet breathing at rest, we inhale about 500 milliliter air and exhale the same amount of air. This volume of air is called *tidal volume* (TV). Only about 350 milliliter of tidal volume actually reaches the alveoli. The remaining 150 milliliter fills the conducting airways and does not come in contact with the blood. As there is no exchange of gases in this space, this volume of air is known as *dead space volume*. The total air reaching the lungs during one minute of respiration is called *minute ventilation*. It is calculated by multiplying the tidal volume by the number of breaths per minute, e.g., if the respiratory rate is 14 per min then minute ventilation will be 14x500 = 7000 milliliter per minute. If we take a very deep breath we can inhale about 2500 milliliter air more. This increased volume of air that we breathe-in deeply is known as *inspiratory reserve volume* (IRV). At the end of the normal exhalation, we can exhale still more with little force. This extra volume of air that we can breathe out after the tidal volume of 500 milliliter is about 1000 milliliter and is called *expiratory reserve volume* (ERV). Even after the expiratory reserve volume is exhaled, some amount of air still remains filled in the air passages. This is called *residual volume* and it is about 1200 milliliter.

Lung capacities are calculated by combining various lung volumes and can be measured by the apparatus known as *Spirometer*. The inspiratory capacity is the sum of tidal volume plus inspiratory reserve volume, i.e., 500 + 2500 = 3000 ml. Expiratory capacity is the sum of TV plus ERV, i.e., 500 + 1000 = 1500 ml. *Vital capacity* is the volume of air that we can inhale and exhale very deeply in one breath. It is the sum of inspiratory and expiratory capacities and is about 4000–4500 milliliter in an adult. Lung capacity is the sum of all volumes.

CONTROL OF RESPIRATION

The respiration is semi-involuntary in nature. It is controlled quite independently and rhythmically without our notice. The respiratory center is situated in the medulla oblongata, which controls the inspiratory and expiratory movements rhythmically. This involuntary control depends entirely upon cyclic excitation of the respiratory muscles by the phrenic nerves to the diaphragm and nerves to the intercostal muscles. Two phrenic nerves start from third, fourth, and fifth cervical (spinal) nerves and pass down on each side of the vertebral column and reach at the diaphragm. Eleven pairs of intercostal nerves originate from first to eleventh thoracic (spinal) nerves. Inspiratory neurons and expiratory neurons are separately working for the inspiration and expiration phases of the respiratory cycle, respectively. The involuntary control depends on the reflex mechanism of chemoreceptors, baroreceptors and stretch receptors. The most important one in regulating the activity of the respiratory center is however the chemoreceptors, which are sensitive to the amount of carbon dioxide in the blood (pCO_2). Increase in carbon dioxide and hydrogen ion concentration in the blood (plasma) stimulates the inspiratory center and increases the depth and rate of respiration. This increased ventilation will promote faster elimination of carbon dioxide from the blood. Fall in blood pCO_2 inhibits the inspiratory center and thus the ventilation is reduced. When carbon dioxide is again accumulated in the blood as a result of continuous metabolic process, up to certain level, the inspiratory center is again stimulated. These chemoreceptors are situated at the bifurcation of the common carotid arteries and in aortic arch quite close to the baroreceptors (Fig. 13). Lack of oxygen in the arterial blood also causes stimulation of the chemoreceptors, which results in the increase of the ventilation.

Distension of alveoli at the end of normal inspiration stimulates stretch receptors situated in bronchioles. The inhibitory impulses travel up to the inspiratory center through vagus nerve and depresses inspiratory center. Stimulation of respiratory muscles is withdrawn and thus expiration takes place due to relaxation of these respiratory muscles. This is known as *Hering-Breuer reflex*. Stretch receptors (proprioceptors) in the intercostal muscles, diaphragm and abdominal muscles also contribute to the regulation of breathing through their stretch reflex mechanism. Increase or decrease in blood pressure stimulates baroreceptors in carotid sinus and thus cause inhibition or stimulation of the respiration respectively. A normal breathing is thus involuntary in nature when we are not paying attention to it. Respiration can also be controlled to some extent voluntarily as per our will. This voluntary control is done from the cerebral cortex. Impulses from the cerebral cortex travel along the descending pathways in the spinal column to the intercostals and the diaphragm. We can hold our breath for a few seconds or minutes. When involuntary stimuli such as elevated pCO_2 or hydrogen ion concentration becomes intense we are forced to withdraw our voluntary control. Within this limit we can however, make necessary changes in depth and duration of inhalation or exhalation volitionally. We can alter our breathing pattern while speaking or singing, in coordination with our other complex voluntary actions.

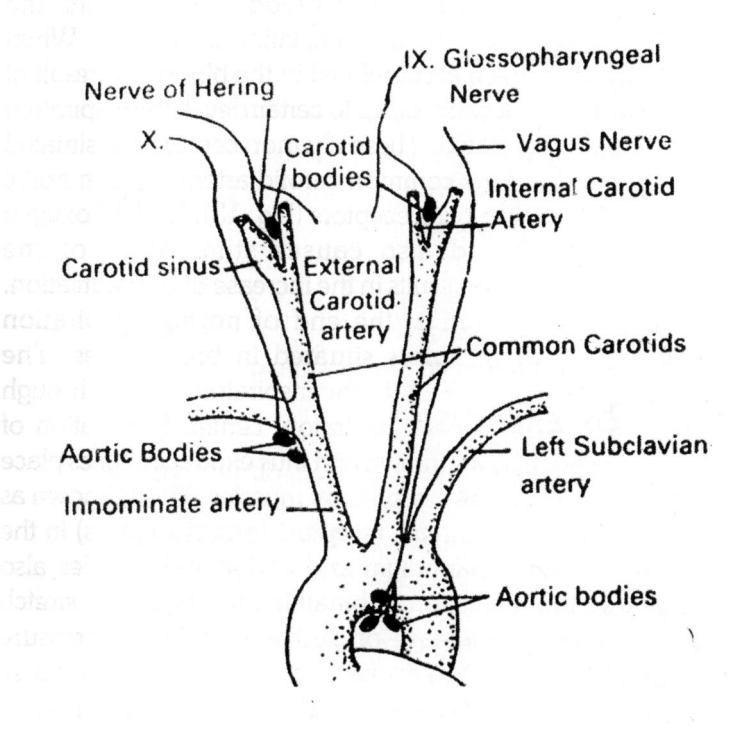

Fig. 13: The Carotid and Aortic Bodies

Thus talking, singing, blowing the air forcefully are the voluntary respiratory acts, which are controlled as per our wish. Sneezing and coughing are involuntary protective respiratory functions carried out as reflexes through the medulla oblongata. Sneezing occurs in response to the irritation of the mucus membrane that is inner living of the nose due to incoming dust or food particles. In these reflex actions, the abdominal muscles and the diaphragm are specially brought into action and the unwanted (foreign) substances are expelled out from the air passages. Changes in the emotional status bring about marked alternation in the respiration, e.g., fright and fear can make the breathing rapid. Excitement can accelerate the respiration, e.g., the psychological tension and anxiety before the athletic event may increase the rate and depth of respiration. Expressions or emotions like laughing and crying require appropriate movement of air in or out of the lungs. Just as emotions and different mental conditions or moods can influence the respiration, we can also control emotions and the mental tensions by modifying our breathing pattern. This is done through the yogic way of breathing, i.e., *pranayama,* in which the respiratory center is controlled voluntarily (through higher brain centers). It is our common experience that we feel more active or enthusiastic when we inhale deeply and we feel relieved of the tensions when the exhalation is prolonged like in sighing.

EFFECT OF EXERCISE

As a result of increased muscular work during exercise, carbon dioxide is produced in larger amount, which accumulates speedily in the joints, muscles and blood. Demand of oxygen is also increased but before chemoreceptors come into action, the receptors in the joints and muscles are stimulated due to increased muscular contractions. Receptors in the joints send impulses to the respiratory center and bring about an increase in the rate and depth of respiration. When chemoreceptors are stimulated, the inspiratory center becomes highly active. The rate of respiration increases. Excess carbon dioxide is expelled out of the body and the level of carbon dioxide is lowered to normal. Besides the gaseous exchange, respiration also contributes to the awareness or alertness of the individual. Changes in the respiratory pattern and consequent gaseous imbalance such as hypoxia (lack of adequate oxygen) may result in altered state of awareness. Various components of the respiratory cycle show variation from person to person due to shifting of awareness and the mental state. These components are, rate and depth of respiration, the ratio of movements of chest to the abdomen, pauses, jerks at any point in the breath, ratio of the duration of inhalation and exhalation. The breathing pattern is normally studied by measuring the movements of the chest and abdomen during the breathing. Yoga has pointed out the relationship between the irregularities in the breathing and disturbances or disorders of physical and psychological functions and vice versa. Now a days many scientists are aware of the fact that the breathing pattern may be an indicator of a predominance of either sympathetic of parasympathetic nervous system and even of the state of arousal, attention and degree of anxiety. Investigations are also being carried out to find out the relationship between the nasal cycle and various physical and psychological functions, which has been explained to a great extent in the yogic text *Shiva Swarodaya*.

From yoga point of view

1. Besides supplying the oxygen, respiratory system also contributes to the state of consciousness, awareness and attention. In pranayama we are dealing with this aspect more. The breathing cycle differs from person to person in respect of the depth, rate of respiration, the movements of the chest and abdomen, pauses, ratio between the duration of inspiration and expiration.
2. This also depends on the postural habits, type of physical and mental activities, behavior, psychological make-up, mood, and emotional condition of the individual.
3. A silent and slow breathing, which is going on easily, without producing any sound is an indication of a good health. However, if suffocation is experienced quite often and some efforts are required for breathing, which may produce a whizzing sound (like in asthma), one should get alarmed and precautionary measures should be taken immediately.
4. We cannot store oxygen anywhere in the body. Oxygen is sufficiently taken from the atmosphere whenever it is needed, automatically. The voluntary breathing is related more to the mind.
5. Respiration is semi-involuntary in nature. Therefore, we can breathe in or out deeply, hold the breath, move our chest or the abdomen voluntarily, up to a certain extent. This is the only system with which we can interfere. No other system can be regulated as per our wish.

6. Most of the time the breathing takes place either from the left or the right nostril. Rarely it is found that both the nostrils are equally open. This is because the congestion (closing) and decongestion (opening) of the nostrils occurs alternately every one to four hours, without our notice. This is known as the *nasal cycle*.
7. Our breathing is related to the life force (*prana*) on one side and the mind, on the other. Therefore, the *pranayama* is like a bridge between the physical existence and the mental activity.

Five

The Muscular System

Movements of all creatures are due to muscular contractions. Muscles are specialized tissues, which can convert chemical energy into the mechanical power and force. Main functions of the muscular system are: (1) locomotion, (2) movement, (3) posture formation and its maintenance, (4) assistance in blood circulation and respiration, (5) protection and support to the viscera, (6) production of a force or the strength and (7) contribution to the functions of digestion, defecation, urination and the process of child birth.

On the basis of the mode of their function, the muscles are recognized under two major groups, (1) *voluntary muscles* such as skeletal muscles that can be contracted as per our will and (2) *involuntary muscles* that are not directly under our control and are further grouped as (i) *Cardiac muscles* and (ii) *Smooth muscles*.

All the muscles possess a remarkable capacity for irritability, conductivity, extensibility and contractility. Irritability is the ability to respond to the stimulation. On stretching, the length of the muscle is increased. The muscle becomes thicker and shorter in length when it contracts. All the three types of muscles differ in their structure, nervous control, mode of contraction and location.

SKELETAL MUSCLES

The skeletal muscles are attached with the bones and cartilages with the help of a *tendon*. Tendon is a strong band of fibrous tissue at the end of the muscle bundle. These muscles, are controlled as per our desire and hence they are called voluntary muscles, e.g., muscles of the head, trunk, hands and legs, tongue, etc. Each muscle is composed of several elongated threadlike *muscle fibers* that are striated. Length of some of the fibers is about 12 centimeter. They lie parallel to each other. Each muscle is well supplied with the blood vessels and nerve fibers. A union of a nerve and muscle is called *myoneural junction*. Motor unit is a basic unit of muscle contraction. It consists of muscle fibers that are supplied with the terminal branches of a motor nerve fiber. The stimulus of an adequate intensity only can cause a muscular contraction. A weaker stimulus cannot bring about a muscular contraction and a very strong stimulus does not increase the intensity of contraction. Thus the motor units follow 'all or none' principle.

When motor nerve impulse stimulates a muscle, a series of chemical changes take place and a muscle contracts. The contraction of a muscle requires energy, which is derived from a high energy compound adenosine tri-phosphate (ATP), present in the muscle fiber. The energy is released when ATP is converted into adenosine di-phosphate (ADP) due to the process of hydrolysis. Thus the ultimate source of energy is the process of glycolysis, i.e., the breakdown of glucose with the help of oxygen.

Glucose + O_2 = Pyruvic acid + ATP + CO_2 + Heat
ATP (hydrolysis) = Energy + ADP + Phosphate
ADP + Phosphate + Energy = ATP

All the voluntary movements are initiated by nerve impulses arising in the motor area of the cerebral cortex. These impulses travel along the spinal cord up to the appropriate muscle and bring about its contraction. Cortex and cerebellum are very well connected with each other.

The prediction of future movements and the position of the body depend on the co ordination between the cerebrum and cerebellum. Further commands from the motor area to the muscle depend on the feedback from the muscle in the form of sensory nerve impulses to the sensory area during various stages of

The Muscular System

muscle contraction. During movements the relative position of the limbs and the trunk are constantly adjusted to maintain balance and stability of the body. Thus the voluntary movements are finely controlled due to neuromuscular co ordination.

The skeletal muscles move the joints with the help of the tendons. The most common type of movements are flexion, extension, abduction, adduction and rotation (refer Fig. 20, page-82). The muscles are known according to their action as follows:

FLEXORS

These muscles bring about the flexion and are situated on the anterior surface of the joints or the body, e.g., biceps muscles of arm on the front side.

EXTENSORS

These muscles are situated at the backside or behind the joints and cause extension, i.e., the movement opposite to the flexion, e.g., straightening of the bent knee.

Generally the flexors are known as *agonists*, which are engaged in contracting or in the actual movement of the part. The extensors are known as *antagonists* and their action is just opposite to the action of the agonists, i.e., extending or unfolding the limbs. Usually when flexors contract, the extensors relax proportionately in coordination and vice versa. This is controlled by the complex reflex system. Other muscles are recognized according to their function, e.g., abductors, adductors, rotators, levators, depressors, etc. The proximal attachment of the muscle (closer to the axial skeleton) is known as the *origin* of the muscle. The distal end, attached to the other bone at some distance is known as the *insertion* of the muscle. When the muscle is contracted, it shortens and becomes thicker in the middle part. This can be observed at the biceps of the arm. When we bend our hand with the force, the girth of the biceps increases and the length is decreased.

The important sense parts that are situated in muscles and tendons are *muscle spindles* (Fig. 15) and *tendon organs*.

They send information to the brain about the state of muscle (contraction or the stretching) so that the muscle is either relaxed or stretched as the case may be. This function is important in order to protect the muscles and tendons in extreme contraction and stretching from being ruptured or damaged. This function is known as a *stretch reflex*. It helps in maintaining the posture.

DIAPHRAGM

It is one of the most important skeletal muscles in our body, which separates the thoracic, and the abdominal cavities, serving as a partition between these two cavities. It is a dome shaped sheet of voluntary muscle. Its convex surface touches the heart and the lungs. Its central part consists of a tendon, known as *tendinous center*.

It originates from the xiphoid process of sternum, sixth lower ribs on each side and lumbar vertebrae. Its end (insertion) merges at the central tendon of the diaphragm. There are three openings in the diaphragm, through which the aorta, oesophagus and the inferior vena cava pass down to the abdominal part. Diaphragm is the principal muscle for respiration. When it contracts, the central tendon is drawn downwards. It descends down with the result that the vertical diameter of the thorax increases and the negative pressure is created in the thoracic cage. As a result the lungs are stretched. They get expanded and the negative pressure is now produced in the lungs. The atmospheric air is inhaled or rather sucked into the lungs due to this sub-atmospheric (suction) pressure in the lungs. The descent of the diaphragm exerts a gentle pressure upon the abdominal parts. This acts as a massage for these parts and maintains proper muscle tone in them. During exhalation the diaphragm relaxes and resumes its former position. Due to this rising of a diaphragm, the vertical diameter of the thorax decreases. This exerts pressure on the lungs and thus the air is forced out during the exhalation. Thus the downward and upward movements of the diaphragm during inspiration and expiration produce relatively positive and negative pressures in the visceral cavities. Functions like micturition, defecation, and inhalation are normally assisted by this mechanism. The breathing in which the movement of the diaphragm becomes more prominent, is known as *diaphragmatic breathing*. During a hiccup there is a sudden and sharp contraction of the diaphragm, causing jerky inhalation, sucking the air quickly and with a typical sound.

ABDOMINAL RECTI MUSCLES

These muscles are also known as *rectus abdominus* muscles. These are the skeletal muscles in the form of bands on the anterior side of the stomach, forming the abdominal wall. They are situated vertically on the right and left sides of the median line (Fig. 14).

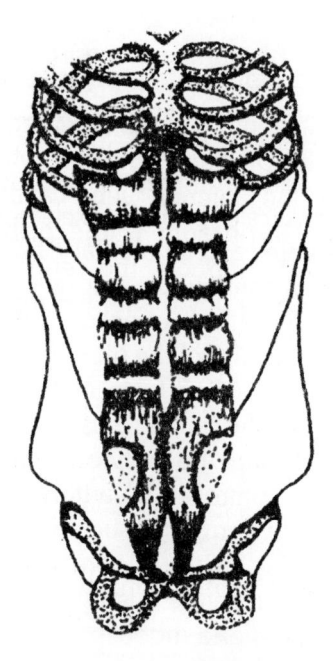

Fig. 14: Rectus Abdominus

The origin of these muscles is at the pubic bone (pubic crest and symphysis pubis) while the insertion is at the cartilage of fifth to seventh ribs and xiphoid process. These muscles possess horizontal tendinous bands or intersections. Rectus abdominus muscles along with other muscles support the visceral parts and hold them in their respective places. The contraction of these muscles causes flexion of the vertebral column, e.g., bending forward. Being strong, these muscles help in vigorous actions that involve flexion. During respiratory phases they are contracted and relaxed in co ordination with the diaphragm and create mechanical pressure on the abdominal parts. If the proper tone or the tension of these muscles is not maintained, their strength is reduced and they become loose. They are now easily pushed forward due to the pressure of the abdominal parts. We shall consider these muscles in the study of *Nauli kriya*.

INVOLUNTARY MUSCLES

CARDIAC MUSCLE

Cardiac muscle is an involuntary muscle, which works quite independently of our will. That means we cannot control them directly as per our wish. Cardiac muscle normally initiates its own contractions and continues to contract rhythmically. It possesses characteristics of both the skeletal as well as smooth muscles, i.e., it is striated and involuntary also. The muscle mass of cardiac muscle is continuous and its cells are intertwined with each other so that the contraction once initiated spreads over the complete structure of the muscle. Refractory period of cardiac muscle is longer (0.30 sec) than the skeletal muscle (0.005 sec). Therefore, the cardiac muscle cannot contract again unless it is relaxed after the previous contraction. Cardiac muscle is also partly controlled by autonomic nervous system and influenced by the hormones such as adrenaline and noradrenaline, circulating in the blood. Although the cardiac function is involuntary in nature, it is influenced due to emotional and attitudinal changes and moods.

SMOOTH MUSCLE

Smooth muscle is also an involuntary muscle, which does not work under our volition. It is controlled by the autonomic nervous system and its own stretch reflex mechanism. Smooth muscle forms the walls of the hollow visceral parts like stomach, intestine, urinary bladder and uterus. This tissue is spindle shaped, having an oval shaped nucleus in the center. Smooth muscle contracts and relaxes very slowly. Its contraction is very powerful; e.g., contraction of uterus during childbirth, and another important aspect in which smooth muscle differs from skeletal and cardiac muscle is that it can remain contracted for a long period without any additional expenditure of energy, e.g., urinary bladder. It can remain in a contracted state for a considerable time during urination. Smooth muscle can stretch without developing tension. The arrangement of smooth muscle tissue in the walls of intestine and blood vessel is typical. An outer longitudinal layer of muscle covers the inner circular layer of smooth muscle. The contraction of these layers help in pushing the food bolus forward during digestion and conducting the blood during blood circulation. Increase in the contents of the organ beyond certain limit causes overstretching which acts as a stimulus for the smooth muscle contraction.

MUSCLE TONE

Muscles are never relaxed completely even in the resting condition. A muscle is usually in a state of partial contraction, showing some amount of tension in it. During resting, the joints are relaxed and the muscles are slightly stretched. This mild stretching initiates a stretch reflex, which cannot cause full contraction of the muscle but makes some of the muscle fibers to contract. This gives rise to some kind of tension, which tightens the muscle. Since different groups of muscle fibers contract alternately a steady tension is maintained in the whole muscle without fatigue. In maintaining this tone the metabolism of the muscle shows negligible increase.

Thus a *muscle tone* is a degree of minimum contraction present in the muscle at rest. It is a sort of a preparation of the muscle that forms the basis for further muscle action. An adequate tone is therefore required for the normal muscle activity. Muscle tone is minimum during sleep. It may be completely abolished only by cutting the nerve supply of the muscle. Muscle tone is an inherent property of a muscle at rest. It is also an example of isometric contraction since the muscle becomes tense without actually shortening.

Cerebral cortex regulates the muscle tone through a simple mechanism. The cerebellum also influences muscle tone. An adequate muscle tone maintains the position of the limbs at rest, supports the viscera and provides a basal level for muscular contraction on which the active movements are superimposed. The strength of a voluntary movement depends also upon the tone of that muscle besides the other factors like initial length and size of the fibers and the number of motor units activated.

During the maintenance of muscle tone, a pumping action on the blood vessels takes place which helps in blood circulation. As each group of muscle fiber contracts alternately, it squeezes the blood out of the capillaries into the veins and thus helps in maintaining continuous flow of blood back to the heart.

The basis of posture is muscle tone. The stability and the position of the body depends upon the presence of adequate degree of muscle tone. The feedback information from muscle spindles (stretch receptors) brings about reflex adjustments in the degree of muscle tone. For example, the neck muscles maintain the position of the head in anatomical position just because the muscle tone of the neck muscles is maintained in a proper degree with the help of this stretch reflex.

Different emotional states influence the muscle tone. Intense emotional excitement, fear, anxiety, happiness, confidence, etc., can give rise to increased muscular tone or strength. This in turn would influence the posture. If the individual is in a sad or depressed or disappointed mood, the muscle tone is decreased and the muscles are greatly relaxed. At this moment if the person were in sitting condition, he would bend forward (flexion). A confident or happy person on the other hand would extend his body. Emotions can interfere with the coordinated movements, making them disorganized. Emotions can also influence the cardiac and smooth muscles and change their tone. It has been

The Muscular System

seen with the help of X-ray studies that on irritation by just a few words, when a person becomes angry, the muscular tone of the stomach is changed and therefore its shape and contour. When the same person relaxes and meditates, the stomach regains its normal shape and size. On the basis of the degree of muscle tone, following conditions are generally observed.

1. Hypotonic condition

In this condition the muscle tone is inadequate and remains on the lower level than what is required. Strong emotions like disappointment, depression, failure, fear, unhappiness, affection, shame, despair, disgust, distress, devotion, etc., can reduce the muscle tone. The person becomes inactive and sluggish in his actions if this reduction in tone is extreme. Muscles will relax too much and the body will undergo a flexion attitude. If this condition persists for longer period under constant influence of these emotions, various abnormal changes will take place at the functional level and the individual may suffer from any disorder such as low blood pressure, lack of confidence, drowsiness, hypoacidity, colitis, obesity, atonicity, headache, flaccidity, inferiority complex, skin troubles, tremors, etc. The person may become passive or slow in action and may develop a tendency to escape from the situation.

While teaching *asanas* to the student or the patient a teacher should consider the muscular tone of the person.

2. Hypertonic condition

In this condition the muscle tone is increased maximum above the required level. Muscles offer strong resistance against any movement due to increased tone and give rise to muscular tension. Muscles become more rigid and the contractions are so strong that there is no proper movement of the joint or the whole body. Strong emotions like extreme happiness, love, anger, jealousy, envy, hatred, hate, hope, and greed increase the muscle tone. Person becomes hyperactive, fast and hasty in his actions. He may possess highly impulsive, agitating and irritating nature. He may be lean, thin, slim or weak in his built, having a superiority complex. His ego may remain inflated and he may also be overconfident. Other conditions, which may be associated with this hypertonicity are hypertension, high blood pressure, muscular tension, tremors, insomnia, spasticity, unsteadiness and a hasty nature.

A yoga teacher must think of the possibility of these conditions for his students and should modify his training accordingly, since the performance of the individuals will depend on such conditions. A yoga therapist should consider these tonic conditions of his patients while planning the line of yogic treatment because the result of the treatment will depend on these basic conditions. If these tonic conditions are not considered while learning and practicing *asanas*, one may cross his limits in bending and stretching the trunk and the limbs. This may be dangerous for the joints and tendons. We would discuss about these conditions again in the chapter on *asanas* to know how yogic practices help to balance these conditions and maintain adequate tone in the muscles.

STRETCH REFLEX

Stretch reflex is an important factor for the posture and the movement. Stretching a muscle little beyond its particular limit causes reflex contraction of the same muscle. We have seen that the skeletal muscle contains highly specialized receptor organ known as muscle spindle (proprioceptor), which is very sensitive to a slight stretching of the muscle.

A simple example of a stretch reflex is the knee jerk. A subject sits in a chair by crossing one leg over the other and the upper leg is kept loose. The quadriceps muscle on the front side of the thigh remains slightly stretched in this condition. Now a tap on the patellar tendon just below the kneecap stretches the quadriceps a little more. As this stretching crosses the optimum limit of it's stretching, the quadriceps contract quickly in response to this overstretching and the leg moves forward with a sharp jerk. The hamstring muscles (flexors of knee) are relaxed in order to allow the extension of the leg in this reflex action.

The Muscular System

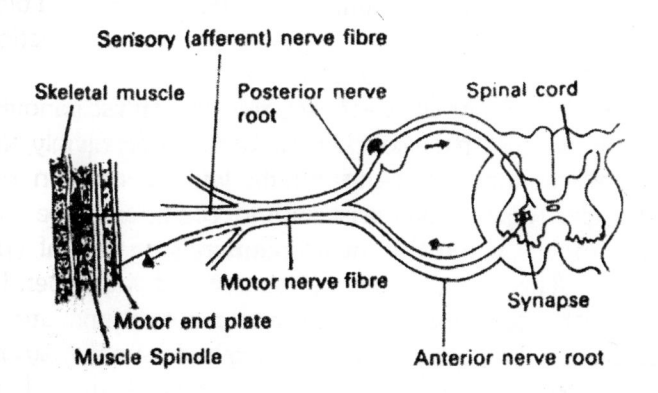

Fig. 15: The Stretch Reflex Arc

When a muscle is stretched, the muscle spindle is stimulated. It sends impulses (information) to the sensory neuron in the corresponding part of the spinal cord through (ascending) sensory nerve fibers. The sensory neuron synapses directly with motor neuron in the spinal cord. A motor nerve impulse reaches the muscle (here quadriceps) through motor nerve and the muscle contracts (Fig.15). Thus stretch reflex is a protective mechanism for the muscle. It protects the muscle from being torn or overstretched. In the absence of this reflex mechanism the muscle would have been damaged. Muscle tone is an example of simple stretch reflex as the muscle is stretched between the bones and in response it is contracted to maintain necessary tension in the muscle.

TENDON ORGAN

This is another type of receptor (proprioceptor) in the tendons of skeletal muscles. Tendon parts are the specialized endings of sensory nerve fiber in the form of knobs. When the stretching of the muscle results into its reflex contraction and increases its tension on the tendon, the tendon may be ruptured or torn if the tension is too much. Thus the tendon organ acts as a safety measure during stretch reflex mechanism, stopping further contraction of the muscle by inhibiting the stretch reflex.

ISOMETRIC CONTRACTION

When a muscle is not allowed to shorten, the contraction merely causes an increase in tension. During such contraction the length of the muscle does not change but the tension is developed in the muscle. This is known as *isometric contraction* of muscle. This happens when the muscle contracts against a strong resistance. The best example of this is the 'bull worker'. One has to push both the ends of this instrument or pull the cords and maintain the position for some length of time. If the muscle is contracted regularly in this way it increases in girth and becomes stronger. However, there is no increase in the endurance, which on the contrary may be reduced because the blood supply to this bulky muscle is inadequate when the workload on it is increased. Such an attractive muscular development is necessary for the body-building contest.

Isometric exercises bring about considerable increase in the heart rate and blood pressure due to which the weak arteries may rupture. Therefore, these kinds of exercises are not recommended for old people, which may be otherwise dangerous for them.

The isometric contraction, however, helps us to maintain a steady posture. Isometric contraction produces less heat than in the isotonic contraction as the muscle does not become shorter. The mechanism of these two types of contractions is otherwise similar. Comparatively, the perspiration is less and the energy consumption is more in isometric muscle contraction than isotonic contraction.

ISOTONIC CONTRACTION

When a contracting muscle is free to shorten the tension does not increase but the length of the muscle is reduced. Its girth is increased. There is no resistance against the contraction. This brings about an easy movement of the body or the part of it.

The Muscular System

The normal movements of the body are dominated by the isotonic contractions. In this contraction more heat is produced with perspiration. All the warming-up exercises contain this type of muscular contraction. Running, swimming, drill, parade are the few examples of isotonic contraction. These isotonic exercises increase the stamina and endurance of the individual. Energy requirement in isotonic contraction is slightly less than that in isometric contraction.

Any complex muscular activity involves finely coordinated isometric and isotonic muscle contractions. We cannot differentiate between these two types of contractions in a given muscular activity. Knowledge of these two types of muscular activities is essential so as to understand the mechanism of *asanas*, which is slightly of a different nature.

OXYGEN DEBT

In a moderate muscular exercise a steady supply of oxygen even up to 2 liters per minute can be maintained, keeping pace with the chemical changes in the muscles. However, during strenuous exercise the energy expenditure exceeds the rate at which oxygen should be supplied to the contracting muscles. When muscles contract without adequate supply of oxygen or in the absence of oxygen (anaerobically), the breakdown of glycogen results in excess production of lactic acid. Lactic acid accumulates in greater amounts as it cannot be removed easily from the muscles. This gives rise to an **oxygen debt**, which has to be repaid immediately after the heavy muscular work is stopped. So the oxygen debt is the amount of oxygen required to convert additional lactic acid into glycogen. The oxygen is supplied to the muscle through the circulating blood. Naturally then the rate and depth of breathing will increase automatically. A prolonged overbreathing after the cessation of the exercise (such as sprint) is well known. Thus oxygen debt is paid back after the anaerobic activity is over.

MUSCULAR FATIGUE

Frequently repeated contractions or sustained contraction of skeletal muscle for a long time, reduces the strength of contraction slowly and gradually. Finally the muscle does not respond to any stimulation. This condition is known as *muscular fatigue*. It results from diminished supply of oxygen and the toxic effects of accumulated lactic acid and carbon dioxide during continuous exercise. The energy is also fully consumed in this situation. If the supply of oxygen and glucose through blood is adequate and prompt, the onset of muscular fatigue is delayed. Short but intensive physical exertion also develops the muscular fatigue rapidly if the muscles are not previously trained. Muscular efficiency also depends on the workload and the duration of work. When a muscle is completely fatigued it fails to respond to further stimulation and ceases to work. In such conditions proper rest, relaxation and supply of glucose are immediate requirements besides the oxygen. No doubt other systems like cardiovascular, respiratory and endocrine system also contribute to the working capacity of the muscles. Psychological factors like motivation (interest), appreciation, mood and anxiety also influence the muscular efficiency. A systematic and regular psychophysical training improves the muscle tone and therefore the endurance, strength, vigor and work output of the individual. Yoga postures also improve the minimum muscular fitness required for day-to-day activities.

From yoga point of view

1. Due to emotional impact muscle tone is affected which in turn disturbs the functions of the body. If *asanas* are performed in a relaxed way the coordination between the nervous and the muscular systems increases, the muscle tone is corrected and thus the emotions are balanced.
2. If the muscle is stretched forcefully beyond its limits and such stretch is maintained, the muscle also tries to contract with force and shows its resistance. This tug-of-war gives rise to tremors in the muscles. With this increased muscular work, the breathing and circulation also increase. Therefore, do not perform *asanas* with jerks or undue force. Know your basic muscle tone and practice *asanas* accordingly.

The Muscular System

3. If the movements are done with minimum force and efforts, the muscular tension or the resistance does not increase. The flexibility and the degree of movement of the joints improve. That is why the warming-up exercises, done prior to *asanas*, are beneficial.
4. When the muscles are relaxed, the muscle tone is reduced and at this moment there is no scope for worries and tensions.
5. During *uddiyan* and *nauli* the diaphragm and the rectus abdominus muscles are contracted and therefore the positive or negative pressure is created in the abdomen.
6. During *bandhas* and *mudras*, specific muscle sphincters are brought into action in order to stimulate related nerve plexuses, e.g., in *Ashwini mudra* the anal sphincters are alternately contracted and relaxed.
7. We can reduce the energy expenditure during *asanas*, by reducing the muscular efforts while practicing them in a peaceful and a relaxed way.

Six

The Nervous System

The nervous system controls the functions of different organs and the activities of the entire organism as a whole. It works through sensation, integration and response, to maintain homeostasis. This *neural base* is responsible for moment-to-moment adjustment, immediate coordination and communication with the internal and external environment from where the stimuli are constantly received. The system responds quickly to the sudden change in internal as well as external environment. It links various organs and systems, coordinates their functions and maintains the integrity of the organism. Any change in the function of one organ or system leads to changes in the functions of other organs or systems. For example, during the vigorous muscular work, large quantity of carbon dioxide is produced which is brought to the lungs to be thrown out of the body. This requires faster blood circulation and rapid respiration. Such necessity is informed to the brain centers, which in turn accelerate the cardio-respiratory function. The blood supply to the working muscles increases and at the same time the heat production and loss of heat also increase. All these rapid but well coordinated changes are brought about by the nervous system.

According to the functions, the nervous system may be divided into two principal divisions:

1. *The Central Nervous System (CNS)*
2. *The Autonomic Nervous System (ANS)*

ANS is further divided into two parts. (i) *Sympathetic nervous system* and (ii) *Parasympathetic Nervous System.*

The Central Nervous System includes brain, spinal cord, 12 pairs of cranial nerves, arising from the brain and 31 pairs of spinal nerves. All the organs and tissues are connected with the brain by numerous branches of these nerves. These nerves and their branches constitute the *Peripheral Nervous System (PNS)*.

The brain and the spinal cord are the large masses of nerve cells (neurons), their processes and neuralgia cells. The cranium encloses the brain. Spinal cord is an elongated structure, which is a prolongation of the brain. It is very well secured in the hollow space of the spinal column. The brain and the spinal column are composed of *gray* and *white matter*. The gray matter consists of nerve cells while the white matter consists of nerve fibers, which are the processes (axons) of the nerve cells. In the spinal cord the gray matter forms the inner part, surrounded by the outer layer of white matter. In the brain it is just reverse, gray matter forms the outer part while the white matter lies on the inner side. Some of the cells of the nervous system perform the function of support and protection to the rest of the parts of the nervous system. These are known as *neuralgia*. They form a protective sheath around the nerves and attach neurons to the blood vessels.

Nerve cells called neurons are the structural and functional units of the nervous system (Fig. 7). *Dendrites* are the highly branched processes of neurons. *Axon* is a single, thin and long process of neuron. The impulse is received by the dendrite and passed on to the cell body of neuron. The impulse is conducted from the neuron to the other neuron through the axon.

Generally speaking, there are two types of nerve impulses, which form the basis of any nervous function. (1) *Inhibitory impulses*, which slow down the function of the concerned organ or stops it completely. (2) *Excitatory impulses* or transmission which facilitates the function. That means the function will be accelerated. For example, the flexion of the elbow requires proper balance in these two types of impulses reaching the elbow so that the biceps are contracted and at the same time the triceps are relaxed. Both the transmissions are properly integrated within the nervous system.

All the nerves, coming from the brain and the spinal cord, spread themselves forming the network of their branches all over the body. Even the area of the body equivalent to the apex of a pin is not left without the nerve endings. The nerve at its origin is connected with a group of neurons, the *nerve center*, which has a special function. Nerve fibers are covered by connective tissue, which forms insulation. The nerves, which conduct impulses (of order) from the CNS to the muscles and the glands, are called *efferent* or *motor nerves*. The nerves, which convey impulses (information) from receptors in the periphery of the body to the CNS, are called *afferent* or *sensory nerves*. Some of the nerves contain the motor as well as sensory nerve fibers. These are known as *mixed nerves*.

CEREBRUM

Cerebrum is the major bulk of the brain, which is well protected inside the skull. It is composed of two halves on the right and the left side, known as *cerebral hemispheres*. The two hemispheres are internally linked by the corpus callosum, which consists nerve fibers. The outer layer of the cerebrum is composed of gray matter, which contains the nerve cells. It is about 2–4 millimeter thick and is known as *Cerebral cortex*. The surface area of the cortex is increased due to convolutions or the folds. Each cerebral hemisphere is subdivided into four lobes by deep grooves (fissures). These are, frontal lobes, temporal lobes, parietal lobes and occipital lobes. Inner part of the cerebrum consists of numerous nerve fibers (white matter), which connect the cortex to various other parts of the brain. Hollow spaces or the cavities within the cerebrum are called *ventricles*, which are filled with the *cerebrospinal fluid*.

Each half of the cerebral hemisphere is controlling the functions of the opposite side of the body. However, there are many functions of the body, like swallowing, breathing, etc., that are controlled by both the hemispheres. *Basal ganglia* are the paired, complicated arrangement of masses of nerve cells. These are deeply situated in each hemisphere. They are connected with the cortex, spinal cord and the cerebellum by an intricate network of nerve fibers and the descending tracts. These structures are connected with the regulation of posture and the performance of habitual and automatic movements of the body for daily activities.

Certain components of the cerebral hemispheres, thalamus and hypothalamus together constitute the *limbic system*, which is concerned with the emotional aspects and behavioral pattern of the individual. It is associated with emotions like pleasure, pain anger, fear, sexual feelings, love and affection.

The cerebrum performs numerous complex functions. The cerebral cortex is divided into sensory, motor and association areas according to their nature of function. The *sensory area* is located at the posterior side of the brain. It receives sensory impulses from the skin sensory organs like eyes, tongue, etc., and other receptors from various parts of the body. The sensory area interprets these sensory impulses into appropriate sensation. *Motor area* lies in the anterior part of the brain. It generates impulses which cause muscles to contract, makes us to speak and at the same time regulate our breathing as per the speech. *Association area* connects motor and sensory areas. It occupies maximum surface on the lateral sides of all the lobes. This area is concerned with our memory, emotions, intelligence, will, reasoning, judgment and personality traits. Consciousness, arousal, awareness, sleep, thinking, imagination, analysis of the sensations, are other important functions of the cerebrum. In short, the cerebral cortex has the supreme control over the whole body.

The *thalamus* is an oval structure, composed of two large egg-shaped masses of gray matter, one on each side of the third ventricle. Thalamus is an important relay station for sensory impulses before they reach the cortex while coming from other parts of the nervous system. Thalamus interprets some of the sensory impulses for pain, temperature, pressure, etc. Thalamus and the hypothalamus constitute the diencephalon. **Hypothalamus** is a small portion below the thalamus, having nuclei in it. Hypothalamus is involved in the integration of the autonomic nervous system, the endocrine system and other bodily functions. It is an important area of the brain to regulate internal environment and to maintain homeostasis (refer page 87). Thus it controls metabolism, heat production and heat loss, arterial blood pressure and cardiac activity. Hypothalamus lies just above the pituitary gland and controls its function. Hypothalamus regulates food intake and thirst. It is also associated with different emotional behaviors of the individual. It controls and integrates the Autonomic Nervous System, especially when it is dealing with the smooth and cardiac muscles and glands.

CEREBELLUM

The cerebellum is located at the posterior side of the medulla and pons, and below the occipital lobes of the cerebrum. Right and left lobes of the cerebellum have a constricted area in the middle part. Cerebrum and cerebellum are well connected with each other and also with the medulla and pons.

Activities of the cerebellum are of reflex nature (below the level of consciousness) and we are not aware of them. Once the voluntary movements are initiated, their coordination depends on the cerebellum. Various proprioceptors are engaged in sending the sensory impulses to the cerebral cortex and inform it about the degree of muscle contraction and the joint movements. The cerebral cortex generates a pattern of impulses and sends them to the cerebellum via pons and the mid-brain. The cerebellum then sends motor impulses (as an action plan) along the spinal cord to the agonist and antagonist muscles and thus brings about smooth and well-coordinated movements. The cerebellum maintains normal muscle tone and controls the posture at the subconscious level, i.e., without our attention. It also maintains the body equilibrium, which depends on the information sent by the internal ear about the position of the body in space. Walking, running, dancing and all other skillful movements are regulated by the cerebellum. The emotions like anger and pleasure influence the cerebellum and bring about the changes in the muscle tone.

The *medulla oblongata* and *pons* form the inferior part of the brain stem. Pons lies above the medulla and anterior to the cerebellum. Pons is a bridge connecting the spinal cord with the brain. It contains the network of the nerve fibers and conducts ascending (sensory) and descending (motor) impulses through them. Medulla contains three vitally important reflex centers for cardiac activity, respiration and vasomotor function. It coordinates swallowing, vomiting, coughing, sneezing and hiccupping. It also helps salivation and digestive activity. The cortex and other parts of the brain influence functions of medulla and pons. An important part—*Reticular formation* or *reticular activating system* (RAS)—lies partly in medulla and partly in pons, spinal cord and diencephalon. The sensory (proprioceptive) impulses activate the RAS. Once the RAS is stimulated, the cerebral cortex is also activated and we experience *arousal*. There is a feedback system amongst the cortex, RAS and the limbic system. Thus a state of *consciousness*, alertness, attentiveness and relaxation, depends on the number of feedback circuits operating at a time. When the sensory inputs are less, the inactivation of the RAS induces a state known as *sleep*.

CRANIAL NERVES

Out of 12 pairs of cranial nerves, 10 originate from the brain stem. First, second and eighth pairs are *sensory nerves*. The third, fourth, sixth, seventh, eleventh and twelfth pairs are *motor nerves*. However, fifth, ninth and tenth pairs contain both sensory and motor fibers and therefore they are known as *mixed nerves*. The cranial nerves mainly innervate the organs in the skull, e.g., eyes, ears, nose etc., while the tenth pair (vagus) which is mixed in nature, innervates visceral organs like esophagus, respiratory pathways, lungs, heart, large intestine, small intestine, stomach and gall bladder and controls their functions.

SPINAL CORD

The spinal cord begins as a continuation of the medulla oblongata. It passes through the spine and extends up to the end of first lumbar vertebra. On its anterior (front) and the posterior (back) side there is a longitudinal groove or fissure which divides it incompletely into symmetrical right and left halves. The spinal cord is well protected by *dura mater*, the tough outer fibrous covering and the inner *pia mater*, the delicate and transparent fibrous membrane around it. The spinal cord consists of outer white matter surrounding the inner H-shaped gray matter. The gray matter consists of nerve cell bodies and un-myelinated (uncovered) axons and dendrites of neurons. The white matter consists of bundles of myelinated axons of motor and sensory neurons. The upright portions of H-shaped gray matter look like horns. The *anterior gray horns* (ventral) represent the motor part of the gray matter. The *posterior gray horns* (dorsal) represent the sensory part of the gray matter. The white matter is also organized into anterior white columns and posterior white columns. Each column consists of bundles of myelinated fibers called tracts. These are the ascending and descending tracts of sensory and motor axons (fibers) respectively.

A *spinal nerve* is a mixed nerve. At the starting point of the nerve near the spinal cord it attaches with the spinal cord by a posterior root and an anterior root. The posterior root contains sensory fibers and the anterior root contains motor nerve fibers. There are 31 such pairs of spinal nerve, i.e., eight cervical, twelve thoracic, five lumbar, five sacral and one coccygeal nerve emerging out of intervertebral foramen.

The ventral branches of the spinal nerves, except thoracic nerves, form networks on either side of the spinal column, by joining with adjacent nerves. Such network is known as a *plexus*. The nerves emerging from these plexuses then innervate the specific structure. The *cervical plexus* is connected with the skin and muscles of the head, neck and upper part of the shoulders, some cranial nerves and the diaphragm. The *brachial plexus* provides nerve supply to the upper extremities, some muscles of neck and shoulders. The *lumbar plexus* is connected with the upper abdominal wall, external genitals and partly the lower extremities. The *sacral plexus* gives off nerves to the buttocks, perineum and lower extremities.

Main functions of the spinal cord are, (1) conduction of nerve impulses and (2) reflex activity. It conducts motor impulses from the brain to the periphery and sensory impulses from periphery to brain, along the descending and ascending nervous pathways respectively. A reflex action is a quick involuntary response to a stimulus coming from the internal or the external environment.

THE REFLEX ACTION

The reflex action is the functional unit of the nervous system. Reflex action is a quick response to the changes in the body or the atmosphere, which helps our body to maintain homeostasis. Such changes in the temperature, potassium, carbon dioxide or oxygen concentrations, pressure, stretch, pain and sensory inputs, etc., act as stimulation. Most of our body functions are controlled by reflex actions, e.g., heart activity, respiration, digestion, urination and defecation. An arc is a circuitry pathway traveled by an impulse to bring about the reflex action (Fig.16). Any reflex arc requires the following components:

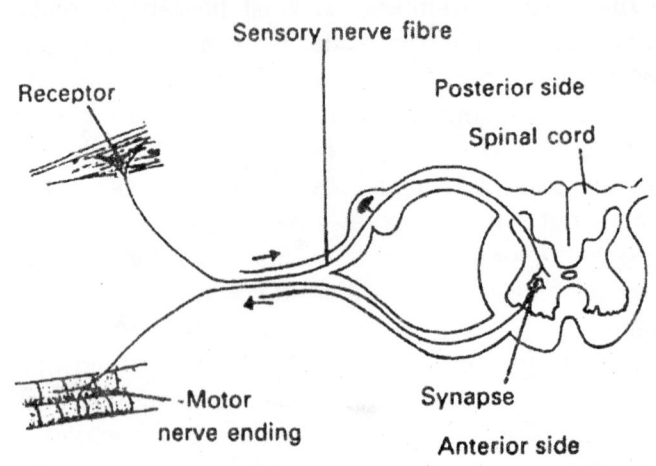

Fig.16: The Reflex Arc

1. Receptor

The dendrites of a sensory structure end in a most sensitive part (sensor), the receptor, which receives and detects the changes in the environment. This stimulation of a receptor initiates an impulse (carrying the information), which travels up to the sensory neuron.

2. Sensory neuron

It conveys the impulse coming from the receptor further to the integrating center or central nervous system through afferent pathways.

3. Integrating center

This is a region in the central nervous system, e.g., in the spinal column, where the motor impulse is generated and passed on to the motor neuron.

4. Motor neuron

It transmits the impulse generated by the sensory neuron or the integrating center to the effector, through the efferent pathways.

5. Effector

Effector is the organ, either a muscle or gland, which works as per the motor impulse (direction or order). Thus the function or the action of the effector is the result of the reflex mechanism. This reflex action takes place below the level of consciousness (without our notice or awareness).

The reflex actions carried out by the spinal cord alone are called *spinal reflexes*. The contraction of the smooth muscle and the glandular secretion in response to the stretching of the alimentary wall (due to food) are the examples of the *visceral reflex*. This may be in association with the autonomic nervous system, as in case of emotional changes. The knee jerk is an example of the *stretch reflex*. Sometimes when the reflex actions are complicated, the cerebral cortex and the cerebellum are also involved for the co-ordination and the execution of the reflex action. Muscle tone is regulated by the stretch reflex. Our postures are maintained due to *postural reflexes* produced due to our peculiar posture.

It may be noted that the reflex action is a part of the nervous system. The stronger sensory impulses are allowed to reach at the higher brain centers to take right type of action with full awareness. If you happen to step on some sharp or pointed material, your leg is withdrawn due to contraction of the flexors. This is a *flexor reflex*, e.g., if the stimulation is repeated or is too intensive, you would become cautious about your steps and would avoid sharp things. Cough reflex is also an example of protective reflex.

Salivation occurs as a simple *inborn reflex* action in response to the presence of food in the mouth. The secretion of saliva also takes place in response to just sight, smell of appetizing food. Even a sound of a dinner bell or even thinking of delicious food will stimulate salivary glands. This is an involuntary activity where the inborn reflex gets associated with the stimulus, which is abnormal or new for the nerve center. This is an example of the *conditioned reflex*. The cortex interprets an abnormal stimulus and if it is appropriate (acceptable), it is adapted with the inborn reflexes. The process of learning is an example of the conditioned reflexes. Conditioned reflexes are acquired during the whole life span of a man, which are strictly individual and are never constant. They may disappear or appear again and again. Once acquired, they take place as if they are inborn reflexes.

AUTONOMIC NERVOUS SYSTEM

A part of the nervous system, controlling the functions of smooth muscles, cardiac muscles and glands is known as *vegetative or autonomic nervous system (ANS)*. It works without the direct control from the brain. However, it is also influenced by the centers in the cerebral cortex, hypothalamus and medulla oblongata. ANS is entirely efferent (motor) in nature. The impulses from the CNS are transmitted by these efferent nerve fibers of ANS to the visceral organs. Hypothalamus, however,

The Nervous System

receives afferent (sensory) impulses from the visceral organs. ANS is divided into two main divisions. (1) *Sympathetic* and (2) *Parasympathetic* nervous system (Fig. 17).

The sympathetic branch consists mainly two chains of ganglia on either side of the vertebral column in the cervical, thoracic and lumbar regions. Some of the sympathetic fibers terminate in the solar plexus. From here the fibers are distributed to the stomach, spleen, liver, kidney and small and large intestines.

The parasympathetic division of ANS includes nuclei located in the brain stem, ganglia and in the second, third, fourth sacral segments of the spinal cord, third, seventh, nineth, and thenth pairs of cranial nerves contain parasympathetic fibers. Both sympathetic and parasympathetic nerve fibers innervate almost all the organs in abdominal and thoracic cavities such as digestive organs, blood vessels, excretory organs, eyes, salivary glands and skull. It may be noted that the hypothalamic region of the brain contains higher nervous centers for ANS.

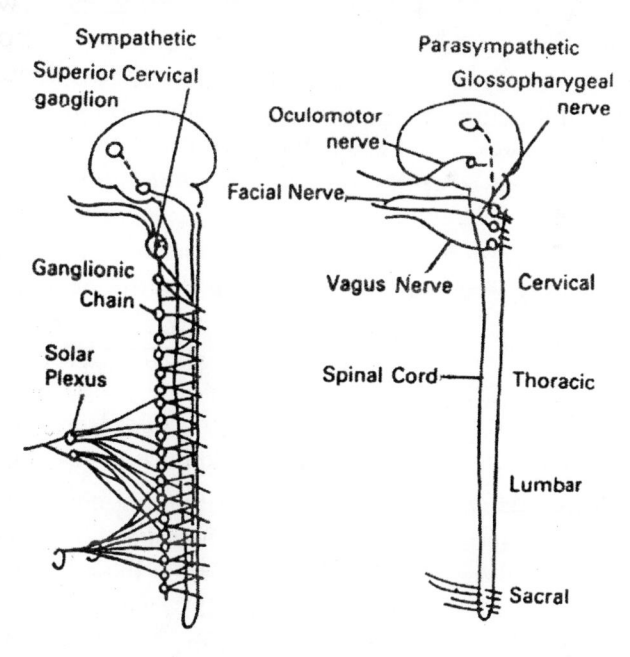

Fig. 17: Autonomic Nervous System

Life processes, which are ever going on in our body without our attention, are all under the influence of ANS. Production of bile in the liver, metabolism, secretion of pancreatic juice, function of heart, micturition (passing of urine), defecation (expulsion of feces), parturition in female (labor), control of diameter of the blood vessels, nasal congestion and decongestion are some of the examples.

Since both the divisions of ANS innervate most of the effector organs, they are finely controlled. Both the divisions work in coordination with each other for smooth functioning of the organs, e.g., sympathetic impulses increase heart rate where as parasympathetic impulses decrease it. Stimulation of sympathetic nervous system brings about the typical physiological responses, collectively known as fight or flight response. It dilates the pupils of the eyes, increases the heart rate, constricts the small blood vessels of the skin and viscera, dilates coronary arteries of the heart, elevates blood pressure, increases breathing, relaxes bronchioles, increases blood sugar level, reduces digestive activity, stimulates adrenal medulla to produce more adrenaline and non-adrenaline that would further intensify the action of sympathetic nervous system. Thus it prepares the individual to face the stressful situations. This is a defense mechanism of the body. Extreme emotions like, fear and anger can also stimulate the sympathetic nervous system. Exercise also stimulates it.

The parasympathetic division on the contrary responds in exactly the opposite way. It constricts the pupils, increases the secretion of salivary glands and lachrymal glands, slows down the heart, increases digestive activity and the peristalsis, constricts bronchi, dilates blood vessels and increases heat loss, etc.

In short, the sympathetic system prepares the body to cope up with the changes in the external or internal environment, e.g., stress or danger. It helps those body activities, which require more energy. The parasympathetic system on the other hand is primarily concerned with functions that restore the resting conditions after the physical activity or the emergency is over and thus conserves the body energy. In normal resting condition or the process of homeostasis, both the divisions counteract each other (and establish a balanced condition) just to carry out the normal processes. ANS is also influenced by various emotional states of the individual, e.g., love, hatred, fear, depression, etc., since the activity of ANS is regulated by the hypothalamus in the brain and hypothalamus is also a center related with emotional changes. In normal conditions a very fine functional balance is maintained in these two divisions of ANS. This is known as *autonomic balance*. This balance gets disturbed due to prolonged (chronic) physical, mental, emotional or hormonal changes in stressful situations.

Consciousness and Awareness

Nerve impulses from sensory organs such as eyes, ears, skin, muscles, joints, etc., reach thalamus and reticular activating system (RAS) and then to wide spread area of the cerebral cortex. The cortical activity is increased and this state is known as *wakefulness* or *consciousness*. During sleep the sensory inputs like bright light, alarm of the clock, touch, any unknown and loud sound, pain, etc., can activate RAS and through it the particular part of the cerebral cortex which causing *arousal* (awakening from sleep). We experience different levels of consciousness such as alertness, attentiveness (attention) or non-attentiveness, relaxation and drowsiness. The feedback system between cortex and RAS, spinal cord and the RAS, slows down or gets inhibited. When RAS is not further activated, some fatigue is accumulated and if the individual is in relaxed sitting or lying condition, a state is produced known as *sleep*.

RAS has connections with ascending and descending tracts in the spinal cord. It is an important relay station to pass ascending inputs to the thalamus and the cerebral cortex. Direct connection of these inputs (impulses) to the cortex produces the state of *awareness* and the impulses going through the thalamus arouse a particular region of cortex so that the *attention* is diverted to the incoming information (inputs). The information received is translated and we experience a *sensation*. When the nature of each and every sensation is analyzed and interpreted in the light of the past experience in appropriate region of the cerebral cortex, it is known as *recognition or perception* (Fig. 18).

The pattern of brain activity can be recorded on the paper with the help of a polygraph or electroencephalograph machine. The electrical potential difference between the two points on the scalp is recorded on the paper in waveform. The graph thus obtained, is known as *electroencephalogram* (EEG). Frequencies of the waves, recorded from different parts of the skull vary. EEG is a useful device to study different levels of consciousness. Relaxation, sleep, mental activity and even the 'eyes open' or 'eyes closed' condition can alter the EEG pattern, indicating different levels of consciousness. *Conscious experience* is a state when a person is thinking, feeling, imaging, dreaming, reasoning or perceiving with full awareness. The conscious experience is a result of co-ordinated interaction amongst many areas of the central nervous system.

The sensory impulses are generated when any of the five sense organs is stimulated due to changes in the external environment. The receptors in the external sense organs like eyes, nose are known as *exteroceptors*. They receive these stimulations and produce nerve impulses, which influence the RAS and cause sensation. Our awareness is drawn outside if the stimulation is strong enough. Similarly the changes in the internal environment (e.g., viscera) are received by the *interoceptors*. Thus, the sensory inputs from the internal organs can arouse internal awareness where our attention is drawn inward. We experience pain or pressure in the stomach in this way. Interoceptors are of two types, (1) *proprioreceptors*, which are present in the muscle spindles, joints, tendon organs and vestibular organs in the ear etc., and (2) *visceroreceptors*, which are sensory nerve endings, situated in the walls of stomach, blood vessels, urinary bladder, lungs, etc. Usually we remain aware of the external environment and rarely pay attention to the internal part of the body. We become aware only when we feel pain, hunger or burning sensation inside the body. When we close our eyes, the external stimulation in the form of light rays is cut off and we can pay better attention to the internal processes like breathing or visceral sensations. Most of the sensory nerve impulses, particularly those produced in posture or the involuntary functions of the body, do not reach RAS or the higher brain centers but give rise to different reflex controls.

An individual must be conscious in order to experience the sensation. When a stimulus is received by the receptor, an impulse is generated and conducted along the afferent nerves or the ascending pathways in the spinal cord to the nerve centers of the central nervous system. The sensory impulses, which are reaching only up to a certain segment of the spinal cord or the brain stem, initiate reflex motor action but cannot produce a sensation. The impulses that are reaching only up to the thalamus, produce *sensation*. When the sensory impulse is terminated in the thalamus, it gives rise to a sensation but its intensity and the location, from where the stimulation originated, cannot be detected. The cerebrum can detect this when the impulses reach the sensory area of the cortex. The sensation is analyzed and interpreted by the cerebral cortex in the light of the previous experience, e.g., a particular visual pattern of sensation is interpreted as 'tree' but it is perceived as a 'mango tree'. Thus the *perception* refers to the conscious registration of the sensory stimulus. Sensations and perceptions are very important for our communication with the environment. We can understand the sensation in terms of:

1. Nature or modality

Pressure, pain, temperature, touch, body position, movement, stretching, suction, throbbing, smell or taste.

2. Location or region

The exact area or the part of the body from where it is coming.

3. Intensity

Whether the stimulus or the sensation is mild, strong or acute.

```
STIMULATION OF THE RECEPTOR
            ⇩
SENSORY NERVE IMPULSE CONDUCTED ALONG
SENSORY PATHWAY (THROUGH SPINAL CORD)
            ⇩
SENSORY AREA OF CEREBRAL CORTEX
            ⇩
TRANSLATION INTO THE SENSATION,
PERCEPTION (STATE OF CONSCIOUSNESS)
            ⇩
AWARENESS OF THE
PARTICULAR SENSATION
            ⇩
ATTENTION TO THE PARTICULAR SENSATION
```

Fig.18: Consciousness and Awareness

4. Duration or period

Whether the stimulation or the sensation persists for a short or prolonged period.

From yoga point of view

1. We rarely become aware of the inner environment like we are not aware of our breathing. In order to turn our attention inward, *Hatha Yoga* has given *Pranadharana* technique, i.e. watching the flow of breath.
2. A potentiality to experience peculiar type of sensations arising during *asanas, pranayamas, dhyan*, etc., is developed gradually by regular and sincere practice with closed eyes and full concentration on the inner happenings.
3. In our day-to-day life our body is working as per our wish (voluntary control by the cerebrum). Thinking, analysis and modifications are constantly going on at the intellectual level. But when we are practicing yoga, such intellectual interference is not expected. Swimming, bicycle riding, typing, etc., once learned, are controlled by reflexes. Similarly after learning the technique of *asanas*, we can focus our attention to the infinite so that lower centers of the brain are free to maintain the posture efficiently and to correct and balance the muscle tone.
4. If strong muscular efforts are slackened and the interference of the cortex is reduced during the yoga practice, the effect of emotions and sympathetic nervous system is also reduced. When tension on the neuromuscular system is reduced, the psycho-physiological relaxation is established. Naturally then the load on the cardio-respiratory system is minimum.
5. Main objective of *asanas, pranayamas, bandhas* and *mudras* is to strengthen the nervous system so as to counter-balance the spiritual power of *kundalini*, when awakened.

Seven

The Endocrine System

This system consists of endocrine glands. There are two types of glands, exocrine and endocrine glands. *Exocrine glands* conduct their secretion to the point of action along the ducts. The endocrine glands pour their secretion, i.e., *hormones* directly into the blood vessels, which supply them blood. Endocrine glands are therefore also known as ductless glands as they have no ducts. Hormones are chemical substances, which act directly on the target cells and influence their physiological functions. This chemical base is responsible for the gradual but permanent or long-term adjustment with the environmental change, inside or outside the body. The balance in the secretion of various types of hormones is maintained indirectly by the nervous system through *negative feedback control*. Exception is the adrenal gland, which secrets epinephrine and norepinephrine in response to the stimulation by the sympathetic nerve impulses. Nervous system and the endocrine system co-operate with each other to maintain a physiological balance, i.e., homeostasis, constantly within the internal environment of the body. It has been experimentally proved that the hormones are also responsible for a particular behavioral pattern of the individual and the secretion of hormones is influenced by intense emotional ups and downs. Hormones bring about marked changes in the neural function and hence the behavior. That is how hormones play their role in the development of a particular mood, attitude, temperament or even the psychological make-up of the individual. This constitutes another branch of science, i.e., *psycho-neuro-endo-crinology*. For example, behavior of a woman at the time of puberty and menopause is typical. The central nervous system, particularly the hypothalamus, plays an important role in controlling hormone secretion. Hormones are of two types. (1) *water-soluble* and (2) *lipid-soluble hormones*. Hormones of the pituitary, parathyroids, pancreas and adrenal medulla are water-soluble hormones, which are the derivatives of proteins or amino acids. Lipid-soluble hormones are steroid hormones, synthesized from cholesterol, e.g., hormones of thyroid, adrenal cortex, ovaries and testes.

If these secretions suffer in quantity due to under (hypofunction) or over (hyperfunction) activity of the endocrine glands, certain pathological conditions in different parts of the body are rapidly established which disturb the homeostasis and may give rise to serious disorders, e.g., on account of malfunctioning of thyroids the hair become gray, nails become brittle and the metabolic processes are disturbed.

PITUITARY GLAND

Pituitary gland (hypophysis) is a small structure like a pea, located in the cranial cavity at the base of the brain and is connected with the hypothalamus by stalk. It has two lobes. (1) *Anterior lobe* and (2) *Posterior lobe*. The anterior lobe constitutes about 75 percent of the total weight of the gland.

The hypothalamus sends regulating factors to the anterior lobe (adenohypophysis). These are the chemical secretions, which stimulate or inhibit the release of hormones from the anterior lobe. The anterior lobe secrets five hormones.

(i) *Growth hormone (GH)*, which regulates general growth of the body.
(ii) *Prolactin (PRL)*, which initiates milk production by the mammary glands (breasts) in females.
(iii) *Thyroid stimulating hormone (TSH)* that controls the thyroid gland.
(iv) *Follicle stimulating hormone (FSH)*, which stimulates the production of eggs and sperm in the ovaries and testes respectively. *Luteinizing hormone (LH)* regulates other sexual and reproductive activities.

(v) *Adreno-corticotrophic hormone (ACTH)*, which stimulates the adrenal cortex to secret its hormones.

Posterior lobe (neurohypophysis) secrets *oxytocin* and *vasopressin (ADH)*. Oxytocin is released in large quantities prior to delivery. It stimulates the contraction of the smooth muscles of the uterus of a pregnant woman at the start of labor. Vasopressin is anti-diuretic in action, regulating the urine formation by increasing the water absorption in the kidneys so that less urine is produced. ADH can also raise blood pressure by causing constriction of the arterioles.

THYROID GLAND

It is located in the neck region in front of the trachea just below the larynx. The right and left lobes lie on either side of the trachea. Both the lobes are connected by a mass of tissue called *isthmus*. The weight of the gland is about 25 gms. Its hormones are *thyroxin, tri-iodothyronine* and *calcitonin*. Thyroxin is a combination of iodine with amino acids. It regulates overall metabolism of the body by controlling the oxygen consumption. It increases concentration of glucose in the blood. Calcitonin helps the normal growth of the body by proper deposition of calcium in the bones. It maintains an adequate level of calcium in the blood. Liver and lungs convert tri-iodothyronine into thyroxine. Hyposecretion of thyroid hormones during the growing age results in hypothyroidism. In children it develops *cretinism*. The skeleton cannot grow properly and the brain does not develop fully. A child thus remains physically and mentally retarded. A cretin child has a yellowish skin, round face and thick nose, protruding abdomen and shows a general lethargy. The condition may be cured in the early stage by administering thyroid hormones.

In adults the hyposecretion of thyroid hormones causes myxedema. A person suffers from slow heart rate, low body temperature, muscular weakness, general lethargy, overweight (obesity) and nervousness. The symptoms are abolished by the administration of thyroxine. This disease is more frequent in females.

Hyperactivity of thyroid gland (over-secretion of thyroxine) gives rise to *exopthalmic goiter*. This is also more frequent in females. The thyroid gland enlarges. The heart rate increases, the eyes protrude out, the person loses weight and becomes irritable and exhibits tremors of the extended fingers. An administration of the drugs that suppress the synthesis of thyroid hormones and other precautionary measures can cure this condition.

PARATHYROID GLANDS

These are four small pea shaped masses attached to the posterior surface of both the lobes of the thyroid. They secret **parathyroid hormone (PTH)** or **parathormone**, which increases the level of calcium ions in the blood by removing them from the bones. It also decreases the blood phosphate level. Thus it helps to maintain the level of these ions in blood. A deficiency of calcium caused by hypoparathyroidism results in muscle twitches, spasms and convulsions. This condition is called **tetany**. Hyperparathyroidism causes more destruction of bones that become susceptible to fracture.

ADRENALS OR SUPRARENAL GLANDS

There are two small cup-shaped structures one on the top of each kidney. Each adrenal gland has an outer major part known as *adrenal cortex* and the inner core, the *adrenal medulla*. These parts differ in structure and function. Adrenal cortex produces number of hormones namely, aldosterone, cortisol, corticosterone, cortisone and gonado-corticoids or sex hormones, i.e., *estrogen* and *androgen*.

Aldosterone is a mineralo-corticoid, which causes retention of sodium chloride in the body and excretion of potassium by its action on the kidneys. Hypersecretion of this hormone leads to increased blood and tissue fluid volume with high blood pressure and edema. Cortisol, corticosterone and cortisone are called *glucocorticoids*. They are concerned with the metabolism and the resistance to stress. They help maintain blood glucose level. These glucocorticoids, during stress (fright,

The Endocrine System

extreme temperature, trauma) raise the glucose level as well as the blood pressure to combat stress. However, their high doses slow down healing of the wounds and depress the immune response.

Gonadocorticoids are responsible for the secondary sexual characteristics in males and females. The quantity of these estrogen and androgen hormones produced by the adrenal cortex is very low. They also contribute to the general growth, healing and maintenance of normal body structure. Adrenal medulla secrets *epinephrine* (adrenaline) and *norepinephrine* (nor-adrenaline). These hormones help us to overcome the stress. Under stress, when these hormones are released, epinephrine increases blood pressure by increasing heart rate and constricting blood vessels. Its action is similar to that of sympathetic nervous system. Thus it prepares the individual for defense or management of the stressful situation.

ISLETS OF LANGERHANS

The pancreas works as both endocrine and exocrine gland. The exocrine portion of pancreas helps digestion by secreting pancreatic juice. The endocrine part consists of clusters of cells called *islets of langerhans*. There are three kinds of cells in these clusters. (1) *Alpha cells*, which secrete the hormone glucagon. (2) *Beta cells*, secreting the hormone insulin and (3) *Delta cells*, which secrets growth hormone inhibiting factor (GHIF) or somatostatin. Glucagon increases the blood glucose level by conversion of glycogen into glucose whereas insulin lowers blood glucose level by accelerating the conversion of glucose into glycogen and increasing transport of glucose from the blood to the cells. Lack of insulin results in a disorder called *diabetes mellitus*. The patient passes large volumes of urine frequently and has excessive thirst and hunger all the time. The blood sugar level increases, which may be dangerous for his life. The excessive sugar then appears in the urine. Normally there is no sugar in urine.

GONADS

The ovaries (in female) produce ovum and the testes (in male) produce sperms. Apart from this function, the ovaries and testes produce hormone from their endocrine cells. Testes produce testosteron, the male hormone that promotes the development of male sexual characteristics, i.e., development of the muscles, their manly shape and size, growth of the penis, axillary hair, moustache and change in voice. Testes also produce hormone *inhibin*, which inhibits secretion of FSH, to decrease rate of spermatogenesis. Testosterone is responsible for the development of the male characters.

The ovaries produce female sex hormones, viz., *estrogens* and *progesterone*. Estrogen (B-estradiol, estrone and estrol) develops and maintains female reproductive structure, secondary sexual characteristics which include development of the breasts, hair pattern, pitch of the voice, fat deposition on the hips and broadening of the pelvis. Progesterone is helpful during pregnancy and prevents normal menstrual cycle and inhibits contractions of the uterus. *Relaxin*, the third hormone produced by the ovaries is particularly helpful during labor as it relaxes symphysis pubis and uterine cervix.

From yoga point of view

1. Emotions, hormones of the endocrine glands, behavior and mental health are deeply corelated with each other. When the function of these glands is maintained at the optimum level by practicing *asanas, bandhas* and *mudras* regularly, physical and mental health are maintained automatically. However, the yogic practices should not be done like exercises.
2. A regular yoga practitioner experiences a feeling of happiness, contentment and a peaceful state of mind all the time and therefore, stress is never felt. Yoga also helps in maintaining the homeostasis. Therefore one can control psychosomatic diseases like diabetes or asthma with the help of yogic practices. However, a suitable change in the lifestyle and diet control is also essential for such results.

3. The influence of yogic practices on the endocrine glands is more evident in females than in males. It is observed by some women that the menstrual cycle may be accelerated or delayed when they start yogic practices particularly *uddiyan bandha, kapalbhati, nauli, dhanurasana, halasana, yogamudra,* etc. Therefore they should practice these on a mild scale and with careful observation.

Eight

The Skeletal System

The bones and their articulations form the *skeleton* of the body. The skeletal system forms the framework of the body. The skeleton supports the muscles and other softer parts of the body. It also protects our brain, spinal cord, heart and the lungs, e.g., the brain is well secured in the skull and the spinal cord is safely lodged in a hollow channel, formed due to well-arranged vertebrae, one above the other. The skeleton helps in the movements of different body parts and the body as a whole. It helps in the respiration. The skeleton also gives a definite form or shape to the body and helps it to take a particular position in space.

THE BONES

Bones are the hardest parts of the body and form the basis of the physical structure. Each bone is supplied with nerves, blood vessels and lymphatic vessels. The bone marrow lies inside the bones towards the end. There are red and yellow type of bone marrows. The red bone marrow consists of reticulo-endothelial cells, which produce blood cells. Skeletal muscles are attached to the bones. In fact the bones remain passive during the movements of the body limbs. Adult human body consists of 206 bones. Following are the four types of bones:

1. Flat bones

These bones are thin like a plate. They protect the organs as they cover them, e.g., cranial bones of the skull, sternum, ribs and the scapulae.

2. Irregular bones

These bones are complex and irregular in shape, e.g., vertebrae of the spine.

3. Long bones

These bones have greater length than their width and are slightly curved for better strength, e.g., bones of hands and thighs.

4. Short bones

These are cubical in shape and are nearly equal in length and width, e.g., bones of the wrists and ankles.

JOINTS

A point where two bones or a bone and a cartilage contact each other is called a *joint* or an *articulation*. Such two bones are held together by a flexible connective tissue. Most of the joints permit the movement within a particular limit while others restrict the movement. The joints are classified as:

1. Fibrous joints

The articulating bones are held very close to each other by a fibrous connective tissue and hence a very limited movement is possible or there is no movement at all, e.g., joints between the shafts of the ulna and radius or tibia and fibula; suture between the flat bones of the skull.

2. Cartilaginous joints

Here the joining material is cartilaginous tissue. Such a joint is immovable in nature, e.g., joint between the first rib and the sternum. The cartilage gets fused with the two bones in adults. A portion of the intervertebral disc is cartilaginous. Vertebral joint is slightly movable.

3. Synovial joints

In this kind of joints the bones move freely upon each other. There is a space between the two articulating bones, known as synovial cavity. A sleeve like articular capsule, which encloses

The Skeletal System

the joint cavity and the cartilage in between the two bones, covers the joint. The outer fibrous layer of the capsule prevents dislocation while inner membrane of the capsule secrets *synovial fluid*, which lubricates and nourishes the joint. Depending upon the shape and style of the articulating surfaces, the synovial joints are divided into six subtypes viz., gliding (carpal and tarsal bones, sternum and clavicle), hinge (elbow), pivot (joint between atlas and axis), ellipsoidal (wrist), saddle (thumb), and ball and socket (shoulder and the hip joints).

VERTEBRAL COLUMN

The spine (backbone) or the vertebral column (Fig. 19) consists of 33 vertebrae. The last four coccygeal vertebrae are fused together in an adult body. Above them, five sacral vertebrae are

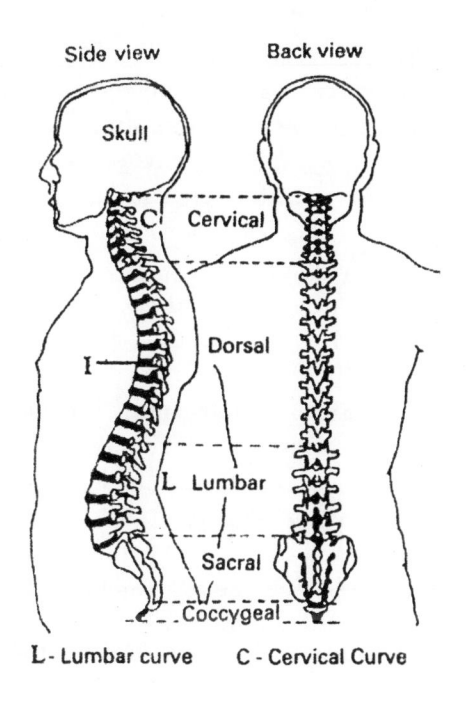

L - Lumbar curve   C - Cervical Curve

Fig.19: Vertebral Column

also fused with each other, forming the *sacrum*. First seven vertebrae are known as *cervical vertebrae* as they are in the neck region. Below these twelve *thoracic vertebrae* are in the upper part of the trunk. The next five *lumbar vertebrae*, in the lumbar region, are the largest and strongest. They support the lower back. The sacrum is situated after the lumbar part, followed by a *coccyx*. All the vertebrae are arranged one above the other and hence a canal is formed in which the spinal cord is safely lodged.

One vertebra is articulated with the other vertebra by means of cartilaginous inter-vertebral disc and is held tight by the strong ligaments. Strong skeletal muscles surround the vertebral column. It is articulated with the shoulder girdle and the pelvic girdle. These articulations are well supported by the strong muscles. They help us in bending forward (flexion), backward (extension), to the right or left sides (lateral flexion) and also in rotating in right or left directions (twisting) in the vertical axis (Fig. 20).

On viewing the spinal column from the sides, four inborn curves in its cervical, thoracic, lumbar and the sacral regions are observed.

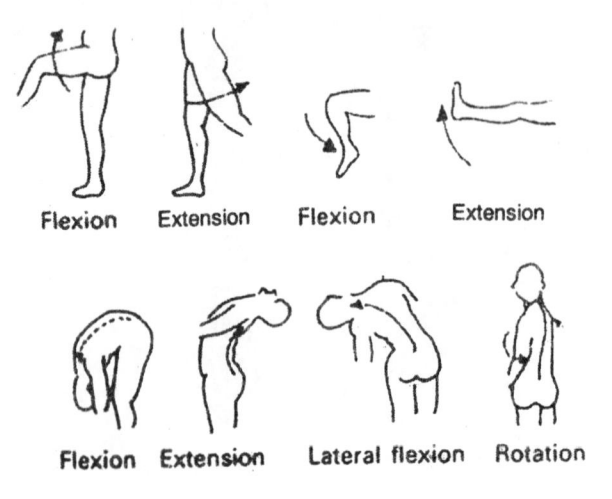

Flexion   Extension   Flexion   Extension

Flexion Extension   Lateral flexion   Rotation

Fig. 20: Basic Movements of the Body

The Skeletal System

These curves increase the strength of the spine, maintain balance in the upright posture, absorb the jerks and the shocks during walking, running and jumping. A faulty development in these curvatures such as exaggerated forward and backward curvatures give rise to the conditions known as *lordosis* and *kyphosis* respectively. Abnormally increased lateral curve produces a deformity known as *scoliosis*. The shoulder girdle consists of clavicle bone and scapula. These bones are attached with the humerus bone of the upper arm. Pelvic girdles are articulated with the sacral part of the vertebral column and with the femur bone of the leg. Ribs are attached to the thoracic vertebrae on the posterior side and the breastbone (sternum) in front. There are twelve pairs of ribs, which form the thoracic cage. Ribs and clavicle bones move with the help of intercostals muscles during inspiration and expiration, by increasing and decreasing the diameter of the chest respectively.

From yoga point of view

1. Flexibility, suppleness and efficiency in the movements of the body depends on the strength and capacity of the joints. Functional efficiency of the joint depends on the nutrition and the regular exercise given to the muscles and the tendons of the joints. By regular practice of *asanas* the flexibility of the joints can be increased. Learning and regular practice of *asanas* in young age offer not only the flexibility but also a proper development of the bones and the joints. Children can increase their height by practicing *asanas* regularly.
2. Spinal column is an important factor of our physical appearance. We are as young as our spinal column. A strong and flexible spine makes our life more comfortable. Almost all the *asanas* are related to the spinal column. It has been observed that those who practice *asanas* regularly, rarely suffer from spinal ailments like lower back pain.
3. Our routine work, including our behavior, depends on the efficiency and the strength of the spinal column.

4. Style and Stature, sitting and standing posture, personality, gesture and an ability to carry weight depend on the condition of our spine.
5. The spine is made healthy and stronger with the help of a regular training through exercises and *asanas*.

Nine

The Excretory System

Metabolism is a continuous process. The products of digestion are converted into the complex molecules of the living matter. This helps in building various tissues (anabolism). When the complex molecules are broken down to release energy (cell destruction), it also produces waste material such as carbon dioxide, water and heat. Protein catabolism produces nitrogenous wastes such as ammonia and urea, which are toxic substances. Other essential ions such as sodium, potassium, chloride, sulphates, phosphates and hydrogen tend to accumulate in the body. All this toxic and excess material must be eliminated from the body. Our body has four main routes of excretion, (1) kidneys, (2) lungs, (3) alimentary canal and (4) skin.

Kidneys are the main organs of excretion. A pair of kidneys controls the water and other body fluid levels. Each kidney is a bean-shaped reddish structure, situated on right and left sides against the posterior abdominal wall in the lumbar region. Each kidney is connected to the urinary bladder by *ureter* through which the urine is passed to the urinary bladder. The bladder contracts during the process of micturition and the urine is expelled through the *urethra*, which opens out through the sex organ. Each kidney consists of millions of *nephrons*, the filtering units, and their capillaries. Blood is circulating continuously through these nephrons where it is filtered. The toxic substances and other waste products are separated from the blood and the blood is sent back to the heart. The urine, thus formed, is collected in the urinary bladder. When the amount of urine rises above 200–400 ml, the stretch receptors in the wall of the urinary bladder are stimulated. The impulses are sent to the lower portion of the spinal cord. This causes reflex contraction of the urinary bladder but it is controlled by our will. This voluntary control is learned right in the childhood. When the pressure on the wall of the bladder increases too much to tolerate, the impulses travel up to the cortical area and the conscious desire for urination is created.

Normally, on an average, about 1.5 liters of urine is excreted in 24 hours. The volume of urine however depends upon the water intake, the environmental temperature and the demand for the maintenance of the water balance and homeostasis. Generally, the specific gravity and the color as well as the constituents of the urine are well maintained in homeostasis but it may be changed in various pathological conditions. The analysis of physical, chemical and microscopic properties of urine helps in the diagnosis of disease.

The respiratory process at the cellular level produces carbon dioxide, which is transported through the medium of surrounding tissue fluid to the blood. The blood is collected back into the capillaries and sent to the *lungs* for pulmonary circulation via heart. During each inspiration, carbon dioxoide is exchanged for oxygen and is eliminated during exhalation. The lungs also eliminate water vapor along with the expired air. The volatile substances like alcohol and anesthetic chemicals are eliminated in the form of vapor, through this route.

Skin excretes water, salts and several organic compounds in the form of sweat. Degree of secretion of the sweat depends on the variation in the environmental as well as the body temperature because the heat is lost through sweating and the body is cooled. *Alimentary canal* eliminates undigested food material, residue of digestive secretions, bile pigments, some bacteria, other undigested coloring agents and little water, in the form of feces.

Ten

Homeostasis

Our body has many organs, each performing a specific function for the body. Coordination amongst all these functions is essential in both, the resting condition and during active exercises. The activities of different systems are adjusted with the changing demands of new situation. This coordination of various activities for efficient function of the body is achieved mainly through two controlling systems, the endocrine system and the nervous system.

Homeostasis is the condition in which body's internal environment remains relatively constant. It is an active process by which the proper hydrogen ion concentration, supply of nutrients, efficient removal of waste products of metabolism, optimum blood pressure, and appropriate blood sugar level are maintained without our notice. Temperature of the body is kept constant at about 37^0 C by balancing heat loss and heat gain processes. This is known as thermo-regulation. If the temperature of the body rises too high or comes down too low then the body cells are unable to carry out chemical actions properly. The tissues are continuously bathed in tissue fluid, which is in contact with the circulating blood. Cells absorb the required nutrients and oxygen from this tissue fluid and give up toxic wastes in return. The blood acts as a transporting system to supply nutrients and oxygen to these tissues and to carry the wastes to the organs of excretion. The composition of this tissue fluid must be maintained all the time. The kidneys, skin and lungs do this job. They also maintain the water level in the body. The hydrogen ion concentration or pH of the blood is accurately maintained at 7.4, i.e., slightly towards the alkaline side. If it becomes acidic, the tissue cannot survive in acidic medium.

Homeostasis is continuously disturbed by any stimulus that creates an imbalance in the internal environment and gives rise to stress. Stress may be produced from increased heat, cold, loud sound, heavy light, lack of oxygen or exertion. Stress may arise within the body due to pain, emotions or unpleasant thoughts. These stressors stimulate the hypothalamus and bring about many changes in the body as the sympathetic nervous system and the adrenal medulla are stimulated. On account of this stimulation the secretion of adrenaline is increased and as a result, heart rate, respiration rate, blood pressure, blood sugar level are elevated and the metabolic rate is increased. This makes a person more alert, aroused and reactive to the situation for the time being. This is actually a defense mechanism of the body. It prepares a person to cope with the stress. After the stressful situation is over, all these functions should return to their normal level. If the stressful situation is prolonged for a long period, the autonomic balance is also disturbed. Disharmony in the body functions results in functional disorders such as diabetes, hypertension, acidity, insomnia, etc. Therefore, one must learn to cope with the stress successfully. Yogic practices can help one in this respect by establishing and maintaining physiological balance (homeostasis) in the body. Proper lifestyle including moderate exercises, proper diet, enough sleep, relaxation and positive thinking will definitely maintain the homeostasis and thus the physical and mental health.

Eleven

Posture

Asana is often translated as posture. Even though *asana* is not simply a posture, in order to understand what is an *asana*, we shall study posture—how it is acquired and controlled. Standing posture, sitting posture and a recumbent (lying) posture are three basic postures, characteristic of human being, developed during the evolution. We can also acquire certain basic postures of animals and birds because of our motor skills. By assuming such postures voluntarily, we may activate certain special areas or the sub-cortical brain centers of coordination. Sages have taken best advantage of this while developing various *asanas*.

Posture may be defined as a particular position assumed by the body with or without the external support. It is the relative arrangement of different parts of the body for a specific purpose. Although natural postures of man are unique, he can adopt several types of postures. Any such posture would involve a well-coordinated action of several muscles, joints and associated nerves. Generally a posture is acquired for stability and equilibrium of the body so as to provide an essential basis for some movements, which are superimposed on it, e.g., sitting posture in a chair, adopted for writing.

IDEAL POSTURE

An ideal or efficient posture is that which fulfils the purpose of the specific activity economically for which it is assumed. Economically in the sense, it should involve minimum voluntary efforts and energy consumption for its maintenance. This is a very easy job for the body, provided the muscle tone is adequate and the other mechanisms coordinate with each other in a healthy manner. A correct or a good standing posture is that where the center of gravity falls exactly on the feet. The line of gravity passes from the highest point of the skull up to the base of the feet through cervical and lumbar vertebrae, center of the hips, knees and ankle joints. The whole weight is thus well balanced and the body does not move forward or backward on and often. Such a good posture is normally maintained with or without our attention. There are many individual variations within this limit.

Many people adopt particular postural styles (habits) in standing, sitting or lying conditions, mostly because of their occupational or job requirements or simply under the name of social etiquettes and develop defective postures. In such *bad* or *faulty posture* the weight falls outside the body in the front or the backside. Natural spinal curves are also disturbed, producing extra curvatures in the spine. This gives rise to disorders like *lordosis* (abnormal forward bending of lumbar region, convexity) or *kyphosis* (excessive dorsal convexity, humpback) or *scoliosis* (lateral curves). The intensity of these disorders increases as the age advances. It can be checked and corrected in early stages with a well-planned exercise program and by developing good postural habits. The foundation of such good habits should be led before the age of twenty.

Mental characteristics are found to be associated with the particular postures. A good or ideal posture exhibits a sound mental and physical health. The posture indicates the attitude or the nature of the individual. Different temperaments, moods, emotions and other psychological factors influence the erect or sitting posture as the muscle tone gets altered. Yogis have taken best advantage of this fact. When the *asanas* are maintained for sometime they help to control our emotional balance. We shall study this aspect in more details later.

CONTROL OF POSTURE

The maintenance of posture and balance of the body is a complex action, which depends on the counteracting reflexes. Basal ganglia, brainstem nuclei and reticular formation are the major

Posture

centers of the brain for such involuntary control. They coordinate with each other and send appropriate motor nerve impulses to the corresponding skeletal muscles through the descending pathways. Their action depends on the afferent (sensory) impulses from the proprioceptors situated in the muscle spindles, tendon organs, joints, labyrinth and the exteroceptors like eyes, skin and ears and also on the visceroreceptors. These receptors convey moment-to-moment information about the position of the body parts and their movement in the space. These sensory inputs are received, integrated and coordinated by these subcortical centers in the brain, below the level of consciousness (i.e., without the control from the cortex) and the motor impulses are sent to the concerned muscle for action. Thus the maintenance of the posture and the equilibrium of the body when it is stable or moving are performed involuntarily without our notice (refer page 92).

The skeletal muscles contract automatically as a result of stretch reflexes, set by the spinal cord or the lower brain centers, depending on the information from the stretch and pressure receptors. Since these reflexes are produced during the maintenance of the posture, they are known as *postural reflexes*. The extensors and flexors of the neck, lower limbs and the trunk, hip muscles are the major muscles that maintain the erect (upright) posture against the force of gravity. These extensors and flexors contract alternately as a result of stretch reflex mechanism. Once the posture is assumed for a particular purpose, it is maintained and adjusted or modified due to other postural reflexes, produced by the sensory receptors in the eyes, skin and vestibular organs (in the ears) as well as the joints. The cerebellum exclusively controls fast movements while the slow movements are managed by the basal ganglia.

Generally a command to adopt a particular posture is sent from the cerebral cortex to the cerebellum and basal ganglia where the actual program of movement is prepared on the basis of the stored patterns of movements, learned earlier. The motor impulses (orders) are sent to the concerned skeletal muscles through the descending pathways in the spinal cord. The basal

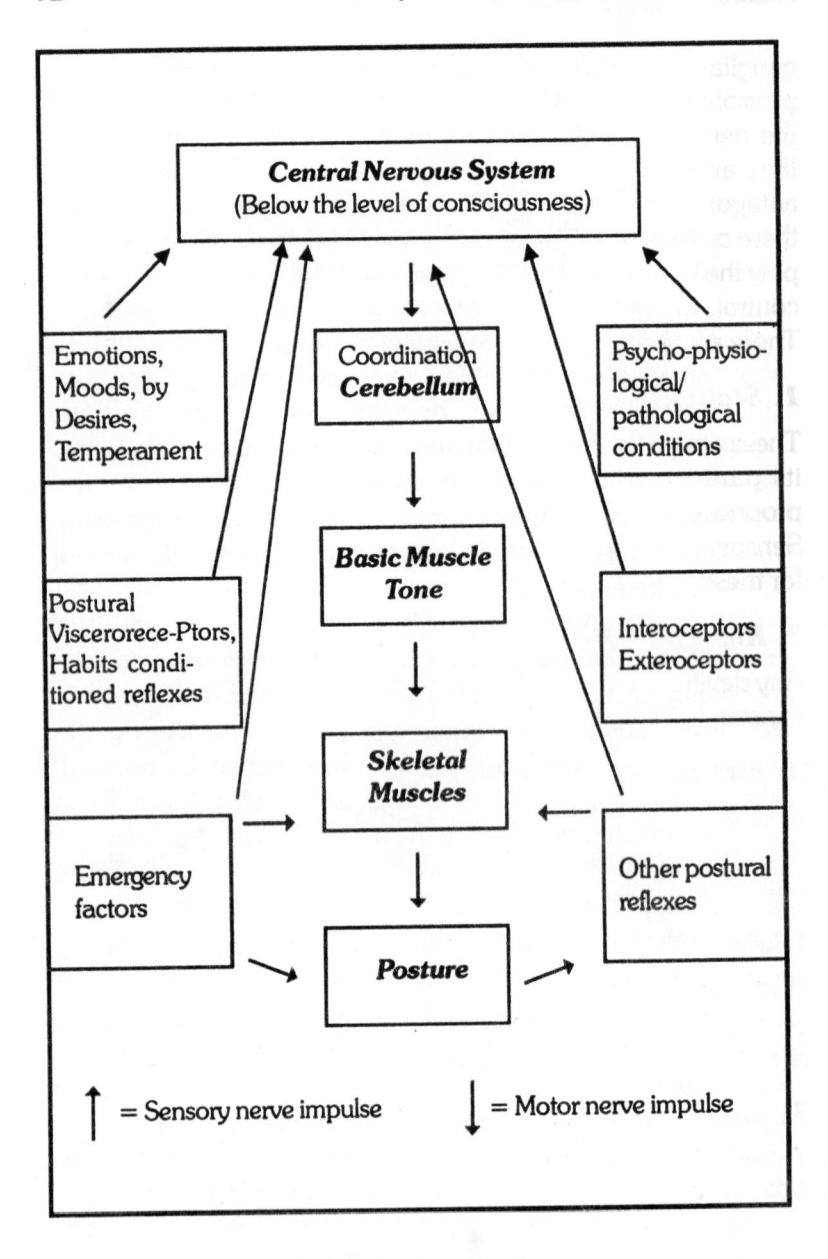

Fig. 21: Control of Posture

ganglia and the cerebellum are informed about the further possible movements. They also receive the information from the periphery or the muscles, tendons about the movements that are taking place. Thus the contractions of agonists, antagonists and other associated muscles are coordinated by these centers. Once the posture is assumed, the postural reflexes play their role in maintaining the posture without our conscious control.

There are three types of postural reflexes:

1. Static reflexes

These are engaged in maintaining the position of the body and its parts in resting condition. These are produced by the proprioceptors, which are sensitive to stretching and pressure. Sensory inputs from eyes and labyrinth are also very important for these reflexes.

2. Righting reflexes

Any deviation from the normal or the basic posture, is corrected constantly by these reflexes.

3. Statokinetic reflexes

In order to bring about a smooth, balanced and progressive movement and to maintain even an abnormal posture, these reflexes are important.

CLASSIFICATION OF POSTURE

Postures can be classified broadly into two groups, (1) *inactive postures* and (2) *active postures*. Active postures are further subdivided into (i) static and (ii) dynamic postures.

1. Inactive postures

These postures are generally adopted for resting or sleeping. In these postures almost all the muscles are relaxed except those required for maintaining the life, e.g., respiration, blood circulation. These activities are however, reduced to a great extent and are minimal, e.g., resting in supine or recumbent position in easy chair in which there are no muscular efforts to maintain the posture against gravity. The joints are also loosen and there is no other activity superimposed on the posture.

2. Active postures

A neuromuscular coordination is required to maintain these postures with voluntary or involuntary muscular contractions.

(i) Static postures: This type of posture is stably maintained for some length of time due to coordinated function of the concerned muscles. Various joints are stabilized and a state of equilibrium is preserved against gravity and other forces. It is controlled semi-voluntarily, i.e., if one is not aware of the posture he has assumed, it is maintained automatically without one's notice. For example, a comfortable sitting posture may be maintained in a semi-relaxed state.

(ii) Dynamic postures: These postures are constantly modified or adjusted to meet the changing demands of the movements that are superimposed on it. Muscles work against gravity in order to maintain equilibrium of the body. Almost all the *asanas* include variety of such postures.

Thus it will be seen that the whole approach in studying the basic principles of anatomy and physiology is to understand the probable mechanisms involved in various yogic practices on the scientific ground. It is obvious that our body responds according to the nature of stimulations from the external or the internal environments. Yogic practices influence the body and mind deeply and bring about necessary changes even in the behavioral pattern of the individual. The individual thus becomes well prepared for the higher practices of yoga. Therefore, our yogic techniques should bear a scientific background along with the traditional support. This scientific background would also help the individual to remove confusion or misconception as well as exaggerated claims about the yogic practices. A yoga teacher with this knowledge would be the best yoga teacher to guide his students on the path of yoga.

PART TWO

ANATOMY AND PHYSIOLOGY OF YOGIC PRACTICES

One

Asana

Traditionally, *asana* means a 'sitting condition' or 'position' of the body, which contributes to the steadiness of the body and mind and a sense of well-being. The term *asana* is also used to indicate a carpet of grass, a square piece of cloth or a mat which is utilized as a comfortable 'seat' on the ground for sitting. *Asana* occupies the first place in *hatha yoga* while it forms the third part of Patanjali's eight-fold (*ashtang*) yoga.

Asanas are often translated as 'postures', e.g., *Bhujangasana* is called cobra posture, *Makarasana* as crocodile posture, *Dhanurasana* as bow posture, etc. It is true that *asanas* are the modified part of the three basic human postures, i.e., standing, sitting or lying postures and bear most of the characteristics of a posture. Yet *asanas* and postures differ in many respects. The term posture does not convey full meaning of *asana*.

In a posture, though it is maintained economically without many efforts, the state of mind is not so important. The mental condition may vary in different postures due to a series of continuous thoughts. For example, even if we relax in a chair quite comfortably, we may remain mentally upset because of some tension or stress. Many postures are developed and maintained below the level of consciousness, i.e., without our attention. A sitting posture is assumed quite easily and comfortably for the purpose of writing even if we do not pay attention (without our awareness). *Asana* is acquired voluntarily, without full concentration on what and how we are doing. Thought process is not allowed but one has to concentrate on the breathing or the infinite during the maintenance of *asana*. This would reduce mental disturbance to a great extent and would make the mind steady or still. No movement is superimposed on any *asana* nor it is expected out of it. The movements for assuming *asana* and to release it are also gone through in a very slow and smooth manner whereas the movements to achieve or to release any posture, may be jerky or quick in nature. Natural standing, sitting or lying postures do not require any special training of the muscles or their associated nerves but in *asanas* we give special exercise to the muscles, joints and nerves when they are maintained for a long time in a steady manner. Postures may need an external support for their maintenance, e.g., sitting in a chair. *Asanas* are maintained without such support (except from the ground).

Sometimes *asana* is also translated as 'pose' but the term pose is not an appropriate translation to explain what is *asana*. Pose is not a natural position of the body. It is assumed artificially to express some emotion or thought. When *asanas* are done properly, the eyes are closed and the facial muscles are relaxed which contribute to the calmness. Such *asana* will further give rise to the emotional stability. Pose, maintained even for a couple of seconds, may lead to a physical or mental strain. Take the example of stage actors. *Asanas* do not cause any exhaustion at any level. On the contrary one feels pleasant at the end of the practice of *asanas*.

The term 'exercise' is often applied to *asana* but *asana* should never be confused with an exercise. The word exercise gives us an idea of quick and forceful movements of the body or its parts and repeated actions, which usually lead to an exertion, tension and fatigue. *Asanas* on the other hand, are practiced slowly and steadily which bring about physical and mental relaxation. The purpose of body-building is absent in *asanas*. We shall study the basic differences between *asanas* and exercises later in more details.

In the light of the above discussion an *asana* can only be defined as a *postural pattern*. One has to achieve this pattern slowly, maintain it for sometime steadily and release it again in a slow and smooth manner. An *asana* is an attitude, which is psycho-physiological in nature. Most of these patterns are based on the natural postures of various animals, birds or even the symbols like tree, lotus, bow and plough, etc. A gradual training is given to the whole body as well as the mind through particular neuromuscular mechanism involved in different postural patterns. This is expected to bring about specific changes gradually in the total personality of the individual, including behavioral changes. Thus it is the pattern of the posture involved in *asana*, which is important and responsible to achieve stillness of body and mind. This is actually a preparation for the higher practices like *pranayama*, *dharna* and *dhyan*. Any *asana* has two aspects, (1) dynamic aspect and (2) static aspect.

1. Dynamic aspect

Some movement is essential in order to assume *asana* or to come back to the initial position. These movements are very slow, smooth and without jerks so that there is no exertion or fatigue and there is no undue strain on breathing. There is no voluntary control on breathing. Generally it is adjusted by the body itself during these movements. However, this dynamic aspect of an *asana* is not so important.

2. Static aspect

Once the 'postural pattern' is assumed, it is maintained for some length of time steadily, comfortably and effortlessly, i.e., without much muscular activity or tension in any part of the body. While maintaining the *asana*, the concentration on inhalation and exhalation or contemplation on ocean or sky (imagery) is done in order to check the flickering mind. This static aspect of *asana* is very important and effective to get maximum benefits from it. For more details read the section titled 'Mechanism of asana'.

CHARACTERISTICS OF ASANAS

It is necessary to quote Patanjali's three very short but important aphorisms dealing with the principles, objectives, effects and also the mechanism of *asana*. It may be noted again that these points are mainly related with the static aspect of *asanas*.

स्थिर सुखमासनम् ।
Sthira sukhamasanam
—*Patanjali Yoga Sutra* II:46

This aphorism gives us an idea about the main characteristic feature of *asana*. It says, *asana* is that which contributes to stability and comfort. Here stability does not mean the stability of body only but the stability of both the body and mind. Even if we remain stable in *asana*, we may remain mentally unstable due to various disturbing sensory inputs. Only the stability of both the body and the mind together would lead us to the sense of well-being. It also does not mean that any position or posture of the body which is easy to attain and comfortable to maintain stably, is an *asana*. In that case perhaps sleeping (recumbent) position would have been the best *asana*, being easiest and most stable one. Since the word *asana* is related more with the sitting condition and also with the stability as well as the feeling of well-being it indicates the conscious state of the individual and not the sleeping condition. Therefore any postural pattern, particularly in a sitting condition, leading towards physical and mental stability as well as a sense of well being is an *asana*. Here it applies more to the sitting pattern, meant for *pranayama* or *dhyana* as it has to be maintained for a long time without any discomfort.

प्रयत्नशैथिल्यानंतसमापत्तिभ्याम् ।
Prayatnashaithilyanantsamapattibhyam
—*Patanjali Yoga Sutra* II:47

This aphorism tells us how the above-mentioned state can be achieved. Slackening of efforts and contemplation on the infinity are the two ways for reaching the above goal. In other words, the relaxed condition or effortless maintenance of *asana* would make the mind free to be attached with the infinity. There is least disturbance from the body as there is no discomfort in

Asana

any part of the body due to easiness and more or less relaxed musculature. The mind is not attracted towards any sensory inputs and can therefore easily be contemplated on the infinite. This further reduces thought processes and the mental activity. As one gets adapted to or established in *asana* there is a negligible amount of involvement of consciousness. When the awareness is directed towards the infinity, no information (input) is likely to come from it. Such postural pattern is maintained below the level of consciousness, i.e., by the lower centers of the brain.

Of course this is rather difficult in the beginning even in case of meditative *asanas* due to the resistance offered by the body itself and the wandering tendency (*vritti*) of the mind. Therefore it is better to cultivate an oceanic feeling, (महाहृदानुसंधानम्) *mahahrudanusandhanam*) i.e., a feeling as if one is just a ripple or a drop of the vast ocean, during maintenance of *asana*. This will reduce the attention toward the tension (or a stretch) in the muscles, joints and tendons.

Another tradition advocates the practice of (प्राणधारणा *pranadharna*). This is done by attending the incoming and outgoing flow of breath or feeling its touch at the tip of the nostrils. Such awareness of breathing helps one to forget about the physical discomfort elsewhere in the body and to relax maximum in the final position of *asana*. In short, slackening of efforts will facilitate the process of contemplation on the infinite or vice versa. Thus the effortlessness, easiness, absence of tensions, undue stretches, minimum muscular activity and absence of thought process by contemplating on the infinite are the characteristics of *asanas*.

ततो द्वंद्वानभिघातः ।
Tato dvandvanabhighatah
—*Patanjali Yoga Sutra* II:48

Really speaking this is the result of the practice of *asana*. When the principles, mentioned above, are followed during the practice, there is no clash between the two opposite forces. On the contrary they work in coordination with each other. These two opposites may be the two types of neural impulses like facilitatory and inhibitory impulses or sympathetic and parasympathetic activities. The neuro-muscular activity is smoothly executed, e.g., contraction of the biceps and the relaxation of the triceps of the arm occur at the same time which helps smooth bending and stretching of the elbow joint. These opposite type of functions or forces are found in every system of the body and a smooth harmonious working of the body and mind depends upon a judicious reciprocity in them. So if the *asanas* are done in a proper way as said above, there would be no clash between these internal opposite mechanisms. *Asanas* help to bring a balance in all such reciprocal functions. The nostril dominance is also one of them.

AIMS AND OBJECTIVES OF ASANAS

Asanas are placed in the beginning of the yogic curriculum. The purpose is quite evident. *Asanas* are psycho-physical practices to culture body and mind for further higher practices of yoga like *pranayama, pratyahara, dhyana*, etc. The body and mind are made healthy and are trained in such a way that a necessary equilibrium (समत्वं) is established in overall functions. One reaches the stage of *asanajaya* (आसनजय), i.e., mastering the *asanas* which is possible after a good deal of practice of *asanas* for a long time. One should be able to sit for hours in a meditative *asana* without any discomfort or internal disturbances. It is nothing but the reconditioning of psycho-physiological mechanisms of the body.

Asanas are expected to counteract the instability (अंगमेजयत्व *angamejayatva*) in the body. This instability or fickleness (tremor) is due to chronic disturbances (विक्षेप *vikshep*) in the muscular tone, which lead to the imbalance in the muscular activity. This tonic imbalance is corrected and diseases are cured by practicing *asanas* (आसनेन रूजोहन्ति *asanena rujohanti*—*Gorakshashatakam*:54). They tackle the root cause of the

Asana

imbalance such as emotional conflicts, stresses, tensions, etc. *Asanas* also overcome the imbalance in other functions of the body, e.g., endocrine secretions. Thus, *asanas* mould our body and mind and make them strong and healthy.

(कुर्यात् तदासनम् स्थैर्यम् आरोग्यम् चांगलाघवम् ।
Kuryat tadasanam sthairyam arogyam changalaghavam
—*Hathapradipika* I:17)

By practicing *asanas* the stability, health and suppleness can be achieved. In nutshell we can say that,

1. Main objective of *asanas* is to promote and maintain perfect health. They reestablish a harmonious functioning of the body and mind as one integrated whole. This reduces stress, strain and tensions arising out of interaction with the external disturbances.

2. To overcome the internal disturbances like tremor and instability (अंगमेजयत्व *angamejayatva*) by reconditioning the psycho-physiological mechanisms and to prepare one for higher yogic practices like *dhyana*.

3. To bring about equilibrium in overall functions at the emotional, behavioral and perceptual level.

MECHANISM OF ASANAS

We know that the central nervous system (CNS) uses its lower centers of integration for the maintenance of posture and equilibrium. These centers are situated in the medulla and pons, mid-brain (brainstem nuclei), cerebellum and basal ganglia. Various reflexes are integrated by these lower centers below the level of consciousness to maintain the posture. This involuntary control depends on the information coming from the proprioceptors, situated in muscles, joints, tendons and soles. Postural reflexes and the muscle tone are very well regulated by the lower centers quite independently and efficiently even when the higher centers in the cortex are not involved.

Any voluntary effort on the part of the body or mind signifies an activity of the higher centers, which dominates the lower centers of integration. This disturbs the usual activity of the lower centers for the postural reflexes. The motor impulses are directly passed on to the skeletal muscles. With the voluntary effort, one may exceed one's own limits to bend or stretch which would cause strong (stretch reflex) contractions, developing more tensions and tremors.

It is our common experience that at least in the beginning when one learns any *asana* for the first time or when he practices it for the first few days to get acquainted with it, a little exertion is caused to the muscles, joints and tendons. This is because the muscles and the joints are undergoing this new type of stretching and bending. One may contract or stretch little more in order to reach the final posture. The joints and the concerned muscles are not that much flexible and therefore would show their resistance. In this condition, the volition plays a dominant role over the lower centers. Such an active stretching, carried on under the influence of the higher centers may lead to undue bending or overstretching, resulting in the damage of the concerned joints, muscles or tendons. Secondly, one always remains aware of the muscular tension, pressure or compression in the abdomen and a slight discomfort here and there. As one progresses in practice and improves his performance of *asana* these feelings gradually disappear and one can now practice them quite easily, without any exertion. The time for holding the *asana* in the final stage is slowly increased. There is a concept of *asanajaya* where one practices the *asana* with great ease and comfort and maintains it stably for longer durations. Of course even from the beginning one can learn and develop a habit of doing *asana* in a very slow and smooth manner. Unfortunately, many people consider *asanas* as exercises and practice them either in the form of isometric or isotonic exercises and continue such practice forever.

Naturally, the results will be different according to the nature of performance. The mechanism of *asanas* when they are practiced with the isometric or isotonic muscular contractions and when they are performed according to the tradition will be different.

In order to achieve the final stage of *asana*, one puts his voluntary efforts, rather forcefully. The muscles and joints are actively stretched and are maintained as such for sometime in that final stage. During such an **active stretching**, the muscles and the joints are actively pulled. As this active stretching is crossing the normal limits of the stretching, the same muscles are actively contracted as a result of stretch reflex mechanism (refer page 46). At the same time the joints offer their resistance as a defense. This strong contraction of the muscles is maintained for sometime. Such sustained and heavy contraction of muscles against the resistance is nothing but the isometric exercise. In 'bull-worker' exercise same principle of isometric muscle contraction is used. One can feel the increased tension in the joints and muscles. If the muscular contraction is too severe in *asanas* it gives rise to unbearable pain and one feels uncomfortable. One remains disturbed due to the pain and discomfort in the body and is unable to concentrate. Fatigue is developed easily and a feeling of exhaustion is often experienced. This may produce tremors in those contracted parts of the body. Such isometric activity puts extra load on the circulation and the respiration as the demand of more energy and oxygen is increased from the muscles. On account of these disturbances one is compelled to release the *asana* early and quickly.

Experimentally it has been observed that when *Paschimottanasana* is practiced like an isometric exercise the heart rate increases up to 32 percent over the initial resting heart rate. Electromyographic studies (EMG) have revealed that in case of *Paschimottanasana* and *Ardhamatsyendrasana*, in spite of an excellence in the performance and maintenance in the final posture, the degree of contraction of muscles was increased due to such isometric element brought into the practice and as a result the duration was also reduced. Such performance would naturally increase the burden on the cardio-respiratory system. That is why the heart rate and the blood pressure would increase. The effortlessness and relaxation brought into the practice of these *asanas* on the other hand could reduce the muscular activity or tension in the muscles as judged by EMG activity. Heart rate did not increase more than 6 percent over the initial resting value and the maintenance phase of these *asanas* also increased by 10 to 50 percent. This indicates that the energy cost of these *asanas* was reduced to a great extent and there was no burden on the cardio-respiratory mechanism during effortless practice of *asanas*.

When *asanas* are performed with lot of tension in the muscles, only the superficial muscles are involved in this practice. Deep muscles do not receive any advantage. Internal pressure changes and proprioceptive mechanisms hardly get any time to influence the lower centers of integration in the brain. Proprioceptive mechanisms are dominated by heavy muscular activity. The active element in the practice will stimulate the sympathetic nervous system more which in turn would give rise to extra psycho-physiological tensions and stress. Now imagine, what would happen if the individual continues to practice in this way for months together. Obviously the symptoms, which are often observed in such individuals are, irritation, tension, inflated ego, offensive and impulsive nature.

However, for the individuals having the hypotonic conditions of the muscles, slight active stretching and sustained isometric contraction will develop necessary tone and strength in the muscles. The individual would feel active, fresh and enthusiastic within a few days of practice with such mild isometric type of performance.

Sometimes *asanas* are also practiced as freehand (isotonic) exercise where each *asana* is repeated three to four times, in a quick fashion even with mild jerky movements. Here the movements are more prominent, leaving no time for the maintenance of the posture. Strictly speaking, this is not an *asana*. The yogic advantages of such dynamic practice (with isotonic muscular contraction) are very much doubtful even though the stamina and endurance of the body is improved. The mental stability in such practice is also questionable. During such practice more heat and sweat would be produced and the sympathetic nervous system would be stimulated more. There will be more strain on the cardio-vascular system with increased energy expenditure. Consequently, the body would be exhausted rapidly. This sort of exercise with slight tightness, purposely maintained in the muscles, would be useful for the hypotonic conditions. However, this practice would yield only physical benefits.

Now let us consider what happens when *asana* is practiced easily with proper relaxation in the muscles, with minimum voluntary efforts and without any tension in the joints and muscles. The movements to achieve the final posture are also very slow and smooth in nature. The attention is focused on the infinite or simply on the breathing process (*pranadharana*) during the maintenance of the *asana*. This attitude of an observer (as a third person) where the awareness is directed towards the breath, further relaxes the body and slackens the voluntary efforts. Since the mind remains engaged in this way (with the infinite or the breath) the thought process is also reduced to a great extent. In this way, in the absence of thoughts as well as the voluntary (motor) actions, the cortical activity (arousal) is also reduced during the maintenance phase of the *asana*. As the dominance (bossing) of the cortex is reduced, the lower brain centers are now free to control the posture and to maintain the equilibrium more efficiently. The type of postural reflexes and their origin as well as the responses from the other systems however, would depend upon the typical pattern of the posture adopted.

It may be noted that most of the *asanas* resemble the natural postures of the animals like crocodile, cobra, peacock, fish, camel, eagle, etc., which are maintained by their lower brain centers involuntarily. It appears therefore that the patterns of *asanas* have been purposely designed to give maximum scope to the lower centers of integration in the brain. By way of *pranadharana* or contemplation on the infinite the cortical influence is minimal and therefore the emotional or the intellectual activity (interference) is also greatly reduced. This in turn reduces various tensions and keeps the individual free from such disturbances at least for a couple of seconds/minutes.

Naturally, with a consistent practice of *asanas* in this way, the emotional and psychological set up of the individual would also be corrected.

In such type of effortless, easy and comfortable maintenance of the posture, various muscles and joints are stretched smoothly without any resistance. This is known as *passive stretching* where the muscles (and therefore tendons) are not stretched beyond their natural limits and the resulting reflex contraction is not so strong. The muscles do not resist the passive stretching, on the other hand they may surrender easily to such passive stretching. When a muscle is easily stretched, the muscular tension cannot be developed. Muscle tone, which is maintained due to a stretch reflex mechanism, either remains at its optimum level or even gets reduced to a great extent, depending upon which muscles are involved in a particular *asana*. We have seen that the muscle tone is the basis of posture and gets influenced by the emotional or the psychological state of an individual. When the muscle tone is reduced due to the passive stretching of the joints and muscles as stated above, the associated nerves are tranquilized and soothed. Naturally, the emotions cannot remain elevated when the nerves are calmed down and are not excited any more. Thus one becomes more and more relaxed as one's emotional tensions are reduced. In this way one's emotional status is set right.

A problem of internal disturbance (*vikshepas*) or clashes (*dvandvas*) or even instability (*angamejayatva*) does not arise because the muscular tensions are reduced and the associated nerves are tranquilized. Cardio-respiratory centers are calmed down as there is no extra demand for energy and oxygen form the muscles. This restores the parasympathetic predominance in the body. Now instead of irritation, ego-inflation and tension, one feels calm and quiet, pleasant, exhilarated, euphoric and relaxed. This makes a long-term effect on the behavior of a person.

Various joints are moved in their maximum range of movement passively. The static but passive stretching of the muscles and ligaments get sufficient time to percolate deeply up to the periosteum (covering at the end of the bone) and the

Asana

capsule and to stimulate the circulation around them. This also causes effective and easy removal of waste products of the metabolism from the joint. The mild stretch reduces the rigidity of the joints. The healthy condition and the flexibility of the joints are thus restored and well maintained by the regular practice of *asanas*. In the beginning of course, for a few weeks, when we try to assume the posture as near to the final stage as possible although in as comfortable and relaxed way as possible, i.e., with least efforts, just as we sit or lie down easily, the mild stretch gives rise to a *pleasant pain*. This pleasant pain is tolerable and it indicates the upper limit of a passive stretch.

The visceral organs are made of smooth muscles. Experimentally it has been observed that the muscle tone of visceral organs is influenced by the emotional state of the individual. When the big muscles of the extremities are undergoing a passive stretch, *asanas* mainly work on the trunk area and the smooth muscles of the visceral organs. The mild, passive and alternate changes of pressure in the internal organs results in stimulation of the autonomic nervous system as the walls of these organs undergo a mild stretching and relaxation alternately. Thus the muscle tone of these organs is maintained at the optimum level. When the muscle tone is regulated through this proprioceptive feedback mechanism, emotions cannot influence as usual. On the contrary due to a fine autonomic balance achieved in this way, the emotional stability is also achieved. Thus the emotional activity of the individual is tackled through the *asanas* when they are practiced effortlessly. The relaxation started at the muscle-joint level is thus important to release the tension at the higher nervous centers. It is therefore obvious that the hypertonic conditions of the muscles could easily be tackled through such static but passive stretch mechanism, which would also have a bearing upon the behavioral aspect of the individual.

CLASSIFICATION OF ASANAS

We can classify *asanas* by considering their anatomico-physiological features and effects, in three major groups.

1. Cultural or corrective *asanas*
2. Relaxative *asanas* and
3. Meditative *asanas*

1. Cultural Asanas

This group includes maximum number of *asanas*, which are meant for reconditioning of the body and mind so as to bring about stability, peace and a sense of well-being. Most of them are working on the abdominal part. Even though the individual looks outwardly normal, his psycho-physiological status may not be suitable for counter-balancing the effects of higher yogic practices and therefore it must be corrected and molded or cultured in a very special way. Thus, these *asanas* would remold and prepare the individual for the practice of *pranayama, dhyana*, etc. The postural defects, disturbed function of various systems, improper muscle tone must be corrected in order to cultivate correct mental attitude. The following sub-divisions of this group are based on their working pattern in this direction.

Sub-group A: Asanas working on the spinal column

Although the action of almost all the cultural *asanas* is on the spinal column, this group of *asanas* work mainly on the joints, ligaments, muscles and the associated nerves of the vertebral column, e.g., *Bhujangasana, Shalabhasana, Dhanurasana, Ardha-matsyendrasana, Chakrasana, Vakrasana, Ushtrasana.*

Sub-group B: Asanas working on interoceptors

1. Asanas working on and through proprioceptors: These *asanas* predominantly work on and through various proprioceptors mechanisms of the skeletal muscles of the body. Stimulation of the prorioceptors gives rise to stretch reflexes, e.g., *Baddhapadmasana, Gomukhasana, Matsyasana, Vajrasana, Trikonasana, Bhadrasana, Padahastasana, Supta-Vajrasana.*

2. Asanas working on and through visceroreceptors: Visceral organs are subjected to the pressure changes brought about in the intra-abdominal cavity. The visceroreceptors in the walls of these organs, on stimulation, send sensory impulses to autonomic nervous centers, e.g., *Yogamudra, Paschimottanasana, Mayurasana, Ardha-matsyendrasana, Supta-Vjarasana, Halasana, Pavan-muktasana.*

Sub-group C: Asanas working on vestibular organs

These *asanas* predominantly work on and through the sense organs of balance including vestibular organs. These organs usually maintain the balance of the body. The *asanas* under this group are *Shirshasana, Sarvangasana, Viparitkarni, Garudasana, Vrishchikasana, Vrikshasana, Kukkutasana, Bakasana, Padhastasana.* They also influence blood pressure mechanism and the circulation.

2. Relaxative asanas

Shavasana and *Makarasana* are two important relaxative *asanas*, which bring about relaxation of the body and mind. They eliminate the physical as well as mental tensions and work at the level of *chitta* (subtle aspect of consciousness). This process of tranquilization further helps in *pranayama, dhyana*, etc., as it contributes in increasing one's concentration.

3. Meditative asanas

These *asanas* provide a comfortable and stable position of the body to make the mind more and more steady for the process of meditation, *dharana, samadhi,* etc., *Padmasana, Sidhhasana, Swastikasana,* and *Samasanaare* meditative *asanas* which are maintained for long duration.

Now let us consider the anatomico-physiological features of these groups of *asanas* so as to understand their probable mechanism in the body.

CULTURAL ASANAS

Important objectives of cultural *asanas* could be summarized as follows:

1. To recondition various joints, the muscles surrounding them, their tendons as well as reflex mechanisms in order to

strengthen them and to develop a stable and comfortable posture for higher practices like *pranayama, dharana, dhyana,* etc. This helps to attain stability and peace of mind as well as a sense of well-being. It also helps to maintain an optimum muscular tone in the body.
2. To train the nervous system, specially the autonomic nervous system in such a way that it could easily bear the interaction of the spiritual forces (like *Kundalini*) when aroused.
3. To establish physiological balance among various systems for their harmonious function. This provides the best organic vigor to the individual.

Anatomico-physiological considerations of asanas

1. The movements, to perform and then to release any *asana*, should be very smooth and slow. The mild exercise at the joints and around the muscles stimulates the proprioreceptors, which bring about mild stretch reflex. This not only increases the blood circulation around the joints but also improves tone of their muscles. The slow movements and the maintenance of the *asana* in a relaxed way require little muscular activity and therefore consume minimal energy. The heart rate and respiration rate remain in the normal range thus putting no extra burden on the cardio-respiratory system.
2. In *asanas* like *Paschimottanasana* and *Halasana* the relaxation in the final posture allows gravity to act as a stretching force and the muscles are passively stretched. In *asanas* like *Vakrasana, Ardhamatsyendrasana, Matsyasana,* the locks and holds help the muscles to remain moderately stretched. In *Bhujangasana, Shalabhasana, Dhanurasana* etc., in an effort to maintain the posture, the muscles are stretched against some resistance from the joints and the tendons. This increases the muscular tension. This is an important aspect of *asanas* if one wants to increase muscle tone. Thus a proper selection of a set of *asanas* could be utilized to correct the tone in the reciprocal group of muscles.

3. It would be easily noted that the exercise of the trunk portion is more emphasized in corrective *asanas*. The action of these *asanas* is more centered upon the vertebral column, particularly the lumbar region, visceral organs and the nerve endings (roots) in this region. Here, the alternate positive and negative pressure gradient will increase the blood circulation. The nerves are toned up as they receive fresh nourishment. Strengthening of the nerves of the viscera including the spinal cord and the branches of ANS is necessary to enable the practitioner to withstand powerful forces of *Kundalini*, when aroused. It has been seen experimentally that the autonomic balance is established by practicing various corrective *asanas*.
4. Cultural *asanas* provide best possible movements for the spinal column like (1) forward-bending (flexion) as in *Paschimottanasan* and *Yogamudra*, (2) backward-bending (extension) as in *Bhujangasana, Dhanurasana, Ushtrasana* and *Matsyasana*, (3) lateral bending on right and left sides, as in *Konasana* and *Chakrasana* (as developed by Swami Kuvalayananda), (4) rotation of the spine in vertical axis in *Matsyendrasana* and *Vakrasana* (as developed by Swami Kuvalayananda) and (5) topsy-turvy and balancing against gravity as in *Sarvangasana, Shirshasana, Viparita karani, Mayurasana, Kukkutasana* and *Bakasana*.
5. The static stretching of the spinal column increases the blood circulation around the spine that tones up its muscles. The trunk movements are also slow and therefore each vertebra is moved gradually and freely in its natural range of movement. The nutrition is improved due to increased circulation around the joints and the toxic waste products are also removed effectively. This prevents the stiffening of the joints and increases their mobility. The vertebral column is bent, stretched or rotated in all the directions in various degrees, in different *asanas*. This exercise and the improved circulation around the spine render it flexible and elastic. The rigidity of the spinal joints is reduced. Growing children above eight and below eighteen years of age, have been

Sarvangasana

Viparitakarani

Halasana

Naukasana

Utkatasana

Fig. 22

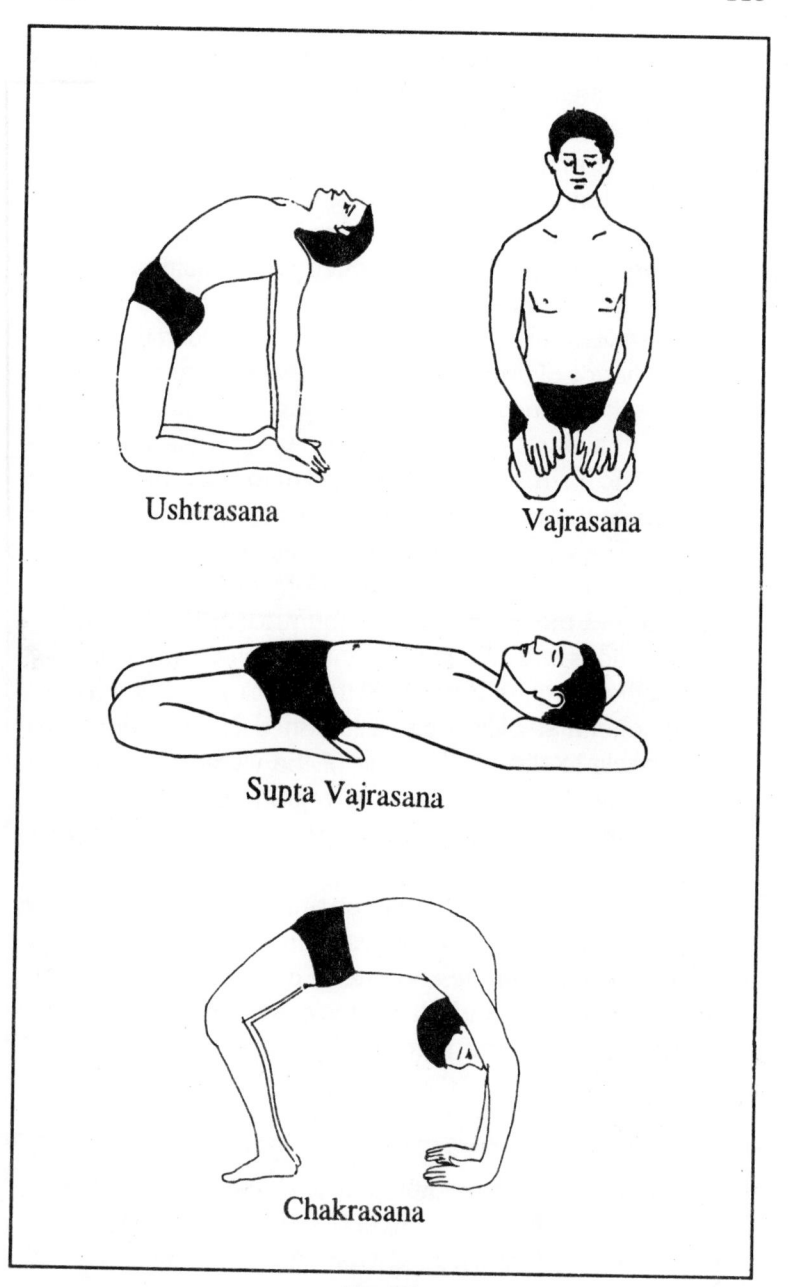

Ushtrasana
Vajrasana
Supta Vajrasana
Chakrasana

Fig. 23

found to increase their height by practicing *asanas* in which the static stretching is maximum.
6. In most of the *asanas* the abdominal region is influenced. During the maintenance phase of the *asanas* the pressure in the abdominal cavity changes, which is reflected on the visceral organs like stomach, colon, urinary bladder, etc. If the normal breathing is continued while maintaining the *asanas* there is an alternate positive and negative pressure on these visceral organs. If the breath is retained during the maintenance of *asana* either after inhalation or exhalation, the positive or negative pressures are also maintained for that much duration. This not only changes the blood circulation in that area but also stimulates the visceroreceptors due to stretching of the walls of these organs. The sensory impulses from these receptors will bring about stretch reflexes in the smooth muscles of visceral organs and maintain their optimum tone. We know that the emotions can influence the muscle tone of the muscular wall of these organs. But now as the muscle tone is improved, the emotional stability is also established. Now the emotions are unable to disturb the tone of the visceral organs and hence the digestive power is regained. This happens particularly when the *pranadharana* is practiced during *asana*.
7. The increased visceral circulation and the alternate positive and negative pressure changes in the abdominal and the pelvic region, promote and preserve the healthy condition of the endocrine glands. It is often observed in women that in the beginning the menstrual cycle is influenced after practicing *asanas*.
8. It may be recalled that the mental characteristics or even the personality is closely related with the posture of the individual. e.g., disappointment or depression results in a total or partial flexion of the body. That means an attitude or the body posture is related to emotional and psychological factors that contribute to the development of one's personality. Typical postural patterns of the cultural *asanas*,

if practiced judiciously as per the tradition, would remove the defect even at the emotional level and thus render balanced and admirable personality. One may therefore experience better emotional stability even after a few days of practice.

We know that the muscle tone of skeletal muscles is the basis of the posture. Muscle tone is influenced by emotions through the cerebellum-hypothalamus functional axis. If the corrective *asanas* are practiced in an effortless (relaxed) and comfortable manner, the cortical activity cannot interfere with this functional axis and that is why new emotional tensions are not developed. On the contrary the muscle tone is reduced considerably due to passive stretch reflex mechanism thus the existing emotional tension is also decreased. The individual feels peaceful and pleasant. The corrections thus made in the tonic background, due to regular practice, are expected to bring about necessary corrections in one's emotional behavior. They may even change one's total outlook towards the life.

9. In topsy-turvy postures, due to upside down position of the body the cardio-vascular reflex mechanisms are stimulated. The venous return becomes very easy as the gravitational force also helps the downward flow of blood. Brain receives sufficient quantity of blood easily. It refreshes the whole central nervous system. But in this condition, in order to prevent forceful blood flow towards the brain, a new pattern of reflex mechanism is set for the circulation in the upper extremity. This type of training to the baroreceptors and the stretch receptors not only checks the forceful blood circulation to the brain during the posture but also maintains the blood pressure at the normal level for all the day-to-day activities of the body.

10. These topsy-turvy as well as the balancing *asanas* stimulate vestibular organs of balance and improve their function. Balancing against the gravity requires one's constant attention as well as a steady mind. A regular training of

Vakrasana

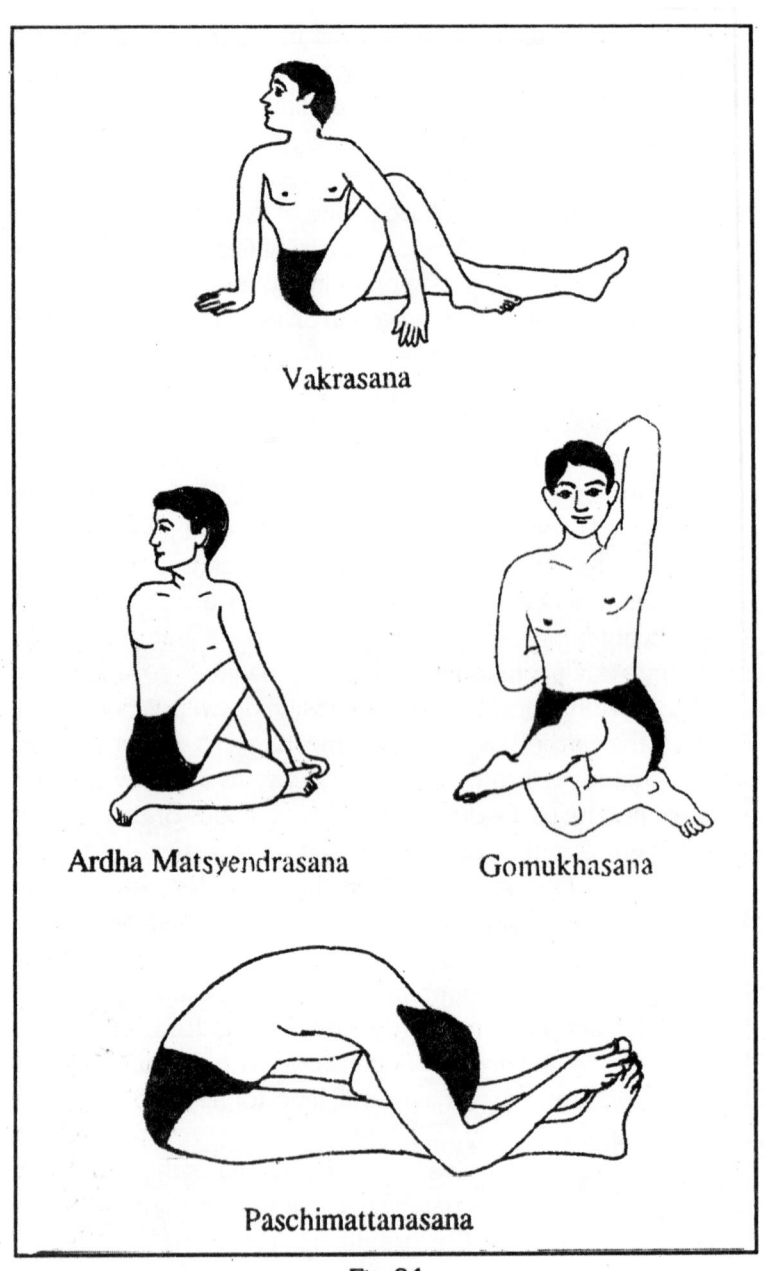

Ardha Matsyendrasana

Gomukhasana

Paschimattanasana

Fig. 24

Bhujangasana

Dhanurasana

Vrikshasana　　　Chakrasana

Fig. 25

these organs in this way through balancing *asanas* would improve mental stability and concentration. This is mainly due to the fact that the external sensory inputs or the internal thought processes are greatly reduced when one remains aware of the balance.

11. Scientific studies have revealed that *asanas* like *Paschimottanasana, Padahastasana, Halasana, Dhanurasana, Ustrasana* influence the nostril dominance and both the nostrils function more or less equally. This is due to decongestion of the mucosal membrane in the nostrils.

Thus these *asanas* recondition various neuromuscular units, including joints, tendons, and other reflex mechanisms and make the body suitable for higher yogic practices.

RELAXATIVE ASANAS

Shavasana and *Makarasana* are the two *asanas* for relaxation, mentioned in *hatha yoga*. They are practiced in supine and prone position of the body respectively. They bring about both physical as well as mental relaxation if practiced properly and sincerely. It should be borne in mind that this is not only a resting posture or sleeping condition but a conscious relaxation. It is also not an idle or a lazy state of mind. On the contrary *Shavasana* makes the individual more fresh and energetic. It overcomes physical as well as the mental fatigue or exertion. Relaxation in *Shavasana* renders the mind more calm and tranquil.

We know that the mental tensions give rise to physical tensions. The mental tensions are the result of our interactions with the external stressful situation or strong emotions. If one fails to cope with them efficiently and easily, the stress is produced. The negative thinking or the analysis and the mental unrest add to these tensions. This is reflected on the nerves and muscles, making them tense. Muscles under such tension remain contracted. They obstruct the normal blood flow and therefore get exhausted very easily. The tense nervous system cannot coordinate various functions of the body and thus a disharmony is produced. Long-term derailment in the vital functions would lead to the 'disease' condition.

Asana

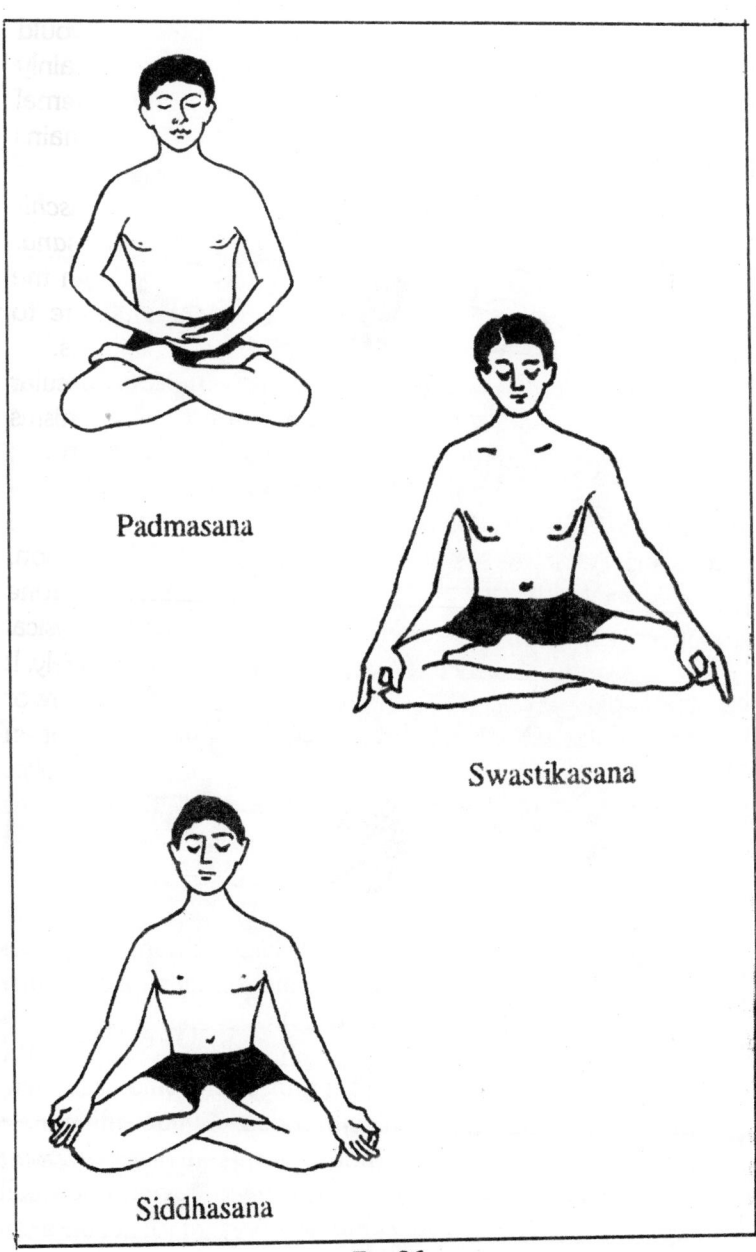

Padmasana

Swastikasana

Siddhasana

Fig. 26

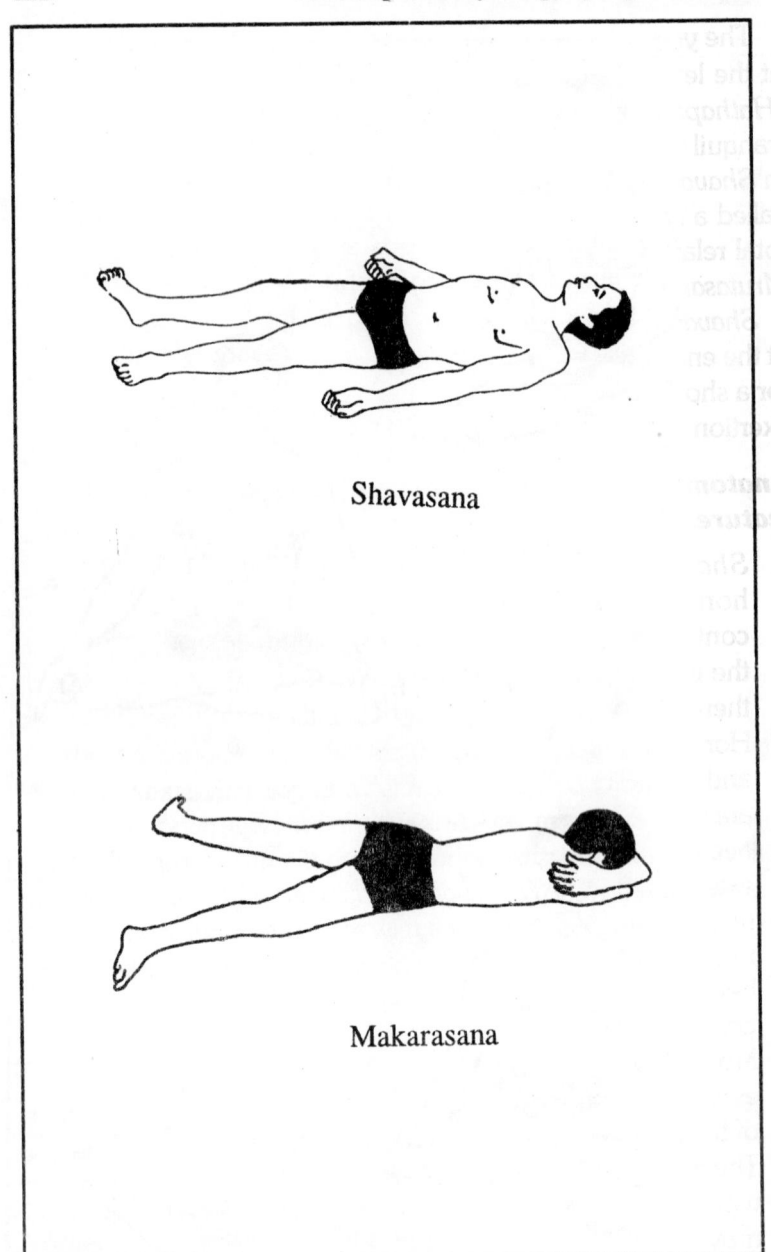

Shavasana

Makarasana

Fig. 27

Asana

The yogic relaxation aims at the release of tensions working at the level of superconsciousness (चित्त chitta). Hatha yoga (Hathapradipika I:32) emphasizes 'Chitta-vishranti' i.e., the tranquil state of subtler mind. The depth of relaxation achieved in Shavasana is compared with the dead body and hence it is called a corpse pose. The name Shavasana thus indicates the total relaxation of the nervous system. It is also mentioned as Mrutasana in Gherand Samhita (II:19).

Shavasana is generally practiced for minimum 10–15 minutes at the end of a session of asanas or even after every 3–4 asanas for a short period from 1–3 minutes, in order to avoid slightest exertion while practicing asanas.

Anatomico-physiological considerations (salient features)

1. *Shavasana* provides the most natural (anatomical), horizontal and comfortable position of the body that contributes to the physical as well as mental relaxation at the first instance. All the joints are consciously loosen and therefore the tension and tremor in their muscles is reduced.
2. Horizontal and relaxed position of the body facilitates efficient and easy blood circulation. Blood pressure and heart rate are reduced and maintained at a minimal level as there is no need to circulate the blood with force. Now the flexor and extensor muscles need not work against the gravity. There is no need to hold the body against gravity. As a result these big muscles relax and the metabolic rate is reduced. Breathing becomes slower, slightly deeper, rhythmic and mostly abdominal in nature, as one progresses in relaxation.
3. Mostly, we are not aware of this abdominal type of breathing even when we are resting but in *Shavasana* the movements of the abdomen are consciously attended in the beginning. The abdomen moves up when we breathe in and sinks down when we breathe-out. Even if one does not feel these movements, he has to correct his breathing by allowing only the stomach to move up and down and by stopping chest movements voluntarily in the beginning. This is

achieved easily if one relaxes his thorax. One starts watching these abdominal movements as a third person (as a witness) rather consciously after a short practice of such abdominal breathing. In *Makarasana*, the abdomen cannot move since it is fixed to the ground and hence one can watch the up and down movement of the lower part of the lumbar and upper hip portion during inhalation and exhalation respectively.

4. During abdominal breathing the diaphragm also moves slowly and rhythmically which has got a soothing effect on the higher brain centers. One immediately feels relaxed. The abdominal breathing gives rhythmic and gentle massage to the abdominal organs, removing their congestion if any. The abdominal muscles are toned up and the blood circulation in the pelvic and abdominal region is increased.

5. Even before watching the abdominal movements in this way, all the body parts and their muscles are relaxed consciously one-by-one or simultaneously. One can experience (with the closed eyes) the difference between the tension and the relaxation in the muscles and joints, e.g., the hip joints, facial muscles, muscles of the lower limbs, etc. This kind of training is required at least in the beginning to relieve muscular tensions as well as to engage the mind properly in such technique so that new thoughts and imaginations are not generated. Otherwise one undergoes a conscious thought process and brings more tensions via memory, intellect and imagination.

6. After this, one can easily practice *Pranadharana* (प्राणधारणा) in which one passively observes the incoming and outgoing flow of breath. One can witness, as a third person, (साक्षीवृत्ति) the current of air moving in up to the chest and again going out through the nostrils. This is the technique by which one can learn to focus his attention consciously.

7. Various stages in the technique of *Shavasana* have been developed upon the principle of progression from gross to subtler level. One is gradually trained to withdraw his

awareness form the gross aspect of the body and to focus it more on the subtler functions of the body and mind. For example, after these steps in relaxation as mentioned above, one develops and remains aware of the touch of air inside the tips of the nostrils. Then one directs his awareness to the feeling of a minute difference of the temperature of the inhaled and exhaled air. One can feel a cooling sensation while inhaling and a warm sensation while exhaling, inside the tip of the nostrils. While doing this, the interference from the cortical region of the brain is reduced and therefore it not only leads the individual to the deeper and deeper levels of relaxation but also helps to reach up to the *chitta* (superconsciousness) and to achieve a state of *chitta-vishranti* (चित्तविश्रांति), i.e., total relaxation. This stage of relaxation however, is not so easy to reach.

8. One realizes the reduction in the number of thoughts entering in the mind particularly when one practices any one of the subtler stages mentioned above. One can easily then develop an attitude of a witness (साक्षीवृत्ति) towards one's own thoughts. In this way, instead of getting involved in any thought process, one observes or watches them, as a third person, coming in and going out of the body-mind complex. As one forgets about the rest of the body, the whole body relaxes completely. The muscle tone is extremely reduced. This resolves the tensions in the nervous system. The mind becomes quieted and one feels very peaceful. One gets gradual training for withdrawal of the mind from all the sensory as well as motor organs (functions) and also for focusing on the thoughts as an observer or seer (दृष्टा). In this condition analytical activities of the cerebral cortex are decreased to a great extent. There is no interpretation and no anticipation. One experiences the thoughtless condition of the mind. This particular training in *Shavasana* helps the individual to focus the mind on the infinity and to slacken the muscular efforts (activity) during the practice of other *asanas*. Thus *chitta* (mind) is going to be relaxed in

Shavasana. Its contact with sensory and motor organs will progressively become weaker and ultimately it could be completely cut off for a time-being. Such functional dissociation of mind from these organs is termed as *Pratyahar* (प्रत्याहार). When the duration of such dissociation is lengthened it gives a momentary experience of *Samadhi* (समाधी) to a practitioner (साधक). Thus *Shavasana* also helps the practitioner to achieve a stage of *Pratyahar*, leading to the higher state of consciousness, i.e., *Samadhi*.

9. Even though sedatives and tranquilizers apparently give a feeling of relaxation, it is temporary. The chemical action of these drugs is to inhibit or to block the neural mechanisms at some level or the other in the nervous system. The mental tensions, worries and anxiety are not felt as long as the chemical influence is there. After the effect of the chemical drug is over, tensions start working again. One gets addicted to these drugs. Day-by-day the doses of the drugs increase. Same thing is true to some extent in case of hypnotically induced relaxation. Only in yogic method of relaxation the whole approach seems to be different. It allows the tensions to come to the surface in an inactivated condition so that they can find their way out without disturbing the individual. The tranquility and peace of mind achieved by the person after the practice of *Shavasana* is of a long lasting nature.

10. The practice of *Shavasana* has been found effective and most suitable in the treatment of hypertension and insomnia since it removes psychological tensions, reduces anxiety, brings about tranquility, rejuvenates the neural functions and establishes balance in all the functions of the body. It gives rise to the sense of well-being and a mental poise. It is therefore really a boon for the patients suffering from high blood pressure. This has been proved scientifically all over the world, by eminent cardiologists. It also acts as a supportive treatment in various diseases like diabetes, asthma, hyperacidity, arthritis, etc. In short it is the most effective therapeutic measure against stress disorders.

A scientific study revealed that persons can relax and restore to the normal resting condition in just 8 minutes if they practice *shavasana* after running on treadmill for five minutes. Where as they required 14 and 24 minutes to become normal when they relaxed in simple supine position and in chair respectively.

MEDITATIVE ASANAS

An uninterrupted process of meditation requires minimum or no disturbance from the external or internal environments. That is, only in the absence of the sensory inputs and their perception, one would be able to concentrate his mind for meditation. *Padmasana, Siddhasana, Samasana, Swastikasana* and *Vajrasana* are important *asanas* for meditation. The aim of these *asanas* is to provide a firm and comfortable posture for the practice of *pranayama, dhyana*, etc., for hours without any physical or mental disturbance. The cultural and relaxative *asanas* in fact make the body and mind stabilized as well as tranquilized which is the basic requirement of meditation. The meditative *asanas* further enhance the practice of concentration and facilitate the process of meditation.

Anatomico-physiological considerations (salient features)

1. Meditative *asanas* provide broad triangular base for the body, formed by two femurs and the pelvis. This broad base gives firm foundation to the body and makes it steady and stable. Even if one looses the body sense during meditation, he remains balanced due to subconscious control of the posture by the lower brain centers.
2. The spine is kept in vertical and straight position and any extra curvature in the backbone is consciously avoided. Four natural curves are well preserved. This is very important for higher spiritual practice. Straight spine prevents compression of the abdominal organs and leaves the abdominal muscles free for the breathing activity. It facilitates easy movements of the diaphragm in breathing.

This also helps alimentary canal to carry out digestive functions including peristaltic movements smoothly. Well-balanced, straight spine requires negligible activity of the flexor and extensor muscles of the trunk to maintain the upright position of the spine. This is sufficient to keep the practitioner semiconscious and to avoid sleep during meditation. The position of hands gives support to the spine like a bracket.

समंकायशिरोग्रीव धारयन्नचलं स्थिरः ॥
Samamkayashirogriva dharayanachalan sthirah
—*Bhagwad Geeta* VI:13

This aphorism from the *Bhagwad Geeta* says that the head, neck and rest of the body should be maintained in balanced (in one line), stable and steady condition (during meditation). Sometimes it is wrongly translated as, erect spine. While making it erect one may disturb its natural curves and put some extra curvature in the spine that requires special conscious efforts to maintain it. The practitioner would get tired and may bend forward. On the contrary, balanced condition of the body, neck and head with all the natural curves intact would stimulate the proprioceptors in the spinal muscles to maintain the equilibrium, without our notice.

In such a balanced condition of the spine the diameter of the thorax is changed during inhalation and exhalation. Therefore the center of gravity shifts forward and backward very minutely but rhythmically. These oscillations of the thoracic part would also stimulate the proprioceptors rhythmically and would bring about their alternate contraction and relaxation through the stretch reflex mechanism. Thus the lower brain centers can easily maintain the position of the body, below the level of consciousness.

This allows the practitioner to focus his attention towards the inner environment and to develop the inner awareness since the disturbances of the external stimuli are greatly reduced. When one is free from the usual sensory feedback and the conscious efforts to maintain the posture, one can attend the inner sensations and feelings arising out of special stimulations of the visceroreceptors and proprioceptors in the coccygeal, sacral and lumbar region. These special sensory impulses are conveyed to the central nervous system where they are integrated by the lower brain centers.

4. Experimentally it has been observed that the energy requirement in meditative *asanas* is less than in normal chair-sitting position. This is mainly because of the low oxygen requirement of the body and reduced production of carbon dioxide on account of negligible muscular activity in the body and reduced burden on the circulatory function. As a result the cardio-respiratory activity is also greatly reduced.

5. The knee joints are not only flexed but also rotated outwardly. This locking of the legs at the knee joints restricts the flow of blood and its accumulation in lower limbs. The muscular activity in the legs is almost zero and therefore the requirement of blood circulation is also negligible. The horizontal position of the lower extremities reduces the vertical distance up to the heart for the venous return. Naturally then the force to return the venous blood against the gravity is reduced. Thus the blood circulation in the lower extremities is minimum. The blood flow is now directed towards the pelvic and the lumbar region. The nerve plexuses in this region get richer blood supply and are therefore toned up and refreshed. It also tones up the lower region of the spine and the abdominal organs. It may be recalled that the sacral region contains network of the parasympathetic nerves. On getting richer blood supply, these autonomic nerves are also toned up and create a peaceful and pleasant attitude.

6. The static stretching and maintained rotation of the knee joints squeeze the blood vessels and press the capsule. When

the meditative *asana* is released the fresh blood supply rushes there and improves its health. Thus the stiffness and the rigidity of the knee joint is gradually reduced. A regular practitioner of *Padmasana* would never experience pain or deformity in the knee joints.
7. The particular angle of femur bones with that of the pelvic girdles facilitates the formation of *Moolabandha* and *Uddiyana bandha*. The muscles in the anal region as well as at the perineum are easily contracted and relaxed. In *Siddhasana* the perineal region is slightly pressed by the heel. It has got a soothing effect on the nervous system that gives rise to calmness.

In this way the meditative *asanas* provide a steady, stable and yet comfortable sitting posture that helps in controlling and concentrating the mind during meditation for considerably longer durations. The *asanajaya* is, in real sense, achieved with the mastery over such meditative *asanas*.

DIFFERENCE BETWEEN ASANAS AND EXERCISES

Many people consider *asanas* as exercises and practice them like exercises. *Asanas* are also employed in the treatment of certain disorders. *Asanas* definitely promote and maintain the physical and mental health. They are preliminary practices to advance on the path of yoga. They are specific postural patterns. If we carefully observe and compare *asanas* and exercises, we would find that they differ from each other in many respects. Let us study these differences one-by-one.
1. Since the aim and objectives of *asanas* and exercises are different, the mode of their performance is altogether different. The movements to assume and release any *asana* are slow, smooth and without any jerk. The maintenance phase of *asana* is more important than the movement part of it. Slow movements always involve the action of deeper muscles and a precise nervous control over them. No force or extra amount of efforts is applied while doing the *asanas*. The whole musculature is rather kept in a relaxed condition. There is no exertion in *asanas*.

Exercises are performed in a fast or speedy manner leading to exertion and fatigue. All the movements are done with a jumpy and jerky element. The maintenance phase is rarely observed in exercises and if it is present it will be for a very short period. The movements in exercise are quick or rapid in nature. Moreover, they are repeated several times. This is why their action will be just superficial.

2. The effect of *asanas* is more on the trunk portion of the body. The proprioceptive and visceroreceptive mechanisms are given free scope to modify feedback control, which is necessary for their healthy functioning. The special patterns of *asanas* when maintained, bring about changes in the pressure in the internal cavities of the visceral organs, which in turn improve the circulation and stimulate autonomic nervous system associated with them. This has a beneficial effect towards balancing the emotional behavior of the individual.

In exercises the movements of the extremities are more prominent and influential. Their effect on the trunk part is secondary. The skeletal muscles of the extremities are powerfully built. The circulation is increased in the periphery. There is a profuse sweating on account of such heavy movements.

3. In *asanas* the spinal column is moved in almost all the directions in its possible range of movements. The vertebrae are stretched in all the directions and also rotated in a clockwise and anti-clockwise manner alternately. The sequence of *asanas* is based on the principle of counter movement for the movement done in the earlier *asana*. The right and left sides are equally considered in *asanas*, i.e., both the sides are stretched or contracted in the same manner. This increases the flexibility of the spine and reduces the stiffness of its joints.

In exercises, on the other hand, only a particular movement is repeated in order to increase strength and skill of that part of the body. Thus only one side is conditioned and developed asymmetrically in many exercises. Sequence is also rarely observed in exercises. The movement of the spine is fast and the counter action is absent. Backward bending of the spine is seldom practiced. The flexibility may be limited or the spinal joints may become stiff in a longer run.

4. Muscle-building is not the aim of *asanas*. Therefore, heavy muscular activity is avoided and hence the energy expenditure is also less than that in exercises. *Asanas* do not put undue load on the cardio-respiratory systems. That is why there is a negligible increase in the rate of heart beats and respiration during *asanas*. Muscular tensions are reduced purposely by slackening the voluntary efforts. Parasympathetic predominance is established during *asanas* and maintained even after the session of *asanas*.

   Heavy muscle masses are built through exercises for more and more muscular strength. These bumpy muscles are cultivated for 'manly' appearance and are considered as a sign of physical fitness and vigor. Really speaking, they do not improve stamina or the physical endurance. After a particular age these over-developed muscles act mainly as parasites, sapping their energy and nutrition from other tissues. In older age, they become loose and give an ugly shape to the body. Heavy muscular exercises increase the strain on the cardio-respiratory system. The sympathetic predominance that is developed during such exercises shows its after effects on the other systems.

5. In *asanas* skeletal muscles are passively stretched and therefore the muscle tone cannot increase beyond a particular level. Even the static stretching during the maintenance phase is also passive in nature. This influences the capsule and the deep ligaments of the joints, stimulates blood circulation around them and ensures their healthy condition. A problem of oxygen-debt or the accumulation of lactic acid in the joints never arises in *asanas*. On the contrary, after the session of *asanas* one feels refreshed, relaxed and energetic since such toxic substances are

effectively removed due to improved circulation. A sense of well-being is developed which is the sign of the perfect health.

In exercises, there are heavy and sustained (isometric) muscular contractions and active stretching of muscles against some graded resistance, e.g., exercise on the 'bullworker' instrument. The muscular tone is tremendously increased. These sustained muscular tensions reflect on the nervous system and give rise to hyper activity of the nervous system. The practitioner of such heavy exercises may become hyperactive and impulsive in nature. When the exercises are finished, one gets exhausted, feels tired and needs rest. The reason is the accumulation of lot of lactic acid in the muscles or the oxygen debt. An elimination of extra carbon dioxide or lactic acid is another workload on the circulatory and respiratory systems.

6. As the voluntary efforts are withdrawn in the final stage of *asanas* the activity of the motor cortex is greatly reduced or even stopped completely. An inner awareness is automatically developed where one can experience special sensations arising in the body due to specific stimulation of the interoceptors. The lower brain centers can effectively integrate these impulses to maintain a proper equilibrium.

In an attempt to achieve the goal in exercises, one makes lot of voluntary efforts. These increased efforts cross the normal limits of endurance and stamina. Success is measured in terms of apparent development of speed, strength and capacities. Naturally more and more external awareness is developed as in case of weight-lifting.

Thus we find that the basic purpose, motivation and therefore the technique of *asanas* and exercises are quite different. Their mechanism and the effects are also different. Therefore there should not be any confusion regarding *asanas* and exercises and their nature.

It is clear that on the physical level, the health and hygiene of the internal organs is primarily maintained by *asanas*. The sensory inputs that are initiated in the trunk region, especially in the lumbar and sacral region due to the special patterns of *asanas* bring about the nerve culture, needed for higher practices like *pranayama*. Proper balance in the neuromuscular system and in the sympathetic and parasympathetic activity of the autonomic nervous system is established. A feeling of exhilaration, freshness, pleasantness, lightness as well as the stability and balance of mind are some of the benefits of *asanas* even to the physical culturist.

One should however, take into account one's limitations due to age, sex, hyper or hypotonic condition of the musculature, rigidity or flexibility of the joints, and the purpose of practicing *asanas*. One should avoid pulling or contracting the body parts by putting lot of efforts (like in exercises) in order to emulate the perfect pattern of *asana*. This may cause physical injury to the joints and muscles by tearing the associated fibrous tissue. The conditions like sprain, muscle pull or spasm may also result. Therefore *asanas* should never be done in a competitive spirit. The violent efforts to reach the final posture should be avoided consciously. 'Pleasant pain' is the limit for the movement and the muscular efforts, which should lead you progressively towards the final stage of *asana* within a few days. According to *hatha yoga*, over-enthusiasm, over-confidence about one's capacity and too much efforts while learning and practicing *asanas* should be avoided. Whenever a need is felt, one should rest and relax for a while so that the cardio-respiratory functions would not be over-taxed. Our aim is to recondition all the regulatory systems by a consistent and systematic practice of *asanas* so that we would be ready to learn higher yogic practices.

The breathing should not be modified unless required for therapeutic purposes. Body would adjust the breathing as per the requirement. Observing same time and the place as well as the direction for the daily practice would enhance the results. The place should be quiet, clean and well ventilated. It should be free from insects and foul smell. In short, a pleasant atmosphere, relaxed body and mind, an attitude of devotion, respect for the teacher or *guru* are the prerequisites for the practice of yoga to reap the benefits on physical, mental and spiritual levels.

Two

Mudra, Bandha and Kriyas

Mudras and *bandhas* are special features of *hatha yoga*. They are practiced to enhance the intensity of the effect of *asanas* and *pranayamas*. Those who wish to achieve spiritual benefits should practice these *bandhas* and *mudras* along with *asanas* and *pranayamas* regularly and sincerely. This will lead them to special experiences and progress towards higher practices like *dharana*, *dhyana* and *samadhi*. However, at the same time it should be borne in mind that the health of the *sadhaka*, in all respects, should be sound enough to tolerate the spiritual force, generated by practicing these *bandhas* and *mudras*. In *Kalika Purana* the importance of *mudras* is described. It says that without *mudras* the practice of *pranayama* as well as meditative *asanas* becomes fruitless.

MUDRAS

Mudra is a skillful technique that helps us in the practice of *pranayama*, *pratyahar*, *dharana*, *dhyana* and *samadhi*. According to *Hathapradipika* and *Shiv Samhita* there are ten *mudras*:

(1) *Maha mudra* (2) *Maha bandha* (3) *Mahavedha* (4) *Khechari* (5) *Uddiyan* (6) *Mula bandha* (7) *Jalandhara bandha* (8) *Viperita karani* (9) *Vajroli* and (10) *Shaktichalana*. *Vajroli* is further subdivided into *Sahajoli* and *Amroli*.

It is surprising that the *bandhas* are also included in *mudras*. Probably the reason is they are only four in number. Usually they are practiced as an essential part of *pranayama*. When they are practiced without *pranayama*, they are *mudras*. Therefore, *mudras*, which are practiced in *pranayama* are known as *bandhas*. They bind and direct the current of *prana* from a particular region and generate specific impulse. When these impulses are understood at the experiential level, the *prana* (vital energy or force) can be directed further through the specific route (*nadi*).

Gherand Samhita speaks about 25 *mudras* in 100 verses. *Tantra* mentions *Ankush mudra*, *Abhaya mudra*, *Kumbha mudra*, *Vara mudra*, and *Shankha mudra*. In *Goraksha Shatak* only six *mudras* are described.

MEANING OF MUDRA

A voluntary neuromuscular action (contraction) or posture with the help of which the *prana* is controlled and directed through a particular *nadi*, is known as *mudra*. That is why *Viparita karani mudra* is practiced as *asana* with a limited objective at the physical level. The other meanings of *mudra* are as follows:

(1) Seal or the cast (mould) (2) stamp, impression, (3) currency, (4) gesture, (5) a body position which gives joy and pleasure, (6) symbol, and (7) acting with some expression on the face.

The word *mudra* is not limited to *yoga*. They are also included in *Tantra* (e.g., *Vijay Tantra*, which saves a person from evil) and the art of Indian traditional dance as well as drama. Unlike in *hatha yoga*, in *Tantra* the importance is given to the special arrangements of the hands and fingers. While in Indian dance and drama, *mudras* are done with the help of eyes and face. The purpose is clearly of an expression or indication of the feelings.

मुदम् आनंदम् ददाति इति मुद्रा ।
Mudam anandam dadati iti mudra (Sharda Tilak)

Here, 'mud' means to rejoice or to be happy and 'ra' means to give. An action that gives us delight or extreme joy. This is an indication that the practice of *mudra* is concerned with sensory aspect.

PURPOSE OF PRACTICING MUDRA

According to *Hathapradipika*, *mudras* are practiced for awakening of the *Kundalini* power (*Kundalini Prabodhana*) while *Gherand Samhita* recommends it for equilibrium and stability (*Sthirata*). *Mudras* are practiced to stimulate a particular neuromuscular area (e.g., anal sphincters as in *Ashwini mudra*) of the body by voluntary muscular contraction maintained for some length of time or repeated with counter relaxation. This generates currents of energy that travel upward. They minimize the activity of mind and the *sadhaka* experiences the mental and emotional stability.

Technique and Effects of Certain Mudras

Gyan Mudra	Contact tip of the index finger with the thumb. This *mudra* removes defects or deficiency in the nervous system. It improves memory and perception.
Pran Mudra	Join last two fingers with the thumb. It removes physical and mental weakness and ophthalmic disorders.
Prithvi Mudra	Join tip of ring finger and the thumb. Muscular and haematic defects are removed by doing this *mudra*.
Surya Mudra	Place tip of the ring finger at the base line of the first node of the thumb. It helps in *Kundalini* arousal. It gives miraculous power.
Varun Mudra	Join the little fingertip with the thumb. It removes dryness and pain from body.
Shunya Mudra	Bend the middle finger and contact the thumb with its nail. Effects of this *mudra* are fast. It removes deafness and other ear disorders.

BANDHAS

Bandhas are included in the technique of *pranayama*. The practice of *bandha* requires more conscious effort. The duration of *bandhas* is lesser than *mudras* because they are practiced mostly with *Antar-kumbhaka* phase. Sometimes three *bandhas* are practiced together to intensify the practice of *pranayama* and to generate a typical sensation.

MEANING OF BANDHA

Meaning of the word *bandha* is to bind, to lock, or to tie. The particular neuromuscular junction is contracted to increase positive pressure and to generate visceroreceptive or proprioceptive impulse that would travel upward through ascending path in the spinal cord. Secondly, there is a specific type of sensation at the contracted area. One has to remain attentive in order to maintain the contraction for a few seconds. One has to develop awareness of these impulses and the sensitivity to experience them.

There are four major *bandhas* in vogue. Their names and the area of action are as follows:

1. *Jalandhara bandha* : Throat (*Kantha mudra*)
2. *Uddiyana bandha*   : Abdomen
3. *Mula bandha*   : Perineum and anus
4. *Jivha bandha*   : Tongue and palate (*Nabhomudra*)

These sensitive areas are stimulated during *pranayama* by practicing these *bandhas* particularly during *kumbhaka*. Then the *pranic* energy passes upwards through *sushumna*, which is to be experienced. Thus it may be said that the *mudras* will awaken the *kundalini* power while *bandhas* will help this serpent power to rise up along the *chakras* to bring about a specific effect.

SIMILARITIES IN BANDHAS AND MUDRAS

1. There is a voluntary contraction of a particular neuromuscular junction or the sphincters of the body in both.
2. This contraction is maintained for some length of time and this is done in a particular posture. Both of them require proper concentration on the technique.
3. Both of them are practiced on the empty stomach.
4. The *sadhaka* who is aspiring to utilize both of these for the higher practices with spiritual aim should be healthy in normal sense.
5. Before learning and practicing them, *sadhaka* should undergo a long and sufficient practice of *asanas*, *pranayamas*, *kriyas*, etc.

6. Both of these practices are concerned with the higher aspects of *yoga* in order to progress on the spiritual path, i.e., both of them activate particular *chakras* (the energy centers) and produce typical sensations, which are experienced by the *sadhaka* (a serious practitioner).
7. Both these practices give rise to the internalized awareness. They increase the concentration of the *sadhaka* more and more on the inner happenings. Thus both of them help to progress in deeper meditation.

DIFFERENCE BETWEEN BANDHAS AND MUDRAS

1. *Bandhas* are used especially during the *pranayama*, particularly during the *kumbhaka* phase. *Mudras* are practiced at other times also or along with other *kriyas*.
2. While applying *bandhas* the breath is held outside or inside. *bandhas* are practiced singly or all together. While practicing *mudras* the breathing is continued. Rarely it is suspended. The awareness may be on the neuromuscular contraction.
3. *Bandhas* are mostly related with the throat and trunk (diaphragm, abdomen and pelvic flour). *Mudras* are mostly concerned with the face, fingers and also the abdomen.
4. *Bandhas* are more related to important *chakras* and do not express any emotion. Eyes are kept closed. *Mudras* are used to express some kind of emotions or gestures. Eyes are mostly open.
5. Effect of *bandhas* is seen immediately. *Mudras* are slow in action.

PHYSIOLOGY OF BANDHAS AND MUDRAS

1. There is a definite voluntary neuromuscular or musculo-skeletal contraction in both, which is maintained for some period from a few seconds to minutes. These contractions are repeated to enhance the effect of *asana* or *pranayama*.
2. Application of *bandhas* not only helps to cut off the connection between the individual and the external environment but also turns the individual's attention inward. In *bandhas* there is an awareness of suspended breathing

movement. This contributes to the tranquility and stability of mind and also helps to detach it from the sensory inputs. In *mudras* the awareness of the breathing movements and/or repeated neuromuscular contractions makes him to perceive sensation from that area which is stimulated to liberate energy.
3. Proprioceptors, visceroreceptors in these areas are stimulated during the contractions, which create special sensation and attract the attention of the practitioner.
4. These stimulations give rise to special kind of nerve impulses, which are sent to the brain centers and translated as new sensations. One can feel and experience various kind of sensations due to these practices, e.g., vibration, throbbing, creeping sensation, feeling of ecstasy, bliss, extreme joy, etc.

UDDIYANA BANDHA

Uddiyana bandha is a technique, which makes maximum use of the diaphragm and the ribs. It is practiced either in sitting or in standing position. This practice also forms the basis for *nauli kriya*. Different technical terms related to this practice are in vogue. Although the technique and the application of these practices vary, they have a common characteristic feature that is the ascending movement of the diaphragm. Following techniques are related to *Uddiyan bandha*.

UDDIYANA MUDRA

The abdominal wall is slightly retracted and maintained in this condition while the normal breathing is continued with the help of chest in sitting position.

TADAGI BANDHA

In the supine position, the knees are folded and kept vertical. Feet are placed near the body (hips). After deepest exhalation *uddiyan* is practiced as usual. Since the abdomen is sucked in, it gives concave appearance like *tadag* (dry pond) to the abdomen.

TADAGI MUDRA

In the same supine position, the abdomen is drawn little inside, maintained as such and the breathing is continued with the chest.

TECHNIQUE OF UDDIYANA

If *uddiyana* is to be practiced in sitting position, one has to sit in *Padmasana* and place the palms on the knees. In standing position one has to bend little forward, bend the knees slightly and rest one's hands either on the thighs or on the knees. Legs are kept apart. Position of the hands is not only important as a support but also because it facilitates the action of the thoracic cage and fixes up the neck and the shoulder muscles properly. After adapting the right type of posture, as described above, for *uddiyana*, exhale deeply. You may take help of strong abdominal contraction for maximum deep exhalation. The breath is held out and a strong mock inhalation is attempted, i.e., the chest is expanded by raising the ribs as if inhalation is taking place. Actually the air is not allowed to flow into the lungs. For this, even nostrils are closed in the beginning. The abdominal muscles are kept relaxed. Thus during the mock inhalation the atmospheric air does not enter the lungs but the chest is expanded like it is inflated in the normal inhalation. Due to this, there is a sharp increase in the negative pressure in the thoracic cavity, which creates a suction gradient towards the diaphragm. The diaphragm is lifted up and the whole abdomen is sucked in towards the diaphragm and the spine, giving it a concave shape. Bending position of the body helps in giving greater abdominal concavity. This condition is to be maintained till one develops a strong desire to breathe in. To release *uddiyana*, the chest is relaxed and the abdominal wall is allowed to come to its normal position gradually and passively and at the same time inhaling slowly. This is one round of *uddiyana*. The optimum duration of one round is possible from 10 to 60 seconds. When one gets mastery over *uddiyana* with a longer duration, *nauli kriya* becomes easier. Such three to four rounds are practiced at a stretch, with or without the normal breathing in between the two rounds. *Uddiyana* is to be practiced on an empty stomach and bladder.

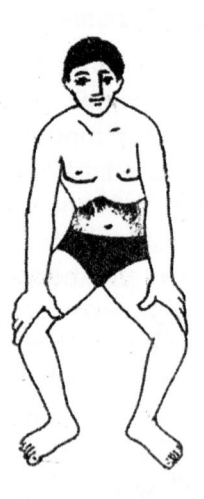

Fig. 28: Uddiyana Bandha

It may be remembered that during normal inhalation the diaphragm moves down when the chest is expanded. But in *uddiyana*, the diaphragm is moving up even though the chest is expanding as usual. Therefore anatomically, *uddiyana* means the rising up of the diaphragm and *bandha* means the neuromuscular locking (action) at the navel region. It is this anatomical position of the diaphragm and the abdominal muscles, which enables one to experience peculiar sensations along the spine, due to stretching of the lower portion of the lumbar part of the vertebral column and the particular angle taken by the sacrum. As stated earlier, the yogic practices thus stimulate the sacral region, which is innervated by the parasympathetic nervous system.

The main physiological characteristic feature of *uddiyana* is, it produces sub-atmospheric (negative) pressures inside the visceral cavities like oesophagus, stomach, urinary bladder and colon. This vacuum creation is mainly due to the ascending movement of the diaphragm, irrespective of the movement of the ribs (Fig. 28) during the expansion of the thoracic cage. The magnitude of negative pressure varies in different cavities from -20mm to -80mmHg. This vacuum production would promote blood circulation in the pelvic region. This will tone up the plexuses in this part and will stimulate the parasympathetic nerve fibers. A sincere practitioner would experience the special type of sensations along the spinal cord. The physical benefits of *uddiyana* are also great. The tone and the strength of the abdominal muscles are well maintained. It prevents congestion in the pelvic region and relieves constipation, as it improves liver function and digestion. It mobilizes the extra fat deposition on the abdominal wall. It has been observed that *uddiyana* produces sinus bradycardia (reduction in the heart rate), which may be due to the negative pressure, created in the thorax.

It has been found that in an enthusiasm and due to lack of appropriate information about *uddiyana*, many people practice some other techniques instead of *uddiyana*. Two types of techniques are possible, namely, Mueller's maneuver (MM) and Valsalva maneuver (VM) which may be practiced by mistake, instead of *uddiyana*. A yoga teacher is expected to know about these techniques in order to be sure that his student is practicing uddiyana and not MM or VM. The technique, mechanism and the effects of these three practices could be explained on the basis of physiological studies on them, as follows.

1. In *uddiyana*, flying up of the diaphragm is the main feature. The mock inhalation is done by expanding the chest after the deepest possible exhalation. Since the abdominal muscles remain in relaxed condition, the whole abdomen is lifted up and inward. Negative intra-thoracic and intra-gastric pressures are created. A suction is felt near the center of the diaphragm, the pelvic region and lower abdomen. The whole technique becomes very easy after some practice and one does not feel exerted. Main objective of the practice is the stimulation of the nerves in the sacral region and to

Valsalva Maneuver   Uddiyan   Muller's Maneuver

⊕ = Positive pressure   ⊖ = Negative pressure

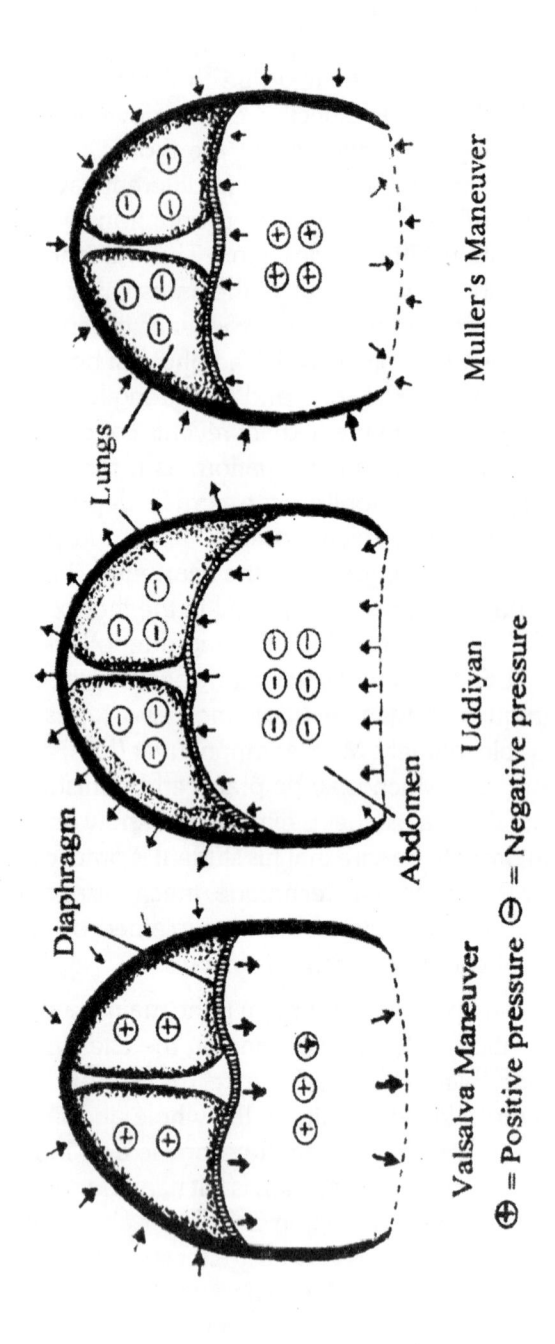

Fig. 29: Difference in Valsalva Maneuver, Uddiyana and Muller's Maneuver

produce typical state of consciousness. Unless this technique is mastered *nauli* manipulation is not possible.
2. In Mueller's maneuver the mock inhalation is attempted with a strong contraction of diaphragm. The lungs are in end-expiratory condition as in *uddiyana* but since the abdomen is deliberately contracted, both the abdomen and the diaphragm remain in a state of isometric contraction. Although there is a negative pressure in the chest, the intra-gastric pressure is positive (Fig. 29), therefore suction is experienced in the neck (throat) region. Since one requires lot of efforts to maintain MM, one feels exhausted after the practice. It is not required to be practiced before *nauli*.
3. In Valsalva maneuver the muscles of the chest and abdomen undergo a sudden and strong contraction after a slight deep inhalation. The whole action is as if one is trying to exhale but no exhalation is taking place since the glottis is completely closed. This technique gives rise to the positive pressure in both the chest as well as in the abdomen. Obviously, this is a strenuous practice and difficult to be maintained for a longer time. Many times we produce such positive pressure during urination and defecation, of course, for a very short period.

Thus it would be clear that the sensory aspect is more important in *uddiyana*. One is expected to perceive these sensations rising up along the spinal cord from the lowermost portion of the trunk. *Uddiyana* should be practiced cautiously since it produces bradycardia due to negative pressures in the viscera, and influences blood circulation as well as the endocrine function. Too much practice of *uddiyana*, may give rise to constipation and the diaphragmatic or the chest pain.

It should also be clear that the technique of *uddiyana* as a preparation to *nauli* and the technique of *uddiyana bandha* practiced during *pranayama* are different. In the former practice one has to exhale and hold the breath while in later one has to inhale and hold the breath. Naturally in the first one negative pressure is developed while in the second the positive pressure is created.

JIVA BANDHA

The tongue is simply lifted up and pressed against the hard palate. The edges of the tongue are turned down, touching the inner sides above the gums. While doing this the frenum and the pharyngeal root of the tongue are pulled, affecting the pharyngeal muscles. One can concentrate on this pull. Mouth is closed. It is difficult to perform *Jiva* and *Jalandhara bandha* together. *Jiva bandha* may be practiced during *antar kumbhaka* as a substitute for *Jalandhara bandha* if one is unable to perform *Jalandhara* lock for some reasons. *Jiva bandha* gives most of the benefits of *Jalandhara bandha* like stoppage of thought process and turning the awareness inward. In addition it improves the health of pharynx, larynx, thyroid and salivary glands. *Jiva bandha* and *simha mudra* together are recommended to treat the problems like chronic tonsillitis, soreness of pharynx and larynx.

JALANDHARA BANDHA

Please refer the page number 176.

MOOLA BANDHA

पार्ष्णिभागेन संपिडय योनिमाकुंचयेद् गुदम् ।
अपानमूर्ध्व आकृष्य मूलबन्धोऽभिधीयते ।।

Parshnibhagena sampidya yonimakunchayed gudam
Apanmurdhva akrushya mulabandho bhidhiyate.

—Hathpradipika II:60

That is, by pressing the perineum (with the heel) and contracting the perineum and anus, one can direct *apan vayu* upward. This is called *moola bandha*.

Some people define *moola bandha* as the contraction of anal sphincters but it is not true. Anal sphincters are also contracted and pulled in and out during *Ashvini mudra*. In *moola bandha* both perineum and anal sphincters are contracted simultaneously. Urination and defecation are the excretory functions of *apan vayu*, controlled by perineal muscles and anal sphincters. One can inhibit the excretory force by contracting these muscles. However this is not the purpose of *moola bandha*. The practitioner is completely absorbed in a typical delighted feeling arising out of sustained contraction of these muscles. Thought process is stopped. Any attempt of thinking will release the *moola bandha*. *Moola bandha* stimulates ANS in the pelvic and genital region, particularly the parasympathetic branch. It improves digestive as well as the sexual power too. By practicing it the quantity of urine and feces is reduced and even old person becomes young. However it should be practiced judiciously otherwise it may cause constipation and sexual disturbance.

NAULI KRIYA

Nauli is one of the *shatkriyas* (six actions) mentioned in *Hathapradipika*. It is an abdominal exercise, meant for cleansing the colon. The characteristic feature of *nauli* is the isolation and manipulation of the right and the left abdominal recti muscles. *Uddiyana* is a basic technique required for *nauli* and *nauli* forms an essential part of the *basti kriya*. One, who maintains *uddiyana* easily for 15-20 seconds, can perform *nauli* perfectly.

While maintaining *uddiyana*, both the knees are pressed with the help of the palms and a forward and slightly downward thrust is given at the same time to the abdominal portion between the umbilicus and the pubic bone. This brings about a contraction of the abdominal recti muscles (Fig.30) between the pubic bone and the ribs and a prominent appearance of these muscles. Since other abdominal muscles are kept in a relaxed condition and only the abdominal recti muscles are contracted, the vertical isolation of these muscles is possible. The equal pressure on both the knees further helps one to achieve the perfect isolation of both the abdominal recti muscles and to make them stand side-by-side in the center. This is known as *Nauli Madhyama* or *Madhya nauli*.

First, one should practice and master the technique only up to *Madhya nauli*. The isolation of both the recti muscles should be complete and their projection should be prominent, compared to the rest of the abdomen. Once the control on *Madhya nauli* technique is gained, the remaining part of *nauli* technique could be practiced easily. The whole practice should be painless. The success in *basti* or *vajroli kriya* also depends on this fine and easy control.

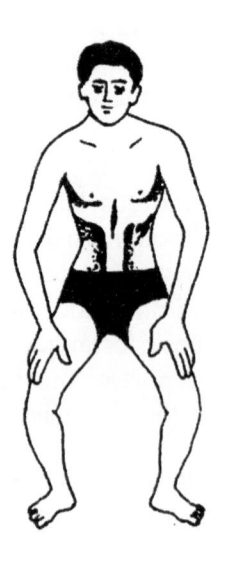

Fig. 30: Nauli Kriya

While maintaining *Madhya nauli*, one leans little more on the right side and relaxes his left side of the abdomen. The pressure on the right knee is increased and at the same time the pressure on the left knee is removed. Thus only the right rectus muscle is contracted and rolled off to the extreme right side. The left rectus is kept relaxed and passive. This isolation and projection of only right rectus muscle is called *Dakshina nauli*.

Now, leaning little more on the left side and simultaneously applying more pressure on the left knee makes the left rectus

Mudra, Bandha and Kriyas 151

muscle isolated and rolled off to the extreme left side. The right rectus is relaxed at the same time. Thus the manipulation of the left rectus muscle on the left side is known as *Vama nauli*. One has to maintain left or right *nauli* for a sufficient time.

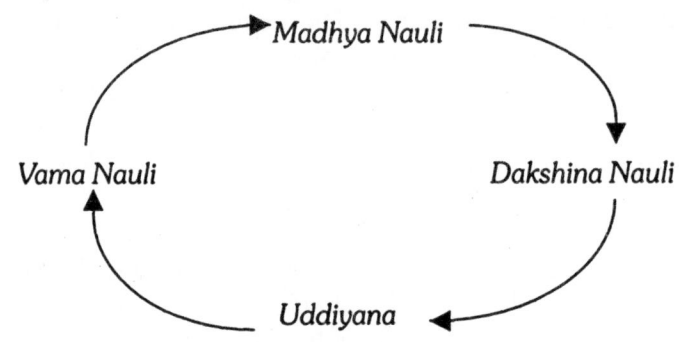

```
          ──►Madhya Nauli
        ╱                  ╲
       ╱                    ▼
  Vama Nauli          Dakshina Nauli
       ▲                    ╱
        ╲                  ╱
          ── Uddiyana ◄──
```

Fig. 31: Nauli Chalan (clockwise)

When one gets full control over this static aspect of *nauli*, i.e., *Dakshin, Vama,* and *Madhya nauli,* one can proceed for *nauli chalan.* The rolling of the recti muscles may be clockwise or anti-clockwise for several times. The whole sequence of rotation is gone through in a quick succession, without any discomfort, pain or strain at any stage. The whole manipulation is continued till one strongly desires to breathe in. In fact, it is not a rotation or rolling as we speak often, but it is the alternate isolation of these three aspects of *nauli* one after the other which appears as if moving from right to left or left to right. The above diagram will help you to understand the whole process better.

Such three to seven rounds are practiced at a time, daily. One may take rest and breathe normally for a couple of seconds between two rounds if necessary. *Nauli* is practiced with an empty stomach.

The main characteristic of *nauli* is the development of sub-atmospheric pressure inside the various abdominal organs like stomach, urinary bladder, colon and esophagus. *Swami Kuvalayananda* investigated the creation of negative pressure in colon during *nauli* for the first time in 1924. He named this partial vacuum in colon as *Madhavdas* Vacuum, in the honor of his guru *Swami Madhavdas Maharaj.* In the beginning, the creation of such negative pressure was thought because of antiperistaltic movement by some authorities. They tried to explain the suction of water in colon during *basti*. But the theory of anti-peristalsis could not explain the water or oil suction in urinary bladder during *vajroli*. The negative or the suction pressure is developed due to ascending action of the diaphragm and the isolation of the abdominal recti muscles. The magnitude of negative pressure during *Dakshina* and *Vama nauli* has been found to be in the range of −20 to −60 mmHg. During *Madhya nauli* it was in the rage of −20 to −80 mmHg. The negative pressure was found in various degrees in different cavities and was maximum in colon. The creation of suction pressure can also be demonstrated by connecting the stomach to the water column in a glass with the help of a rubber tube. The water is immediately sucked inside the stomach when *nauli* is performed. The water is sucked inside the colon during *basti* because of vacuum creation inside the colon during *nauli*. Same is the case with *vajroli* where even viscous liquid (oil) is sucked inside the urinary bladder with the help of *nauli kriya*. The X-ray studies on *nauli* have revealed that the right and the left domes of the diaphragm move up independent of each other in *Dakshina* and *Vama nauli* respectively. Different parts of the colon also move due to rolling manipulation in *nauli* and thus cause redistribution of the colon contents. The lumbar portion of the spinal column is stretched during *nauli*.

Thus *nauli* is an excellent exercise for the abdominal viscera. It maintains the optimum tone of the abdominal recti muscles by their repeated contraction and relaxation. The recti muscles become stronger and support the internal organs well. The abdominal wall cannot bulge out. It is claimed that *nauli* relieves constipation, indigestion and improves functioning of the liver. *Nauli* promotes the blood circulation in the pelvic region due to high negative pressures and tones up the nerves in this area. Increased circulation of blood removes the waste products more effectively and prevents congestion in the lower abdomen.

Thus it also acts as a cleansing process on the physical level. It helps to mobilize fat, deposited on the abdominal wall and maintains the shape of the abdominal muscles. The nerve plexuses and their fine terminals in the pelvic region are stimulated mechanically. The nature of sensation may vary from individual to individual. Thus *nauli* renders gastro-intestinal system healthy by acting powerfully on the abdominal organs. The endocrinal glands in the abdominal area are also stimulated. Since the gastric cavities are affected due to the negative pressure and are stretched or relaxed alternately, the autonomic nervous system associated with them is also stimulated. One forgets the external disturbances and is totally concentrated upon the technique. The autonomic nervous system then becomes able to establish optimum level of physiological functions. We have seen that the emotions are working on the smooth muscles of the visceral organs and disturbing their normal function, e.g., anxiety can alter the tone of the stomach muscles and gastric glands secrete more acid. So it is quite possible that we are tackling our emotional make up while practicing *kriyas* like *nauli* and *kapalbhati*. One should therefore relax sufficiently after practicing *kriyas* and should drink milk to calm down.

The blood circulation is increased in the abdominal area due to negative pressure development. The negative pressure and the increased blood supply to visceral organs can stimulate the hormone secretions. Similarly in females, the uterus is also subjected to the negative pressure. Therefore they should practice *nauli kriya* cautiously.

KAPALBHATI

भस्त्रावल्लोहकारस्य रेचपूरौ ससंभ्रमौ ।
कपालभातिर्विख्याता कफदोषविशोषणी ।।
Bhastravallohakarasya rechapurau sasambhramau,
Kapalbhatirvikkhyata kafadoshavishoshani
—Hathapradipika II:36

Dhauti, basti, neti, trataka, nauli and *kapalbhati* are the six cleansing processes mentioned in *hatha yoga*. They are the techniques of purification. The specific organs or the parts of the body are cleaned by these practices. The metabolic process is a continuous process. There are also other functions of the body where the end products are toxins. These poisonous substances are to be removed from various parts and thrown out of the body. Yoga believes that there are not only these physical but mental or psychological impurities (*malas- ey*) also, which cause blockages in the function of the nervous system, if they are not thrown out, they would create imbalance in different functions and ultimately prepare a base for various diseases like asthma, insomnia, acidity, and kidney stone. In short, these *kriyas* remove the impurities and help us to maintain the health. According to *hatha yoga*, one should remove all these toxins and the disorders of phlegm by means of these six purificatory processes, before starting *pranayama*. Literally, *kapalbhati* means an exercise that makes the forehead shining. It is one of the six cleansing processes (*shatkriyas*) described by *hatha yoga*. This purificatory process involves the breathing apparatus, nasal passages and the sinuses in the skull that are cleansed effectively. *Gherand Samhita* mentions three varieties of *kapalbhati* having a chief characteristic feature of cleansing the nasal passages in the skull. We shall, however discuss the technique of *kapalbhati* as given in *Hathapradipika*.

TECHNIQUE OF KAPALBHATI

Padmasana is the best *asana* to practice *kapalbhati*. After sitting in *padmasana*, the palms are pressed moderately on the respective knees and the hands are kept straight. By doing this the vertebral column automatically becomes straight. The upper part of the chest and the shoulders are slightly elevated. Due to this position, the movement of the abdominal muscles is easily controlled during the practice of *kapalbhati*. *Padmasana* provides a firm foundation to the practitioner with a broad triangular base. The vibrations or the mechanical jerks produced during vigorous practice of *kapalbhati* are easily absorbed and counterbalanced by this foundation. The force created by the abdominal muscles is properly directed up, towards the chest.

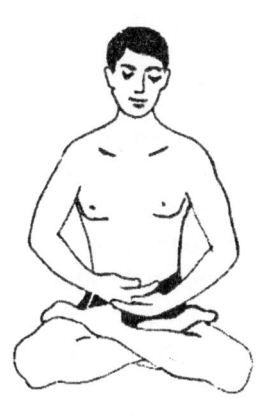

Fig. 32: Padmasana for Kapalbhati

Kapalbhati is essentially a voluntary abdominal breathing. *Puraka* and *rechaka* are gone through in a quick succession with the help of the abdominal muscles. The thoracic part is more or less unmoved as there is no usual expansion of the thoracic cavity. There is no retention of breath in *kapalbhati*. *Rechaka* is more important part of this practice. In normal breathing the process of inhalation is active and the phase of exhalation is passive but in *kapalbhati*, *puraka* is passive and *rechaka* is active in nature.

Puraka

After raising the chest slightly up, to start with, one just relaxes the abdomen and inhales passively so that the abdomen protrudes out. Immediately after every quick exhalatory stroke of *rechaka*, one relaxes the abdomen and allows it to bulge out due to the pressure from the abdominal organs. At the same time the diaphragm descends easily, increasing the vertical diameter of thorax. The intrapulmonary pressure is lowered and the atmospheric air rushes in the lungs. Approximately 100–200 ml air is inhaled in such a quick but passive and shallow inhalation. No frictional sound is produced in *puraka* as the air enters passively in the lungs without any force.

RECHAKA

Rechaka consists of active contraction of the abdominal muscles and at the same time a forceful and rapid exhalation. The abdominal muscles are contracted quickly and vigorously around and slightly below the navel region. This gives a strong inward push to the abdominal organs, which in turn, pushes the diaphragm upward in to the thorax. Diaphragm now exerts an active (positive) pressure on the lungs and the air is expelled out quickly and forcefully. Of course the volume of exhaled air is same to that inhaled in *puraka*. In *kapalbhati* there is no resistance to breathing, i.e., both the nostrils are used and the glottis are wide open. The muscles of the neck and the face are kept relaxed so that the air escapes smoothly. Although the friction of the air is avoided in the interior and upper nasal passage and the throat, little friction takes place at the opening part of the nostrils, producing a sound just like one produces during moderate blowing of the nose.

The thoracic part is little elevated and maintained in a relatively fixed condition. It is not expanded with every stroke of the abdomen. If the chest moves with every exhalation, then the air would not be blown properly and the work of breathing muscles would increase unnecessarily. When the chest is maintained in an expanded condition, the force created during *rechaka* by the quick abdominal contraction, gets an axial direction. The blowing strength of diaphragm increases and the air passage is cleaned more effectively due to the forceful air current. This powerful air current also exerts a suction pressure on all the crevices of the nasal passage and on the opening of the sinuses. This expels the mucous contents and other secretions from this part.

When the abdomen is actively contracted and pushed inward, the pelvic region is also automatically contracted. This results in a strong contraction of the anal sphincters. It is desirable that at least in the beginning one should avoid the formation of *moola bandha*. One may introduce *moola bandha* voluntarily with *kapalbhati*, after a long practice.

Mudra, Bandha and Kriyas

When the contracted muscles of the abdomen are relaxed or loosened, the abdomen bulges out and *puraka* is done passively. Again for the next *rechaka*, the abdominal muscles are contracted rapidly and strongly. Thus *puraka* and *rechaka* follow each other, moving the abdomen forward and inward alternately. Blowing sound is also produced with each *rechaka*. The whole process appears like a bellow of a blacksmith.

Thus one cycle of *kapalbhati* consists of only *puraka* and *rechaka*, which are done rapidly, emphasizing more on *rechaka*. The standard frequency of breathing in *kapalbhati* is 120 times per minute. The breathing is rhythmic and the speed is acquired slowly by bringing proper coordination of the abdominal contraction and relaxation with exhalation and inhalation respectively. This voluntary control is learnt by conscious practice in the beginning. Normally 10-20 expulsions are gone through in each round in the beginning. The number of breaths per minute are gradually increased over a long practice. After mastering the technique, the recommended speed is achieved. Such rhythmic and well-controlled speed, in this vigorous abdominal breathing, is essential. For all practical purposes, the practice of *kapalbhati* in this way for half to one minute is sufficient. There should be no undue strain on the breathing mechanism at any stage. The force of expulsions, the speed, the number of expulsions at a stretch in one round, the number of such rounds in one sitting, uniform pitch of frictional sound are all properly adjusted consciously, according to one's purpose and capacity.

Now let us observe some of the physiological effects of *kapalbhati*. The respiration obviously becomes shallow in nature. The tidal volume decreases. In normal breathing it is 450-500 ml per breath while in *kapalbhati* the tidal volume has been found to be only 150-200 ml per breathing cycle. Minute ventilation (MV), however, increases about three times more than that in the normal breathing due to increased breathing rate. In normal breathing MV is 7.5 liters per minute, while in *kapalbhati* MV is about 20.5 liters per minute. Thus the Oxygen consumption increases due to increased work of breathing. Consequently, Carbon dioxide is eliminated in large quantity from the blood. Oxygen consumption increases by 10–40 percent over a normal breathing and then decreases by 3 percent, after the practice is over, compared to the normal values. As large quantity of carbon dioxide is washed out from the blood during *kapalbhati* the respiratory center is not stimulated for breathing, on the contrary it is inhibited and one experiences a quiet or a tranquilized state of mind. Experimentally it has been observed that the duration of *antar kumbhaka* (holding the breath internally) increases, if practiced immediately after *kapalbhati* of 30–45 seconds. An apnea like condition is automatically established. This helps one to hold his breath comfortably for a longer time. It may be remembered that *kapalbhati* for 20–40 seconds included in the first part of *Bhastrika pranayama* by Swami Kuvalayananda seems to be quite reasonable.

The heart rate increases slightly by 15–20 beats per minute and systolic blood pressure also increases by 7–10 mmHg. The diastolic blood pressure remains more or less the same. Although these cardio-vascular changes are mild in nature, a hypertensive or a heart patient is advised not to practice *kapalbhati*. It may be remembered by the readers that in all most all the yogic techniques the lower abdominal and the pelvic region is the target area of their action. A practitioner feels more energetic and fresh after even a short practice of *kapalbhati*. It brings about a slight sympathetic tone in the body followed by a parasympathetic predominance after the practice. That is why one feels relaxed and tranquil after little prolonged practice of *kapalbhati*. This is also supported by the fact that during *kapalbhati* the peripheral blood flow is reduced (as seen through plethysmogram tracing).

Thus *kapalbhati* not only clears the respiratory passage and keeps it free from impurities and mucous etc., but also stimulates the nerves in the abdominal (navel) region and in the skull. It produces a peculiar awareness in the forehead region and enhances the effects of *bhrumadhya drishti* (gazing between the two eyebrows). It also helps in awakening the *kundalini* power. It gives excellent massage to the abdominal organs and improves digestion. As one is required to attend and synchronize the breathing with the abdominal force at least in the beginning, consciously, it reduces the alertness for the external environment and induces inner awareness. For all these reasons it seems very practical that the practice of *kapalbhati* precedes the *Kumbhaka* phase of *Bhastrika pranayama*.

TRATAKA

निरीक्षेन्निश्चल दशा सूक्ष्मलक्ष्यं समाहितः ।
अश्रुसंपातपर्यन्तमाचार्यैस्त्राटकं स्मृतम् ॥

—*Hathapradipika* II:32

Meaning: With steady eyes one should gaze at the smallest object comfortably until tears roll down.

मोचनं नेत्ररोगाणां तन्द्रादीनां कपाटकम् ।
यत्नतस्त्राटकं गोप्यं तथा हाट्कपेटकम् ॥

—*Hathapradipika* II:33

Meaning: *Trataka* cures eye diseases and prevents laziness but it should be respected and preserved like one cares for the casket of gold.

Trataka is one of the six cleansing processes (*Kriyas*) of *hatha yoga*. It is performed with the eyes. Traditionally there are three types of *trataka*, available for the practice.

1. Antar trataka

With closed eyes one has to experience as if he is gazing in between the two eyebrows (*Bhrumadhya drushti*) or heart, navel or any other such internal organ.

2. Madhya trataka

Still gaze on *bhrumadhya* or *nasagra* (tip of nose) or any near object made of metal or stone or even on *Aum* written on paper, or single dot in black color, with open eyes.

3. Bahya trataka

Fixing the gaze on the distant object like Moon, rising Sun or illumined planet.

TECHNIQUE OF TRATAKA

Trataka is done preferably in *padmasana* (lotus posture) or *ardha-padmasana* on the ground. It can also be done in *sukhasana* (comfortable sitting posture) but with the straight back or spinal column. A *ghee* lamp is placed in the level of the eyes at about one meter distance. Now with the relaxed mind one should gaze at the bright portion of the flame, without blinking, till tears appear in the eyes and roll down on the cheeks. This is the endpoint of *trataka*. After this eyes should be closed gently. The practitioner then should sit quietly for 3-5 minutes and then open his eyes slowly. If required, one may repeat the technique once again. It is recommended that after this the practitioner should wash his face and eyes with water. The duration of *trataka* from the beginning till the appearance of tears varies from person to person. It also depends on the state of mind of the individual. The duration of *trataka* is less if the practitioner is relaxed and if the practitioner is tensed or disturbed, he may take more time to finish. Generally in normal individuals *trataka* is finished within 3-5 minutes. Some individuals have been observed to take even more than 12 minutes.

BENEFITS

Hatha yoga mentions that by performing *trataka* regularly the eye disorders are cured and the lethargy is overcome. Such regular practice of *trataka* facilitates practice of *Shambhavi mudra*, which leads to the process of *Dharana* (contemplation) and the practitioner gets the great vision. This description from *Gherand Samhita* (I:53) indicates that the *trataka* is closely concerned with the training of the nervous system in a particular direction. Mental tensions are also reduced after the practice of *trataka* and one feels very calm and quiet. Peacefulness or pleasantness is the feeling normally experienced by the practitioners after *trataka*. The sleep pattern is improved within a few days practice of *trataka*. The period of elimination of emotional tensions as well as the magnitude of relaxation depends upon the basic nature and composition of the person. Sincere and severe practice of *trataka* is mandatory for those who are desirous of learning hypnosis.

Mudra, Bandha and Kriyas

PHYSIOLOGY OF TRATAKA

It has been found that soon after *trataka* is over, the parasympathetic predominance is established as indicated by lowering of heart rate and respiration rate as well as an increase in amplitude of plethysmogram (vasodilatation). That means a peripheral blood circulation is increased after *trataka*. Emotional balance or stability is restored and a degree of relaxation is increased as indicated by the production of well-modulated train of alpha frequency after *trataka*. *Trataka* acts as a catharsis, bringing out repressed or suppressed wishes or desires and eliminating them from the subconscious level. This is the process of purification. After this, the practitioner experiences psychophysiological relaxation and a feeling of calmness and lightness. One pointed concentration is improved, and attention fluctuations are reduced. It has been found that the neurotic tendencies such as anger, short temper, suspicion, irritation and resentment are reduced after *trataka* practice is done for one month. Anxiety is also reduced. In this way *trataka* is very important practice to remove impurities or blockages in the neural network and to prepare the individual for meditation.

CAUTION

1. Avoid candle or other lamps.
2. Use *ghee* lamp and cow's *ghee*. Do not perform *trataka* on flickering flame.
3. Hypertensive persons should perform *trataka* after the practice of *Shavasana*.
4. Persons having too much emotional or mental disturbance should not practice *trataka* unless they go through other preliminary *asanas* and *kriyas*.
5. Never rub your eyes after *trataka*.
6. Do not repeat *trataka* more than three times in one sitting.
7. Do not try to read or watch TV immediately after *trataka*.

Three

Pranayama

Pranayama occupies second place in *hatha yoga* while it constitutes the fourth step of Patanjali's *Ashtanga yoga*. A serious student of yoga is expected to start practice of *pranayama* when he becomes well versed in *asanas*, i.e., when a stage of *asanjaya* is achieved so that one can sit for hours together, steadily and comfortably.

The word *pranayama* is formed by two words i.e., *prana* and *ayama*. *Prana* means a subtle life force, which provides energy to different organs (including mind) and also controls many vital life processes (e.g., circulation, respiration, etc.). *Ayama* signifies the voluntary effort to control and direct this *prana*. Breathing is one of the vital activities governed by *prana* on a gross level. This is the only *pranic* activity available to us, which can be regulated voluntarily. Secondly, the breathing system (*pranic* activity) is linked with the nervous system (base of the mental activity) on one hand and the mind (consciousness) on the other. Yoga has taken best advantage of this situation, considering that the mind could be controlled effectively with the voluntary regulation over breathing. This is expected to manage the materialistic inclinations and instincts of *chitta* (superconsciousness).

Therefore, *pranayama* essentially becomes a process by which the mind is controlled by voluntary regulation of the breathing. For our understanding, *prana* is simply a 'breath' and *ayama* means a control over it. Just like we have speed-breakers on the road to control the flow of traffic, we bring a 'pause' in breathing. So *pranayama* means a voluntary and temporary pause in the movement of the breath. From yogic point of view it is a door between our physical existence and the spiritual path.

तस्मिनसति श्वासप्रश्वासयोर्गतिविच्छेदः प्राणायामः ।
Tasminsati shvasaprashvasayor gativichchedah pranayamah
—Patanjali Yoga Sutras II:49

The meaning is that the pause, brought in the movement of inhalation and exhalation, is nothing but *pranayama*. Rishi Patanjali has explained four types of *pranayama* (*Patanjali Yoga Sutras* II:50 and 51) on the basis of the nature of the 'pause' (स्तम्भ वृत्तिः *stambhavrutti*) that is a temporary suspension of breath viz., (1) pause after or at the end of the prolonged (दीर्घ *deergha*) and very slow (मन्द *manda*) exhalation (प्रश्वास *prashvas*). (2) pause after or at the end of deep and prolonged inhalation (श्वास *shvas*) (3) pause is brought any time one wants to bring for a considerable time. It may be somewhere in between the usual inhalation or exhalation. This is a prolongation of a break in the breathing (*stambhavritti*) and (4) the practitioner experiences pause at any time without his voluntary efforts, after a long practice of above three types of pauses.

According to yogic literature, when the breath is held after exhalation, it is called *Bahya kumbhaka*, when the breathing is stopped after inhalation, it is known as *Abhyantara kumbhaka* while the fourth type of pause as mentioned above which comes automatically after a long practice of *pranayama*, is known as *Keval kumbhaka*.

Svatmaram Suri, the author of *Hathapradipika* mentions eight varieties of *pranayama* (*Hathapradipika* II:44) not on the basis of nature of *kumbhaka* but on the basis of nature of inhalations and exhalations, which are gone through before and after the *kumbhaka*. The technique of all the eight type of *kumbhakas* is similar but the technique of inhalations and exhalations before and after *kumbhaka* is different for each type of *pranayama*. Effect of each type of *pranayama* is also different on the physical, mental and of course on the spiritual level.

According to Patanjali, a slightest change brought in the normal speed of breathing (*gati vichchedah*) is *pranayama*. Also systematically controlled and prolonged inhalations and exhalations constitute *pranayama*. Obviously to do this a voluntary control is necessary. In normal breathing also, there is a pause between inhalation and exhalation that may be only for a few milliseconds. Therefore voluntary control brought on any one of the three, i.e., inhalation, exhalation, the pause, or on all three, will be called *pranayama*.

CHARACTERISTICS OF PRANAYAMA

Pranayama essentially consists of a voluntary control on the breathing and probably due to this fact; many people refer it to as a breathing exercise. Various breathing exercises have been developed with the purpose of providing more oxygen to the system. In *pranayama*, on the contrary, the emphasis seems to be given on the practice of *kumbhaka*, a controlled phase of holding the breath.

Pranayama is normally done in a relaxed sitting condition in which the demand for oxygen from the body is minimal. When the hemoglobin is fully saturated with the oxygen, no more quantities of oxygen can be accepted. Our body cannot and does not store oxygen anywhere in the body. During *kumbhaka* phase more time is available for the exchange of gases between the blood and air. Naturally then, more carbon dioxide is accumulated in the blood and the lungs than that in the normal breathing. If we calculate the amount of oxygen, available in one minute of normal breathing and compare it with the amount of oxygen we are getting in one minute of *pranayama* it will be clear that the amount of oxygen, available in *pranayama*, is even less than that of the normal breathing. It is therefore wrong to say that in *pranayama* one gets more oxygen. It will be clear by now that *pranayama* has no oxygen value, as compared to the deep breathing. Practice of *pranayama* requires a conscious control over the breathing. One remains fully aware of what he is doing during different phases of *pranayama*. In other words, *pranayama* is never done mechanically. Awareness of breathing is most important while practicing *pranayama*. No other bodily action is associated with *pranayamic* phases.

Talking and singing are also voluntarily controlled respiratory acts but they cannot be compared with *pranayama*. Singing or talking involves some kind of emotions or expressions and more over they are the acts of communication. *Pranayamic* breathing does not produce any emotion nor it expresses any thought or desire. Simply holding a breath during underwater swimming is not a *kumbhaka* as swimming involves some physical and mental activities. During *kumbhaka* phase a total stand-stillness is necessary, even at the mind-intellect level. That is, while practicing *kumbhaka* no imagery or thought process is allowed.

Each cycle of *pranayama* is a complex voluntary act, consisting of three distinct phases, i.e., *puraka, kumbhaka* and *rechaka*. Three types of *kumbhakas* are possible.

1. Abhyantara or purna or antar kumbhaka

This is a controlled suspension of breath after *Puraka*. Since the inspired air is compressed in the alveoli during this retention, the intra-pulmonary pressure is raised and maintained for some length of time. When duration of *antar-kumbhaka* is more, *Jalandhara bandha* is recommended.

2. Bahya or shunya kumbhaka

This is a controlled retention of breath after *rechaka* phase. The intra-pulmonary pressure is lowered and maintained for some length of time.

3. Keval kumbhaka

The suspension of breath appears automatically somewhere in a mid stage of respiratory acts, after a long practice of *pranayama*. This stage is characterized by equal atmospheric and intrapulmonary pressure.

Hatha yoga recommends some *bandhas* to be applied along with each cycle of *pranayama*. *Moola bandha* is practiced during *puraka*, *uddiyan bandha* is done in *rechaka*, while in *kumbhaka*, all the three, i.e., *moola, jalandhara* and *uddiyana bandhas* are advocated.

Thus the technique of *pranayama* includes specific rules regarding the method of breathing, in terms of: (1) force of breathing, (2) the duration of each phase of breathing, (3) number of rounds of *pranayama*, and (4) attention on breathing. When the force of breathing is reduced, it increases the duration of that particular phase. Tradition advocates definite proportion of time for these phases of *pranayama*. We shall deal with some of these characteristics while studying the mechanism of *pranayama*.

The following important features are commonly observed during the practice of almost all types of *pranayama*.

One has to sit in any suitable meditative *asana*, keeping the spine in a straight and well-balanced condition. Eyes are closed gently so that at least the powerful external stimulation is cut off. This helps one to pay attention to the inner happenings. Inhalation in *puraka* and exhalation for *rechaka* is slow, smooth and without any haste. The flow of air is kept uniform having same force all throughout. That means both the phases are gone through in a most controlled way.

Every *puraka* and *rechaka* must end quietly. The habit of expanding the chest or contracting the body musculature violently at the end of *puraka* and *rechaka* respectively is consciously avoided. An attempt of snatching the air at the end of *puraka* and forcing out some more air at the end of *rechaka* would disturb the next cycle of *pranayama*. Therefore, *puraka* and *rechaka* should end easily, pleasantly and smoothly, without any strain.

Rechaka is always given longer time than *puraka*. The orthodox proportion between *puraka* and *rechaka* is 1:2. In an effort to give double time for *rechaka* one should not prolong it too much, which may otherwise hasten the following *puraka*. Best way is to first judge the duration for which one can prolong the *rechaka* easily and then to allot just half of the time for *puraka*.

An orthodox practice of *pranayama* consists minimum ten rounds at a stretch. Traditional text like *Hathapradipika* however, recommends 80 rounds in one sitting and such four sittings in a day, i.e., in the morning, afternoon, evening and at night. That means the total cycles will be 320 per day.

Moola bandha, jalandhara bandha and uddiyana bandha are applied during kumbhaka. Of course it is a strenuous exercise and one should have a long practice of pranayama before introducing these bandhas in the practice. Only jalandhara bandha may also be employed during kumbhaka and the abdomen may be contracted little inward and maintained in this condition through out the practice of pranayama. This helps one to remain aware of the inner happenings or the breathing, and to prevent the flow of diverting thoughts.

Increase in the airway resistance is another peculiarity of pranayama. Inhaling or exhaling through only right or left nostril at a time as in anulom-vilom pranayama or partial closure of glottis to produce sound as in Ujjayi pranayama, reduce the air passage. Naturally, the volume of air reaching the lungs and going out of the lungs will be controlled. The ratio between the volume of air and the volume of blood reaching the lungs will change as the ventilation is approximately reduced to 50 percent.

AIMS AND OBJECTIVES OF PRANAYAMA

Any activity, which requires a total concentration of our mind will also control our breath and may even stop it for a while, e.g., while threading the needle, our breathing is stopped for a few moments. This shows clearly that there is a correlation between our mind and breathing, a pranic activity. In an example given above, we often experience that the thought processes are also stopped for a couple of seconds as the mind is engaged and is well concentrated on the action of passing the thread through the hole. It is our common experience that when we become angry or emotionally upset, our breathing is markedly changed in its rate, depth and the whole maneuver. The emotions and the mental activities are related to the nervous system and through it they change our breathing. This means if we try to manipulate our breathing voluntarily we tackle the life force which is deeply connected with the mind (nervous activity) and therefore with the emotions. Pranayama aims primarily at the control on the mind. When the mind is at a standstill, no thought processes or emotional disturbance is possible. Thus by controlling the mind we would be able to control different emotions and as a result, the temperament, moods, desires and natural instincts of mind (*vrittis*) would also be controlled automatically.

चले वाते चलं चित्तं निश्चले निश्चलं भवेत्।
योगी स्थाणुत्वमाप्नोति ततो वायुं निरोधयेत्।।
*Chale vate chalam chittam nishchale nishchalam bhavet
Yogi sthanutvamapnoti tato vayum nirodhayet*
—Hathapradipika II:2

So long as breathing is continued and the air is moving in and out of the body, the mind remains unstable. When the breath is stopped, the activity of the mind is also controlled and it becomes standstill. Thus a yogi attains a complete motionless state of *chitta* (consciousness). One should therefore restrain one's breath.

ततःक्षीयते प्रकाशावरणम्। धारणासुच योग्यतामनसः।।
Tatahkshiyate prakashavaranam. Dharanasucha yogyata manasah
—Patanjali Yoga Sutras II:52-53

By practicing *pranayama* the ability to perceive, to know the reality, is intensified. The mind is trained and made capable for the process of *dharana*. Since the mind becomes steady and peaceful after the practice of *pranayama*, it becomes suitable and capable to be concentrated on one object at a time. Such 'one-pointedness' (एकाग्रता *ekagrata*) is a pre-requisite of *dharana*.

Different *nadis* (नाडी) are also purified by practicing *pranayama*. This is known as *nadishuddhi pranayama*. Nadis in yoga, are the subtle channels or the passages for the transmission of nerve impulse, or the conduction of the *prana*, for the circulation of the blood or lymph or even for the flow of air (वायु) through them. Most important *nadi*, which opens when both the nostrils are equally open, is *sushumna*. By cleaning these *nadis*, *pranayama* eradicates all types of *malas* from the body and mind. *Mala* in yoga is a toxic factor that gives rise to an imbalance in the body and mind by obstructing or blocking the normal functions of *nadis*.

Psychologists have shown that the particular type of personality corresponds with a typical breathing pattern. It has been shown experimentally that the state of arousal, attention, mental task, emotional disturbance and behavioral pattern influence and modify our breathing pattern. During *pranayama* the breathing is consciously made slow, deeper and rhythmic. This brings about noticeable relaxation, tranquility, balance, and sense of well-being to the mind. In this situation, one's ego-consciousness, which is the seat of all instincts and desires, is checked or controlled and therefore, cannot interfere with the mind as usual. When ego is controlled, the behavioral pattern can also change. Thus the practice of *pranayama* also contributes in transforming the total personality. This helps one in controlling his non-yogic tendencies, instincts and urges arising in his mind (*chitta vritti nirodhah*). This leads one to further stages like *pratyahara* and *dhyana*. We can observe such changes after a long practice of *pranayama* in a serious practitioner of yoga (*Sadhaka*).

In recent years the scientists have admitted the role of psyche in so-called somatic diseases and the term psychosomatic diseases is given to such diseases where the cause is not the infection but the psychic tensions and disturbances. *Hatha yoga* claims to cure all these diseases when *pranayama* is practiced properly. It also warns that if *pranayama* is not practiced judiciously then many diseases may arise, e.g., asthma, constant hiccup, pain in head, ear and eyes, etc. It seems possible since the breathing is associated with the autonomic nervous system (ANS) and ANS is related on the other hand with mental and emotional reactions. By judicious practice of *pranayama* one attains sound health, steady and peaceful mind, slim and lustrous body (*Hathapradipika* II:16–18) and can eradicate all the diseases.

DIFFERENT TIME RATIOS

In order to maintain uniformity and rhythm in all the rounds or cycles of *pranayama* and to allow one to practice within his limitations, different time proportions (ratios) are followed during the practice. Such time ratios provide best proportion and the combination of *puraka, kumbhaka* and *rechaka* phases as far as their duration is concerned. The purpose behind this seems to:

1. provide one some means to measure one's own capacity so that one may not transgress and over-step one's own limitations and wreck the delicate and vital mechanism of respiration and
2. stimulate ANS and other breathing reflexes in most rhythmic, regular and systematic manner so as to condition them for higher spiritual forces, and to render them tough against day-to-day stresses and tensions.
3. increase span of inward flow of attention. The concept of fixed time ratio is probably the answer to the commonly arising question in everybody's mind as to how much and how long one should inhale, how long one should retain the breath and how much one should prolong the exhalation. When we follow the time ratio and prolong the breathing accordingly, the force of breathing is automatically reduced and adjusted uniformly for all the cycles.

The most favored view is to have the proportion of 1:4:2 for *puraka, kumbhaka* and *rechaka* respectively. Of course it is hard to reach this ratio right from the beginning. According to this ratio if *puraka* is done for five seconds, *kumbhaka* should be done for twenty seconds and *rechaka* should be prolonged for ten seconds. However, after a long practice it is possible to reach this ratio in which *Jalandhara bandha* must be practiced during *kumbhaka*. Another tradition advocates the ratio of 1:2:2. In this proportion *kumbhaka* and *rechaka* are given just double time than that of *puraka*. This proportion is found rather easy and comfortable to be adjusted and hence one is advised to start with the second ratio, i.e., 1:2:2. While introducing the time ratios one should however see that phases are gone through smoothly without any feeling of suffocation at any stage. These time ratios are not rigid rules but they serve as guidelines for conscious but rhythmic and uniform control over the breathing mechanism for all the rounds of *pranayama*. One has to avoid any jerk, strain, discomfort, violence and haste while following the time proportions.

Another tradition (*Goraksha Samhita,* II:4) suggests *matras* in a ratio of 6:8:5 for safe and convenient practice of *pranayama*. To start with, maintain a ratio of 1:1:2 and then gradually increase the ratio to 1:2:2 and so on. A feeling of distress or air hunger at any stage indicates some strain in following the proportion. One has to reduce the time for *puraka* in this case so that other phases are also reduced in their duration and then the whole practice becomes easier.

All these proportions can also be practiced easily by counting numbers or chanting *mantras* in mind. In the beginning, for proper time sense, one may take help of a watch and adjust all the phases. The phase of *kumbhaka* should be introduced just in the form of a small pause between *puraka* and *rechaka* and then its duration may be increased gradually, and cautiously.

MECHANISM OF PRANAYAMA

We know that the respiratory system works involuntarily through various reflex mechanisms. The depth and the rate are maintained automatically according to the oxygen requirements of the body from moment to moment. Now when we bring so many changes in the breathing during *pranayama*, the whole mechanism of breathing gets altered. We shall now consider the physiological changes occurring due to modifications in breathing during different phases of *pranayama*.

PURAKA PHASE

Shvas is the natural involuntary process of inspiration, regulated by the respiratory center in the medulla oblongata. *Puraka* is the voluntary prolongation of the inspiratory phase. It is well controlled in terms of time, force, ventilation and depth as per the proportion. Inhalation in *puraka* is done in a very smooth way by keeping the force uniform. The speed at which the lungs are filled is thus regulated. When we increase the duration and prolong the phase of inhalation the force is automatically decreased. In *bhastrika pranayama*, however one breathes in and out very rapidly, giving just half a second for one cycle, consisting of *puraka* and *rechaka*, for the first part of *bhastrika* (120 cycles per minute). In *Anulom-vilom* and *suryabhedan pranayama puraka* is done through only right or left nostril at a time. In *Ujjayi* and *Bhramari pranayama*, the contraction of the glottis and the throat muscles reduces the ventilation. Thus the mechanics of inspiration is modified voluntarily during *puraka*.

During the phase of *puraka* the lungs are expanded considerably and the walls of the alveoli are stretched maximum. After a particular degree of stretching, the stretch receptors situated in the alveolar walls are stimulated. In the normal breathing, at this stage or even before this, the inhibitory impulses would have been sent to the inspiration center and the phase of exhalation would have been started in a reflex. But as we continue the phase of inhalation by our strong voluntary control, the normal stretch reflex is inhibited and therefore no exhalation is possible. The chest continues to get expanded under cortical control. The stretch receptors are thus trained to withstand more and more stretching.

As we continue to inhale, the intra-pulmonary pressure is also raised. The diaphragm does not move freely as the abdomen is kept slightly inward and controlled. Therefore the alveoli in the upper pulmonary part are filled with air. One uses his inspiratory capacity for prolonged phase of *puraka*. This has a beneficial effect on the gaseous exchange, which then works efficiently throughout the day.

Normally we finish our inhalation in 1.5 seconds during which the exchange of gases is almost completed. Now although the need of oxygen is very less, we are prolonging our inhalation from 2–5 seconds. Instead of usual 500 ml air, we are now inhaling 1–1.5 liters of air and the volume of blood reaching the lungs is also more. The exchange of oxygen/carbon dioxide is very effective. During the *puraka* phase, which is a conscious act, the filling of the lungs is done as per one's limit and is well attended. In order to bring necessary proportion in *puraka*, *kumbhaka* and *rechaka* the duration of *puraka* is adjusted. When *puraka* is well adjusted and made shorter, *kumbhaka* and *rechaka* are also gone through smoothly without a feeling of suffocation or a pressure in the chest. Thus *puraka* is not merely a mechanical prolongation of inspiration but it is done with full concentration of mind.

KUMBHAKA PHASE

Here we would consider only *antar kumbhaka*. *Kumbhaka* is a voluntarily controlled suspension of breath. After a particular stage in *puraka*, as per the time ratio observed, one stops inhalation and retains the inhaled air in the lungs for proportionate time. The intra-pulmonic pressure (in alveoli), which is raised to one's optimum capacity, is maintained during *kumbhaka* stage. The alveoli and the bronchioles are stretched to their optimum level. The stretch receptors, however, cannot bring about the reflex contraction of the lungs, and the respiratory muscles cannot relax as they do normally, due to strong motor control.

The ideal duration of *kumbhaka* is that which would enable one to give double time for *rechaka* than that of *puraka*. The duration of *kumbhaka* is gradually increased over a long practice of *pranayama* so that the respiratory center is gradually acclimatized and trained to withstand higher carbon dioxide concentrations in the alveoli and in the blood.

The metabolic processes continuously produce carbon dioxide which is picked up by the blood. Under normal respiration this carbon dioxide is promptly thrown out of the body. But now when we retain the breath for a considerable time, the carbon dioxide level (concentration) is going to increase in the blood. For example, if we hold the breath for 20 seconds, the blood volume reaching and being circulated in the lungs for exchange of gases would also increase as the heart would pump the blood for nearly 25 times during such retention of breath. The ratio between volume of inspired air and the blood is thus changed. Obviously the exchange of oxygen and carbon dioxide across the thin walls of the alveoli and the blood capillaries would take place more efficiently as they get more time. However, the exchange of gases will not be possible after a particular stage when there is a saturation of the gases on both the sides, i.e., in the alveoli and in the blood.

In the normal breathing of one minute duration we inhale and exhale about 7.5 liters of air where as we have just one to two rounds of *pranayama* in a minute, providing us only about 3–5 liters of air. If we calculate 20 percent oxygen from the air, it would be clear that oxygen available for the exchange is less in *pranayama* than in the normal breathing. Therefore, it is a misunderstanding that oxygen uptake increases in *pranayama*.

The chemoreceptors, located in the medulla oblongata, near the entry of the IXth and Xth cranial nerves, are sensitive to the amount of carbon dioxide in the blood. The increasing concentration of carbon dioxide in the blood stimulates these chemoreceptors, which in turn send the impulses to the respiratory center. The respiratory center, which would have otherwise started exhalation, is now helpless against the strong voluntary control from the cortex. So in a way we are training these chemoreceptors to tolerate more and more tension of carbon dioxide during *kumbhak*. After some stage in *antar kumbhaka*, an inner urge, to exhale, arises for the first time (*pratham udghat*), which is generally neglected by our volition. The second inner urge to exhale (*dvitiya udghat*) is still stronger than the first one, which is also sometimes ignored. The third and the strongest desire (*trutiya udghat*) cannot and should not be neglected. Now *rechaka* should be started without any delay. This way without crossing the limits one can increase his capacity to perform *kumbhaka* for longer durations.

Two important principles of *pranayama* are, concentration and awareness. *Pranayama* is never done mechanically. One is expected to remain aware of 'fullness' of the lungs or the pressure of the inspired air in the lungs. One may even experience a stand stillness in the mind or the thoughtless condition of the mind during *kumbhaka*. In order to avoid any functional damage to the delicate respiratory mechanism and the nerve centers, tradition advocates *Jalandhara bandha* during *kumbhaka* phase.

The peripheral chemoreceptors, which are sensitive to lower level of oxygen in the blood, would also send powerful stimulation to the respiratory center to start exhalation. As the carbon dioxide goes on accumulating during *kumbhaka*, the chemoreceptors report it promptly to the pneumotaxic center, which in turn tries to stimulate expiratory center. The autonomic or the reflex mechanism of respiration is fortunately far more powerful than the control from the higher centers. That is why after a particular stage it is not possible to hold the breath further. Regular practice will however acclimatize the receptors gradually to the increasing concentrations of carbon dioxide.

Role of Jalandhara Bandha in Kumbhaka

Bandha means a tie or a lock. In *Jalandhara bandha* (chinlock) the head is bent and the chin is pressed firmly on the jugular notch. Due to this sharp bend of neck, the internal and external carotid arteries, carotid sinuses and sinus nerves are pressed. This specific neuromuscular action around the front side of the neck will influence the circulation, nervous function and the glandular (thyroid) secretion. It is claimed that when *Jalandhara bandha* is applied, the heart rate slows down and the blood pressure reduces. *Jalandhara bandha* also induces a particular (trance like) state of awareness, which helps in the mental abstraction from the external things. It helps to maintain an inward projection of mind, producing typical consciousness of the inner happenings. In the beginning one may remain aware of the fullness of the lungs or the increased pressure in the lungs, since *Jalandhara bandha* also adds to the intra-thoracic pressure from the upper side. The vertebral column in the thoracic region near neck is also pulled up and one may remain aware of the stretching in upper back portion in the beginning.

When *Jalandhara bandha* is applied, the blood flow towards the head is restricted. It prevents extra blood supply to the brain. The vagus nerve is stimulated, which brings about a soothing and calming effect on the higher nervous centers. The central chemoreceptors in the medulla, which are sensitive to increased pressure of carbon dioxide in the blood, will not be stimulated so strongly as the blood flow is reduced. Similarly the stimulation of the peripheral chemoreceptors, which are sensitive to reduced oxygen level in the blood, will not be so strong. Thus *Jalandhara bandha* helps in reducing the strength of the autonomic (involuntary) chemoreceptor reflex mechanism which otherwise is very strong in regulating the depth and the rate of breathing. This facilitates the voluntary control over holding the breath. One holds the breath and retains deeply inspired air under pressure easily with the help of *Jalandhara bandha* since it minimizes the inner urges which otherwise would force one to start exhalation while practicing *kumbhaka*.

If *Jalandhara bandha* is not applied during *kumbhaka*, the respiratory center is strongly stimulated by the chemoreceptors and one has to build-up still stronger volitional force against it. Other involuntary centers, like cardiac and temperature regulating centers, are also influenced. It may result in the increased heart rate and blood pressure, sweating and giddiness. If one practices *kumbhaka* in this way without *Jalandhara bandha*, it may damage or wreck the fine autonomic balance between these functions. One may become a permanent victim of unbalanced blood pressure, heart rate and the breathing pattern.

When *Jalandhara bandha* is applied, the inspired air, which is compressed in the lungs, will not be allowed to rush out with force. Delicate eustachian tubes are also protected from the increased air pressure in the pharynx during *kumbhaka*.

Thus a judicious practice of *kumbhaka* along with *Jalandhara bandha* would give us the expected results from voluntary control over breathing such as concentration, balance in the autonomic functions, conscious control on the mind, etc. which are necessary for higher yogic practices like *dhyana*.

RECHAKA PHASE

After retaining the breath for sufficient length of time as per the time ratio, in a comfortable manner, the *Jalandhara bandha* is released by moving the head up and *rechaka* is started. *Rechaka* is a voluntarily controlled exhalation as compared to the normal exhalation (*prashvas*). The time (duration), force, ventilation and the flow of air are controlled in order to increase the duration of *rechaka* as per the time ratio. The exhalatory force is reduced and the air is allowed to escape slowly. For this purpose, exhalation is carried out through one nostril only (as in *Ujjayi, Suryabhedan* or *Anulom-vilom pranayama*) or through both the nostrils by contracting the glottis partially at the same time (another variety of *Ujjayi*). Thus by creating a slight airway resistance, one can regulate the volume of air to be expelled out per unit of time. This helps in prolonging the exhalation and to reduce the force of the outgoing air. In *rechaka*, one uses his expiratory reserve volume for exhaling completely before starting the next *puraka*.

Now the intra-pulmonary pressure is slowly reduced and the alveoli are gradually deflated. By this time when one is exhaling slowly, the percentage of carbon dioxide is still increasing in the blood and the chemoreceptors in the medulla are trying to inhibit exhalation and to start inhalation by stimulating the inspiratory center. Similarly the peripheral chemoreceptors are also trying to bring about inspiration in a reflex as they are sensitive to the lower oxygen concentration in the blood. But both of these reflexes are defeated by our strong volition and we continue to breath out. The purpose seems to acclimatize these receptors to higher concentrations of carbon dioxide in the blood, as stated above in *kumbhaka*. It may be noted that carbon dioxide has got calming effect on the nervous system up to certain limits and has been found to reduce anxiety when administered in the form of a mixture containing 65 percent carbon dioxide and 35 percent oxygen. This would help the mind to undergo a state of meditation.

The duration of *rechaka* is however so adjusted that there is no feeling of 'air hunger' at any stage. If it is not well adjusted in proportion, the following *puraka* is hurried and the whole proportion of the *pranayama* is disturbed.

Significance of Double Time Proportion For Rechaka

One is supposed to follow 1:2 ratio for the duration of *puraka* and *rechaka*. Even when *kumbhaka* is given four times more duration in 1:4:2 time ratio, *rechaka* is given double time than *puraka*. Really speaking *puraka* is a true measure as other phases depend on it for the proportion. Therefore, it is better to adjust *puraka* so as to give double proportion to *rechaka*. This is possible after knowing one's capacity to prolong the phase of exhalation. For example, if one is able to breathe out for eight seconds comfortably, he should adjust his *puraka* only for four seconds. Let us consider the significance of double duration for *rechaka* on the basis of psycho-physiological principles.

1. Normally, the instinct of inhalation is always stronger than that of exhalation. This is due to increase in carbon dioxide level in the blood at the end of normal expiration. When we prolong the phase of exhalation we tackle this chemoreceptor reflex and discard the urge of inspiration. Thus prolonged duration of *rechaka* facilitates such training of the chemoreceptors to withstand more and more concentrations of carbon dioxide in the blood. This is actually a preparation for *keval kumbhaka* to appear one day, which is nothing but an arrest of respiration in the mid stage, during or in between the inhalation and exhalation for some time.
2. It is our common experience that we feel relaxed whenever we exhale deeply and smoothly. The experiments have shown that various tensions as well as the anxieties are reduced during prolonged exhalations. Prolonged *rechaka* would then liberate more psycho-physiological tensions and one would feel calm and quiet. Usually, the higher degree of physiological arousal is required for receiving any emotional impact. Prolonged exhalation gives rise to the parasympathetic tone in the body and reduces the level of excitation and therefore emotions cannot influence the nervous system.
3. In order to observe a particular time ratio in each cycle of *pranayama* total concentration is necessary. When *rechaka* is prolonged smoothly we remain aware of the force, flow of the air and the time (duration), thus keeping our mind

away from (perception of) the external stimulations and the thought processes for maximum time.
4. Increased duration of *rechaka* makes the exhalation most complete. As one is using his expiratory reserve volume, the expired air containing increased percentage of carbon dioxide is thus completely squeezed out of the lungs (except dead space volume and residual volume). When we inhale for *puraka* of the next cycle of *pranayama* we get maximum quantity of a fresh air equivalent to 75 percent of our vital capacity. This offers better scope for effective gaseous exchange. If the *rechaka* phase is not sufficiently prolonged, some amount of air remains in the alveoli at the end of incomplete exhalation. This volume of air, which contains accumulated carbon dioxide, would be mixed with the incoming fresh air, and the amount of oxygen reaching the alveoli will be less in every cycle. One may not be able to keep proper ratio of time as he may feel suffocated after a few rounds. Therefore double proportion for *rechaka* seems to be appropriate.
5. Since we are maintaining *uddiyan bandha* during *rechaka* and prolonging it for a long time, we are also maintaining intra-abdominal pressure for such time. This pressure reduces the blood circulation in the lower abdominal region, which may be diverted to the sacral region. Thus by prolonging the duration of *rechaka* the sacral nerves (parasympathetic branch of ANS) are provided with more nourishment, which would be toned up and made stronger.

In short, during the practice of *pranayama* we tackle all the respiratory reflexes on account of our volitional control on the respiration. The impulses from both the CNS and ANS are better integrated due to rhythmic and proportionate stimulation of the proprioceptors and visceroreceptors as well as the vagus nerve. The emotions are positively influenced due to this rhythmic and smooth breathing pattern adopted everyday. Like emotions, the mental activities are also related with the breathing. As the mind is engaged fully in the breathing, unnecessary thought processes are checked. As the cognitive, intellectual and the ego-based analytical processes of the mind are minimal or even absent, the mind becomes more balanced which enables us to experience higher levels of consciousness or to get into the state of meditation as the power of concentration also increases. *Pranayama* has not been developed to supply oxygen. It is meant for controlling and balancing CNS and influencing the autonomic functions as well.

DEEP BREATHING AND PRANAYAMA

Many people have wrong ideas or impressions about *pranayama* and they consider it as a deep breathing. Fundamentally *pranayama* and deep breathing are quite different techniques and should never be confused for each other. Let us see how they differ from each other, although both are voluntary in nature.

1. Although both *pranayama* and deep breathing are voluntarily controlled, their aim and objectives are quite different and therefore the technique of both is also different. *Pranayama* aims at tackling autonomic nervous system through the conscious control from the cerebral cortex. It brings the mind under control. *Pranayama* is done when one is relaxed. It is not practiced after any muscular exercise.

    Deep breathing may be voluntary or even sometimes involuntary when it is resorted to overcome the fatigue, as a secondary process. Deep breathing is aimed at providing more oxygen and to get rid of accumulated carbon dioxide from the blood or to overcome oxygen debt.

2. Three distinct phases, i.e., *puraka, kubhaka* and *rechaka* constitute one cycle or round of *pranayama*. The phase of *rechaka* is always prolonged than *puraka*. A particular time ratio is followed to make it most rhythmic and proportionate. The number of cycles per minute in *pranayama* may be just one or two. For practicing *pranayama*, a proper posture is adopted and the eyes are closed to reduce sensory inputs

from the external environment. This helps to produce a particular inner awareness.

In deep breathing there are only deep inhalations and deep exhalations. There is no question of retention of breath. Both the phases are almost equal. No time ratio or any proportion is observed. Rate of breathing in deep breathing may be 10–15 per minute and two rounds or cycles may not be identical. There is no need to close the eyes.

3. In *pranayama*, proper posture is to be adapted, e.g., *Padmasana* or *Siddhasana*. It is to be practiced at a particular time in the morning on an empty stomach. All the phases are gone through very smoothly and slowly. At least ten rounds of *pranayama*, two or three times a day, are usually recommended for a normal practice. *Hathapradipika*, for example recommends eighty rounds four times a day.

In deep breathing there is no restriction on the number of cycles. One may stop anywhere if the purpose of getting more quantities of oxygen is fulfilled. There is no need of any particular posture or time proportion for deep breathing. Empty stomach is also not an essential condition.

4. Breathing against airway resistance is a peculiarity of *pranayama*. The airway passage is narrowed (contracted) and the flow of the air is restricted. The degree of such airway resistance varies in different *pranayama* during *puraka* and *rechaka*, e.g., breathing through one nostril at a time as in *Anulom-vilom* or partial contraction of the glottis as in *Ujjayi*. The purpose behind this seems to change the ratio of air and blood volume in the lung. The volume of air reaching the lungs is reduced while the amount of blood being circulated at the same time is almost same as usual. The volume of blood is more than the volume of air, reaching the lungs. As the phase of inhalation is prolonged in *puraka*, the scope and efficiency of gaseous exchange is also more. After practicing *pranayama* one feels fresh and energetic throughout the day.

In deep breathing, we can use both, the nostrils as well as the mouth. The volume of air certainly increases than that of the blood since the time allotted for inhalation is less. This provides larger quantities of oxygen to be readily absorbed in the blood. The blood is quickly saturated with the oxygen and at the same time maximum quantity of carbon dioxide is washed out from the blood. Deep breathing is thus a breathing exercise, purely meant for providing more quantities of oxygen to the body for the time being.

5. The lower abdominal and pelvic muscles are maintained in a slightly contracted condition throughout the practice of *pranayama*. This not only prevents congestion of the abdominal organs in that region but also maintains the diaphragm slightly at a higher level so that one does not exceed the limit of his inspiratory capacity during *puraka*. One uses upper (clavicular) part of the lungs for inhalation. The elevated condition of diaphragm also helps one to develop sufficient intra-pulmonary pressure.

In deep breathing on the other hand the position of the diaphragm or the abdomen is not important and one can use any or both the regions for deep respirations as the main purpose is to provide maximum amount of oxygen to the body.

6. In *pranayama*, certain bandhas like *Jalandhara, Uddiyan*, and *Moola bandha*, i.e., neuromuscular locks as well as gazes like *nasagra drishti* (नासाग्रदृष्टी) and/or *bhrumadhya drishti* (भ्रूमध्यदृष्टी) are to be employed during the practice. These make the *pranayama* more effective in controlling autonomic functions of the body.

In deep breathing no such neuromuscular contractions or gazes are observed during the practice. In fact there is no control on the technique of breathing except on the depth of respiration.

7. One has to be completely aware of his breathing technique in order to maintain a proper ratio amongst *puraka, kumbhaka* and *rechaka* phases. A particular sound from the throat (*Ujjayi pranayama*) is produced (even if *kumbhaka* is not practiced) for which a conscious control on the force

of breathing and the vocal cords is required. The mind remains engaged in the breathing process in the beginning. In advanced stages of practice one is expected to perceive special sensations along the spinal cord or to experience the meditation state.

Deep breathing is done mechanically and without proper concentration or the conscious control. The external stimulations or the thought processes may be continued during deep breathing. There is no consideration of the emotional state of the individual.

8. Increased concentrations of carbon dioxide in the blood during *pranayama* stimulate various psyco-neuro-endocrinal mechanisms. Due to rhythmic and regular practice of *pranayama* the sub-cortical centers, which are related to emotional and mental aspects, are well organized and integrated for their functions. Thus *pranayama* cultures the nervous system and makes the individual more peaceful, balanced, and attentive for the inner happenings. It increases the parasympathetic tone.

In deep breathing, as the large quantities of oxygen are provided to the system, one becomes physiologically aroused or excited by increasing the sympathetic tone in the body to carry out more physical and mental work. This may give rise to new tensions in the body and mind.

Thus the mechanics of breathing, the immediate and long-term effects, techniques of breathing and the very purpose of *pranayama* and deep breathing are quite different and therefore *pranayama* should never be considered as deep breathing exercise or vice versa.

ANULOMA-VILOMA PRANAYAMA

This *pranayama* is also known as *Lom-viloma* (लोम विलोम), *Nadishodhan* (नाडीशोधन) or *Nadishuddhi* (नाडीशुद्धि) *pranayama*. The main characteristic feature of this *pranayama* is the alternate breathing through the left and the right nostril with or without *kumbhaka*. Actually speaking this is not a regular *pranayama* but the prior breathing practice to prepare oneself for the practice of *pranayama*.

SWARA YOGA

Many of us may not be aware of the fact that we breathe mostly through only one nostril at a time and even the force of breathing is also not equal for both the nostrils. *Swarayoga* (स्वरयोग), the science of breath claims that there is a natural, rhythmic and alternate change in the dominance of one nostril to another, occurring after every one hour. It also believes that a particular type of nostril dominance is preferable for preparing one mentally, emotionally and physiologically for a particular activity of day-to-day life. This is because certain physical activities and psychological conditions were observed to be associated with the predominant flow of breath through a particular nostril. For example, the right nostril dominance is associated with the digestion of food, outward directedness, more vigorous activity, more active and aggressive nature and more alertness for the external happenings; whereas the left nostril dominance is related to more passive psychological state, more quiet and receptive mood which helps one in getting easily directed towards the inner environment.

Yoga not only recognized this one-nostril dominance from the beginning but also has correlated certain psychological changes and behavioral tendencies with it.

Modern science has revealed several chronic functional disorders ranging from simple intellectual asthenia to visceral dysfunctions like asthma, peptic ulcer, cerebral palsy, dysmenorrhea, etc., associated with permanent single nostril dominance on account of the septum deviation or some other obstruction in the nostril. Various mental and emotional disturbances have been observed to influence the natural rhythm of the alternate nostril dominance, by bringing about the nasal congestion and changing the secretions. Physical factors like temperature, humidity, irritants, breath holding as well as exercise are known to alter nasal airflow and to establish equal dominance in both the nostrils.

For many years the modern science did not pay much attention to this natural phenomenon but recently many scientists, in India and abroad, have contributed to explore this interesting subject in more details. Physiologically, our body tries to adjust itself with the environmental temperature changes through alternate vasodilatation and vasoconstriction mechanism. It is an autonomic function and is more marked at the extreme terminals like tips of fingers, toes, earlobes and the nose. As there are many cyclic changes in the external environment, like day and night cycle, various body activities are governed by cyclic functions of the autonomic nervous system (ANS). One such periodic function is the *nasal cycle*, i.e., regular alternation in nasal congestion from one nostril to the other, thereby shifting the nasal airflow resistance from right to left and left to right nostril several times a day. Such nasal cycle also exists in rabbits, rats and pigs but evolutionary significance of this biorhythm is still unknown to the modern science. *Swarayoga* also claims a particular *Swara* (see table on page 189) on a particular day (*tithi*).

The human nose is composed of two parallel chambers, separated by a thin septum. The inner wall of these chambers is lined with a covering called *mucous membrane*. The chambers extend into the skull and just above the posterior part of the hard palate. The inner side of the nasal cavities contain horizontal shelve like turbinate bones which are covered with erectable tissues. This is a spongy and thick tissue, which can be filled with large quantities of blood (vasodilatation), and expanded in size. This engorgement of the erectable tissue, due to vasodilatation, causes congestion and produces resistance to the airflow in that nostril. At the same time, the blood flow to the other nostril is reduced due to vaso-constriction of the blood capillaries, the erectable tissue shrinks and thus the airflow resistance is decreased in this nostril, increasing the volume of air passing through this nostril. There is a rhythmic alteration of degree of congestion and decongestion of mucous membrane of each nostril. If the left nostril is less congested and offers less resistance to the airflow, that means a greater air volume is flowing through the left nostril and hence this condition is referred to as 'left nostril dominance'.

Both sympathetic and parasympathetic efferent nerves of ANS innervate the nose. The sympathetic stimulation causes vasoconstriction and thereby decongestion of the nostril which increases the airflow through that nostril. At the same time the parasympathetic action results in the increased blood flow (vasodilatations) to the erectable tissue in the other nostril, causing congestion, and blocking the nostril. Thus a rhythmic shift in ANS tone is responsible for alternate nostril dominance. There is no wonder then if the emotional and psychological states are found to affect and disturb this natural rhythmic function since the emotions and tensions are related with the ANS and its centers in the limbic portion of the brain.

It has been found that the nasal cycle exists in about 85 percent people, in the form of left or the right nostril dominance. Remaining 15 percent people will show either equal partial blockage or equal wide opening of both the nostrils. This may be for a short time when one nostril is opening and the other is getting blocked at the same time. It is now an established fact that the blocked nostril can be opened by the use of *Yogadanda* (crutch like 'Y' shaped wooden bar). For example, if the right nostril is congested or blocked and if one places *Yogadanda* under the left arm pit and presses it little bit against an axilla, the left nostril will start getting blocked slowly and the right nostril will be decongested or opened within a short time. Similarly, if one lies comfortably on left side, distributing the weight on exactly lateral side, the right nostril will be opened and at the same time the left nostril will be blocked. This is not only due to the gravity but the vascular and the nervous reflexes are also involved in shifting the dominance. Thus recumbent lateral posture plays an important role in nasal cycle during sleep. Such laterality was first explained by *Swarayoga*, the science of breath.

It has been observed that the human performance also depends on the particular nostril. The endocrine function has been demonstrated to be related to the change in the nostril dominance. The cerebral hemispheric activity of one side as judged by EEG technique was also found to be correlated with the nostril dominance on the contra-lateral side. In short our ancient yogis knew the fact that the nasal cycle is the only medium in our hand to control and balance the autonomic functions of the body. The balanced function on all the levels of the nervous system is essential for the maintenance of a good health.

Swarayoga believes that the left nostril breathing dissipates more heat from the body or in other words, it has a cooling and calming effect on the body. Left nostril is known as *Ida nadi* (इडा नाडी) or *chandra* (moon) *nadi*. *Ida nadi* represents the constructive, anabolic or energy conservation aspect of the *pranic* (autonomic) function. The right nostril is known as *Pingala nadi* (पिंगलानाडी) or *Surya* (sun) *nadi*. It has got heating, activating and strengthening effect on the body. It represents destructive, catabolic or energy consuming aspect of the body. The main purpose of *anuloma-vilom pranayama* is to purify these principal subtler channels (*nadis*) of the body for easy flow of the energy through them. It is believed that because of our irregular schedules of meals, sleep, stresses, pollution, infections and other disrupting forces, the *nadis* are filled with impurities or the toxic substances (मल] *malas*) and are therefore blocked. The flow of '*prana energy*' (*shakti*) is obstructed. *Gherand Samhita* advocates that one should perform the alternate nostril breathing before the main *pranayama* to cleanse these *nadis* (*Gherand Samhita* V:38-42, 53). *Hathapradipika* II:7-10) gives a detailed technique of this *pranayama* in order to remove different *malas* from the body (*sharir mala*) and the mind (*chitta mala*). When both the *nadis* work evenly and simultaneously the third *nadi* starts functioning. This *nadi* is known as *Sushumna* (सुषुम्ना) *nadi* (नाडी). *Prana* (vital force) is supposed to travel through this *nadi* during *pranayama*.

Fortnight	Nostril Dominance (Swara) and Days (Tithi)				
Full moon days (Shukla paksha)	Left Nostril 1, 2, 3	Right Nostril 4, 5, 6	Left Nostril 7, 8, 9	Right Nostril 10, 11, 12	Left Nostril 13, 14, 15
No moon days (Krishna paksha)	Right Nostril 1, 2, 3	Left Nostril 4, 5, 6	Right Nostril 7, 8, 9	Left Nostril 10, 11, 12	Right Nostril 13, 14, 15

For this purpose it is necessary to purify all these *nadis* with the help of *anulom-vilom pranayama*, so that the vital force will flow through them. This cleansing of the *nadis* may be accomplished in three months or even earlier, according to *hatha yoga*, by practicing *anulom-vilom pranayama*. Now let us see the technique and the mechanism of *Anulom-vilom pranayama* in brief.

TECHNIQUE OF ANULOM-VILOM

Sit comfortably in *padmasana* or in any suitable meditative *asana*. The spine is maintained in a balanced and straight position and the abdomen is controlled after moving it slightly inward. After this form a special *mudra* of the right palm by folding and supporting the index and middle finger together at the bottom of the thumb (Fig. 33). The ring finger and the small finger are used for closing the left nostril. The right nostril is closed with the help of the thumb. This *mudra* is known as the *Pranav mudra*.

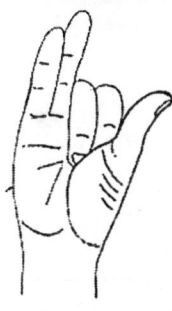

Fig. 33: *Pranav Mudra* of the Right Palm

Inhale slowly and deeply through the left nostril. The force and the flow of breath is maintained uniform till the inhalation is complete. This is *puraka* phase. At the end of the *puraka*, the left nostril is immediately closed with the help of ring finger and little finger. Since the right nostril was already closed before *puraka*, now both the nostrils are closed. *Jalandhara bandha* is applied and breath is retained according to one's capacity (*yatha shakti*-यथाशक्ति). This is *kumbhaka* phase. When there is moderately strong desire to release the breath, one opens the right nostril just by removing the thumb from it and starts exhaling slowly and smoothly through the right nostril for proportionate duration. This is *rechaka* phase. Now, the next *puraka* is done through the right nostril. After doing *kumbhaka* as before, the *rechaka* is performed through the left nostril. This is considered as one round of *nadishuddhi pranayama*. Such 3, 7, 10 or even more rounds are gone through at a stretch. *Puraka* phase is deeper and slow (दीर्घ एवं मन्द *deergha and manda*) while *rechaka* phase is still more prolonged and slower (प्रदीर्घ मन्द *pradeergha and manda*) in nature. This helps to maintain a ratio of 1:2:2 or 1:4:2 for *puraka*, *kumbhaka* and *rechaka*. Breathing is however very smooth and without any frictional sound.

LEFT NOSTRIL   RIGHT NOSTRIL

1. Puraka ⟶ 2. Kumbhaka ⟶ 3. Rechaka

↑   ↓

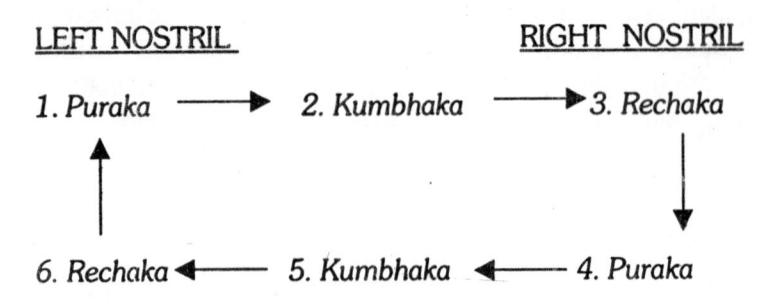

6. Rechaka ⟵ 5. Kumbhaka ⟵ 4. Puraka

Fig. 34: Sequence of Breathing Phases in Anulm Vilom Pranayama

The beginners should, however, practice only *puraka* and *rechaka* phases through the left and the right nostrils alternately (without *kumbhaka*) with the time ratio of 1:2. Even this much voluntary control will slowly train the nervous system associated with the breathing mechanism. *Kumbhaka* phase should be introduced in the form of a pause, to be expanded gradually over a long practice. Number of rounds also should be increased gradually.

Since the breathing is done through only one nostril during *puraka* and *rechaka*, the minute ventilation is reduced. Another reason for this is, the controlled prolongation of both the phases as per the ratio. The amount of air reaching the lungs is restricted while the volume of blood being circulated in the lungs remains unchanged. That is, the ratio between air and blood volume in the lungs is altered. The gaseous exchange, therefore, takes place more efficiently. The other breathing reflexes are tackled as described in the chapter on mechanism of *pranayama*. The awareness is directed towards the breathing process, which reduces the perception of the disturbing sensory inputs from the external environment. This helps one to become more sensitive to and conscious of the flow of the air in the beginning and later on of the inner happenings. This will also restore the natural, regular rhythm and balance in the nasal cycle phenomenon.

As we know that the nostrils are supplied with both sympathetic and the parasympathetic branches of ANS. ANS is also related with other autonomic functions of the body as well as the opposite forces working with mental, emotional and psychological activities of the individual. It is also related to right and left hemispheric activity and the autonomic control on the endocrinal function. During the practice of this *pranayama* the cortical activity in relation with the intellectual planning, analysis, ego-consciousness and the thought processes is greatly reduced to a minimal. It therefore appears that the rhythmic and proportionate as well as consciously controlled breathing through two nostrils alternately, brings about a harmony in the two oppositely working neural activities and establishes the balance in them.

It brings tranquility and peace to the mind, making it more balanced and stable. The mind is better concentrated. The soothing effect of this *pranayama* on the nervous system reduces various emotional tensions and one feels relaxed and light. This will have a bearing upon the emotional behavior of the individual if one practices it over a long period. Calmness and mental relaxation are easily felt immediately after the practice of this *pranayama*. This *pranayama* has also been reported to improve the function of digestion and sleep. Thus, *anulom-vilom pranayama* produces suitable environment for the development of proper inner awareness. As the practice gradually increases, the *sadhaka* becomes able to perceive special sensory inputs from the interoreceptors in the spinal area starting from the sacral region. It removes blockages in the nerve conduction and corrects all the neural functions and therefore it is essentially practiced before other *pranayamas*.

UJJAYI PRANAYAMA

मुखं संयम्य नाडीभ्यामाकृष्य पवनं शनैः ।
यथा लगति कण्ठात्तु हृदयावधि सस्वनम् ।।

*Mukham samyamya nadibhyamakrushya pawanam shanaihi
Yatha lagati kanthattu hrudayavadhi sasvanam*

Meaning: By closing the mouth, inhale slowly through both the nostrils as if you are sucking it (like a straw). It will reach up to the heart, touching the throat.

Ujjayi pranayama is one of the eight types of *pranayamas*, described by *Svatmaram*, the author of *Hathapradipika* (II:51–53). The chief characteristic of this *pranayama* is the audible hissing sound produced due to the partial closure of the glottis, during *puraka* as well as *rechaka*. This simple variety of *pranayama* can be practiced in sitting or standing position or even while walking. One should, however, practice *kumbhaka* very carefully or avoid it when *ujjayi* is to be performed while standing or walking.

Padmasana or any other suitable meditative *asana* is assumed and palms are gently pressed upon the knees. This prevents extra anterio-posterior curvatures in the vertebral column and makes it straight. It also prevents bulging of the abdomen and helps one to contract the abdominal muscles easily. It becomes easy to raise the chest up and maintain it as such, throughout the practice. Eyes are closed moderately, keeping the surrounding muscles relaxed. The mode of breathing in *ujjayi* is slow and smooth.

PURAKA PHASE

The abdominal wall is slightly contracted and is held in this little retracted condition throughout the practice of *Ujjayi pranayama*. The controlled condition of the abdomen is advantageous in many respects than the protracted or relaxed abdomen as follows.

1. The diaphragm is pushed up due to the constant abdominal pressure and is held in this elevated condition all through out. The lower abdomen cannot bulge out during the inhalation, as the descent of diaphragm is not possible now. Thus the breathing is mainly thoracic and slightly diaphragmatic in nature. The lower ribs expand and one can feel the expansion of the lower rib portion even at the backside. The clavicular musculature is also brought into action and the upper portion of the lungs is easily filled with the air. In this respect slightly elevated condition of the shoulders help further. The intra-pulmonary pressure falls more and allows more quantity of the air and consequently larger amount of oxygen in the lungs than when the abdomen is protruded out. The contracted condition of the abdomen also helps one to exhale completely in *rechaka*.
2. The X-ray studies have revealed that the lowermost (sacral) part of the spine is pulled up when the lower abdominal muscles are contracted. The intra-abdominal pressure is also raised. The peripheral nerves, the nerve plexuses, the sacral part of the autonomic nervous system as well as the visceroreceptors in this region are thus stimulated, mechanically, to generate peculiar sensory impulses in this region.
3. It has also been observed experimentally that the duration of *kumbhaka* increases slightly, when the lower abdomen is

maintained in a 'contracted' state than when it is protracted or relaxed. The maintenance of the abdominal muscles in the contracted condition requires proper conscious control. This helps the practitioner at least in the beginning to divert his attention from the external things and to focus it inside the body. The wandering tendencies of the mind are thus checked.

Just like one sips a cold drink through a straw, the air is drawn (sucked) slowly through both the nostrils. A hissing sound is produced due to partial closure of the glottis in the throat. One should feel the touch of the air from throat to the cardiac region in the chest. The friction of the air is expected in the throat region only. Some of the nervous disorders as well as the dryness and pain in the upper nares are caused due to the damage to the olfactory region. Therefore the friction of the air in the upper region should be avoided. Conscious relaxation of the facial muscles would help in avoiding friction in the upper nasal passage.

The partial closure of the glottis increases the airway resistance and reduces the ventilation. The amount of air reaching the lungs is thus controlled. When the air flows over this constricted air passage, it produces a sound like sibilant 'sa' due to the friction. In order to produce the sound in a low but soft and uniform pitch, the air is allowed to flow slowly and smoothly. The force of breathing is reduced. The sensation of filling and emptying of the lungs can easily be felt. A proper awareness is required for producing this hissing sound in a uniform pitch and to control the airflow. Thus mind remains engaged in the breathing.

The proportion of *puraka* phase constitutes the real measure for fixing the time proportion of *kumbhaka* and *rechaka*. One can reduce the time for the phase of *puraka* so as to give double proportion to the *rechaka*. Even though the limit of inhalation in *puraka* has been advocated until the air is felt in the throat, one should however, fix the proportion of *puraka* according to his capacity so that the proportion of *kumbhaka* and *rechaka* phases is same (double) for all the rounds of *Ujjayi pranayama*.

KUMBHAKA PHASE

At the end of *puraka* the glottis is completely closed and *Jalandhara bandha* is applied by bending the neck forward and fixing the chin in the jugular notch. If one requires, both the nostrils are closed with the help of thumb and the last two fingers as in *anuloma-viloma*. Now the inspired air cannot escape through the air passage.

The beginners should, however, resort to only *puraka* and *rechaka* phases in the ratio of 1:2 along with the distinctive sound. The *kumbhaka* is introduced in the form of a short pause between *puraka* and *rechaka* and the duration of this pause is gradually lengthened by regular practice. When the time proportion is followed as per the tradition i.e. 1:2:2 or 1:4:2, the *kumbhaka* is comfortably performed if, (1) no sense of suffocation is experienced at any stage in *kumbhaka* and (2) no discomfort or strain is felt during *rechaka* that follows *kumbhaka*.

Along with the *Jalandhara bandha*, an advanced student of yoga also applies *uddiyana bandha* and *Moola bandha*, during *kumbhaka*. Due to *Jalandhara bandha*, the dorsal portion of the spinal column, and the muscles of the neck and upper back are stretched upward. This adds to the intra-pulmonic and intra thoracic pressures. *Uddiyana bandha* increases the intra-abdominal pressure and pushes the diaphragm up. Thus these pressures are deliberately raised and maintained during *kumbhaka*. On account of increasing pCO_2 and decreasing pO_2 in the blood, the chemoreceptors are stimulated. This reflex is however, inhibited because of our voluntary control. The purpose behind all this seems to generate peculiar sensory nerve impulses by stimulating visceroreceptors and the chemoreceptors. The tolerance of these receptors is to be gradually increased by applying more and more strong voluntary control. One becomes aware of these sensations in the beginning that make him better concentrated on the breathing. After a long practice of *kumbhaka* in this way, one also experiences the stand-stillness (*stambha-vritti*) in the mind. This helps one to enter into a typical meditative state of mind. *Jalandhara bandha* is first released when one wishes to terminate *kumbhaka* and to start *rechaka*.

RECHAKA PHASE

Traditionally, *rechaka* is done through the left nostril but for the convenience and to avoid complexity and confusion, it is done through both the nostrils. When *rechaka* is to be done through the left nostril, the right nostril is closed with the help of right thumb. The abdominal wall is further contracted a little, so that the diaphragm is pushed up maximum and as far as possible, to complete voluntary exhalation. Contraction of the chest is consciously controlled for uniform outgoing flow of breath till the end of *rechaka*. Friction of the air in the nasal part is avoided. The glottis is partially contracted and a frictional sound, approximately similar to that in *puraka*, is produced in a low, soft and uniform pitch. It is rather easy to contract throat and to produce frictional sound in *rechaka* than in *puraka*. It is quite natural. When we speak, the exhalatory phase is controlled. Sound is rarely produced during inhalation. Therefore it takes time to gain control on the hissing sound during inhalation. If one attends the friction in the throat carefully and consciously in order to produce uniform sound it helps one to reduce awareness of the external environment. Sometimes one experiences accumulation of mucous in the throat, which is drained out due to exhalatory force against the narrow air passage. Sometimes dryness is also experienced in the throat. The duration of *rechaka* is always longer than *puraka*. The orthodox proportion between *puraka* and *rechaka* is 1:2. That means if *puraka* is done for five seconds, *rechaka* should be done for ten seconds. Traditional way of exhalation through the left nostril seems to have been designed to bring 1:2 ratio without much efforts, e.g., logically exhalation through one nostril will require double time than the inhalation through both the nostrils, provided the force of breathing is constant. *Rechaka* should, however be performed with proper care so that *puraka* of the next round is in no way hurried. In fact all the phases and their ratios should be well adjusted so that there is no strain or suffocation felt at any stage of *pranayama*, irrespective of the number of rounds one wants to undergo. Usually 10–20 rounds are practiced at a stretch in one sitting, depending upon the capacity and need (purpose) of the individual.

It has been observed experimentally that the cardiac output is increased in *Ujjayi pranayama*, compared to deep breathing and normal breathing. This is mainly due to the intra-thoracic and intra-pulmonary pressure changes in *Ujjayi pranayama*, which influences the heart and its blood vessels. For instance, negative intra-pulmonary pressure during *puraka* phase for 4–5 seconds, increases the venous return to the heart while positive pressure maintained during *rechaka* for ten seconds causes better emptying of the blood vessels. A mild increase in heart rate has been reported in the beginners when they introduced *kumbhaka* in their practice. There was a reduction in heart rate when they practiced only *puraka* and *rechaka*. We know that various interoceptors are stimulated due to increased stretching of and pressure in the alveoli and the changes in pCO_2 and pO_2 in the blood during *pranayama*.

In *Ujjayi* also these interoceptors send the sensory nerve impulses to the respiratory center as well as thalamus and hypothalamus in the brain. The prolonged exhalation in *rechaka* produces predominance of parasympathetic branch of ANS and therefore one feels calm and relaxed as well as balanced in mind, after this *pranayama*. The hypertensive person can also practice this *pranayama* since anxiety is reduced due to soothing effect of this rhythmic and evenly controlled breathing. The external stimulations and the thought processes are not attended. On the contrary the mind is fully engaged in the controlled breathing process, e.g., controlled production of sound, which creates necessary inner awareness. This increases one-pointed attention and induces a typical state of consciousness and also increases the power of concentration, which is a prerequisite for *dhyana*. When the mind is tranquilized and brought under control, the analytical process of the intellect and ego-consciousness are also controlled. In a longer run it will cultivate right type of emotional and behavioral pattern.

A practice of *Ujjayi pranayama* without *kumbhaka*, has been found to relieve depression. One feels energetic and vitalized immediately after the practice of this *pranayama*. The oxygen consumption has been found to increase in the beginners but in regular practitioners the oxygen consumption did not increase. Therefore it may be said that *Ujjayi pranayama* can provide better chances of oxygen absorption as and when required, depending upon the metabolic rate of the body. That is why *Ujjayi* can be practiced even in standing or while walking. This *pranayama* has also been found to improve voice. One can correct his defective breathing pattern that is associated with his emotional responses. As this *pranayama* tackles the autonomic nervous centers and sub-cortical centers by reducing 'arousal' of RAS (reticular activating system) and establishes more parasympathetic tone in the body, other autonomic functions such as regulation of blood pressure, gastrointestinal activity and the endocrinal secretions are also properly regulated. It may be remembered that these functions are properly balanced if one is not emotionally disturbed. *Hatha yoga* claims that the diseases of *dhatus* (the basic elements or tissues of body construction, according to *ayurveda*) and the disorders of throat caused by excessive phlegm are removed by this *pranayama*. *Hatha yoga* also claims that the gastric fire is increased and the diseases like dropsy can also be cured by this *pranayama*. Thus *Ujjayi pranayama* is an important *pranayama* in *yogic* curriculum.

SITKARI PRANAYAMA

सीत्कां कुर्यात् तथावक्त्रे घ्राणेनैव विजृम्भिकाम् ।
एवमभ्यासयोगेन कामदेवो द्वितीयकः ।।
*Seetkam kuryat tathavaktre ghranenaiv vijrumbhikam
Evamabhyasayogen kamadevo dvitiyakah*
—*Hathapradipika* II:54

Meaning: Producing 'sit' sound while breathing in through the mouth (for *puraka*) and exhaling through the nose (for *rechaka*) is *Sitkari pranayama*. By doing this *pranayama* practitioner becomes another *Kamadeva* (God of sex).

In the real sense this description of the technique of Sitkari *pranayama* is very short and incomplete. There is no explanation for *kumbhaka*. But we can understand that the nature of *kumbhaka* is same in all the *pranayamas*. The difference lies only in *puraka* and *rechaka*. So we can practice *kumbhaka* as we did in case of other *pranayama*. That means, same rules will apply for use of *bandhas*, time ratios, etc.

TECHNIQUE

Sitting in *Padmasana* and keeping the spine straight is a prerequisite. Close your eyes. Stretch out your lips in the side like we do when we laugh or smile with our teeth closed together. Place the tip of the tongue where upper and lower teeth meet. Naturally the inhalation will be done through the space available in between the teeth and the tongue.

While doing *puraka*, suck the air along with the sound 'si'. At the end of *puraka*, press the tongue more on the teeth. This will create a sound like 'ta'. Both the sounds together will appear like 'sit'. That is why it is called *Sitkari pranayama*. Set the time ratio for *puraka* and *rechaka* as per your capacity and need. *kumbhaka* is done as usual. *Jalandhara bandha* is applied first, then *uddiyana bandha* and lastly *moola bandha*. The duration of *kumbhaka* will be as per the selected (decided) time ratio, i.e., 1:2:2 or 1:4:2. To start *rechaka* the *bandhas* are released in the same order and exhalation is done slowly without producing any sound, through both the nostrils. The duration of *rechaka* will be double than the *puraka*. This is one round or cycle of *sitkari pranayama*. One can practice ten or even more cycles in one sitting.

BENEFITS

While doing *puraka* one can feel cooling touch of the air. This feeling can be extended up to throat and lungs in the chest. If one attends this feeling continuously, it has a calming and relaxing effect on mind. Those who have complaint of hypertension, excessive bile secretion, acidity, extreme heat or burning sensation in the body, can take best advantage from this *pranayama*. Benefits like increase in the lung capacity, concentration are same like *Ujjayi pranayama*. *Hathapradipika* claims that the practitioner will look like *Kamadeva*. This means that *sitkari pranayama* has got anabolic effect on the body. Good luster and glow on the face, internal strength and a handsome look make the practitioner more attractive if *Sitkari pranayama* is practiced regularly. Naturally the resistance power will also increase. This *pranayama* removes lethargy and makes the practitioner more enthusiastic.

CAUTION

In hot season (summer), as the atmospheric temperature also increases, this *pranayama* can be practiced in the early morning in the open air. But in other seasons when the temperature is less than 20°C it will be harmful to practice it in the open air. One may catch cold easily. In the closed room when there is lot of smoke or there are too many people, do not practice this *pranayama* as the air is inhaled in *puraka* through the mouth. There is a possibility of infection.

SHITALI PRANAYAMA

जिव्हया वायुमाकृष्य पूर्ववत् कुम्भसाधनम् ।
शनकैर्घ्राणरन्ध्राभ्याम रेचयेत् पवनं सुधीः ।।

Jivaya Vayumakrushya purvavat kumbhasadhanam
Shanakairghrana randhrabhyam rechayet pavanam sudhihi
—*Hathapradipika* II:57

Meaning: Air is drawn in over the tongue and *kumbhaka* is performed as before. The wise practitioner then breathes out slowly through both the nostrils. This is known as *shitali pranayama*.

It is obvious from the name of the *pranayama* itself that it gives cooling effect to the body. The technique of this *pranayama* as given by *Hathapradipika* seems to be incomplete but *Shiva Samhita* (3:85) and *Jyotsna Teeka* describe it in details.

TECHNIQUE

Padmasana or *Ardha-padmasana* with straight spine is the

essential condition of sitting and thoracic breathing with the contracted lower abdomen are same for this *pranayama* as in other *pranayamas*.

Before inhaling for *puraka* the tongue is drawn out and by lifting its sides voluntarily, a structure like a channel is formed. *Shiv Samhita* describes it as 'beak of a crow'. This is however possible only for 50–60 percent population. Those who cannot do this, may turn the tongue upward, form the horizontal channel and then inhale. Now hold the tongue between the lips and inhale through it. A sound like 'si' is produced. Inhale slowly so that more cooling sensation is experienced. After this proportionate *puraka*, start *kumbhaka*. Rules for the *kumbhaka* are similar like other *pranayama*. For *rechaka* exhale through both the nostrils slowly for double time than *puraka*. Perform ten rounds or more.

BENEFITS

The technique of this *pranayama* is simple and easy to do. As the name suggests, one experiences cooling sensation in the whole body. During the normal breathing the air becomes immediately warm as soon as it enters through the nose. In *Shitali pranayama* the air is sucked through the wet channel of the tongue and therefore gets cooled. In summer this *pranayama* is helpful in reducing the temperature of the body. *Hathapradipika* claims (II:58) that the diseases of spleen, fever, inflammation, over production of bile and the consequences of poisonous food consumption are cured by this *pranayama*. One attains fine control on his thirst and hunger due to this *pranayama*. One experiences calmness and peace in mind. The mental steadiness, pleasant and 'energetic feeling' after this *pranayama* are experienced through out the day. Other benefits like increase in lung capacity and stamina are same as in other *pranayamas*.

CAUTION

Do not perform this pranayama in open air when the temperature is as low as 5–10 centigrade because the air is directly entering into the lungs. One may catch a cold. Similarly avoid the practice in the hall where too many persons are gathered.

SURYABHEDAN PRANAYAMA

आसने सुखदे योगी बद्ध्वा चैवासनम् ततः।
दक्षनाडया समाकृष्य बहिस्थं पवनं शनैः॥
आकेशादानखाग्राच्च निरोधावधि कुम्भयेत्।
ततः शनैः सव्यनाडया रेचयेत् पवनं शनैः॥
कपालशोधनं वातदोषघ्नं कृमिदोषहृत्।
पुनः पुनरिदं कार्य सूर्यभेदनमुत्तमम्॥

Asane sukhade yogi baddhwa chaivasanam tatah
Dashanadya samakrushya bahistham pawanam shanaihi
Akeshadanakhagrachchya nirodhavadhi kumbhayet
Tatah shanai savyanadya rechayet pawanam shanaihi
Kapalshodhanam vatadoshaghnam krumidoshhrut
Punah punaridam karyam Suryabhedanamuttamam
—Hathapradipika II:48–50

Meaning: After sitting comfortably on a soft *asana* (mat), inhale slowly through right nostril. Perform *kumbhaka* until you feel it up to hair and nail ends. Then perform *rechaka* through left nostril slowly. This *suryabhedan pranayama* is the best *pranayama* and should be done again and again to cure disorders of vat, warms and to cleanse the forehead.

In *hatha yoga* surya means right (side) and *chandra* means left. Therefore *surya nadi* means right nostril and *chandra nadi* means left nostril. Here *Daksha nadi* and *Savya nadi* means right and left nostrils respectively. In *Gherand Samhita* (5:58–63) this *pranayama* is called as *Sahit pranayama* and one has to perform it till he experiences sweating up to hair. *Prana, Apana, Samana, Vyana* and *Udana* are five different parts of *prana vayu* (subtler energies) having different qualities and functions and are related to *surya* (sun principle) and the *nabhi kendra* (umbilicus). Therefore *Suryabhedan* means when one inhales air through the right nostril, it is mixed with these five *pranas* at umbilicus, which is the main center of energy.

TECHNIQUE

Sit comfortably and steadily in any meditative posture out of *Padmasana, Siddhasana* or *Swastikasana* with the straight spinal column. Form the *Pranav mudra* of the right palm (finger 25). Close your eyes. Close your left nostril and inhale deeply and proportionately through the right nostril. The ratio of *Puraka, Kumbhak* and *Rechaka* should be 1:1:1 in the beginning and increased up to 1:2:2 or 1:4:2 gradually, over a period of month.

Gherand Samhita stresses on applying *Jalandhara bandha*. It is purposely done to increase the pressure in the thorax. The intensity of this pressure should be such that it is felt up to the nails of the fingers or the root of the hair. This means, it is expected that *kumbhaka* should be more intensive and for maximum duration. Of course one should perform *kumbhaka* as per his capacity, practice and the purpose. Otherwise it may be dangerous to increase the intensity rapidly and without proper practice. The breathing reflexes should be trained gradually. Exhale slowly through the left nostril for *rechaka*. No sound is expected to be produced during any phase of *pranayama*. This is one round. Start second round again from the right nostril. Such 5–10 rounds or even more can be practiced in one sitting.

BENEFITS

Hathapradipika claims that the regular practice of this *pranayama* clears sinuses in the forehead, cures vat (nervous) disorders and eradicates worms or the diseases their off. The speed of the aging process is reduced and therefore one remains and looks younger for years. That means youth, endurance, enthusiasm, freshness is well maintained by this *pranayama*. Other benefits like increase in lung capacity, good resistance power, more steadiness of mind, better concentration power is same as for other *pranayamas*.

One thing is clear that by practicing *Anulom-vilom pranayama* Hatha yoga wants to establish a harmony and balance between the body and mind and it also wants to provide better nutrition and anabolic action in the body. Recent research findings show that the oxygen absorption is increased when it is done without *kumbhaka*, increases heart rate and physical work capacity. The weight is expected to reduce when 25 or more rounds of *suryabhedan* are practiced four times a day.

CAUTION

Increase the intensity and duration of *kumbhaka* gradually by practice. Those who have complaint of high blood pressure, biliousness, insomnia and those have different shifts of work with irregularity in daily routine, should practice *Anulom-vilom pranayama* instead of *suryabhedan pranayama*. This *pranayama* stimulates metabolic activities. Therefore, to maintain vital energy level and vigor, practice *Anulom-vilom pranayama* in proportion. For spiritual purpose, practice *suryabhedan* under the guidance of a yoga expert who will advice you as per your constitution and nature.

BHASTRIKA PRANAYAMA

यथा लगति हृत्कण्ठे कपालावधि सस्वनम् ।
वेगेन पूरयेच्चापि हृत्पद्मावधि मारुतम् ।।
पुनर्विरेचयेत्तद्वत पूरयेच्च पुनः पुनः ।
यथैव लोहकारेण भस्त्रा वेगेनचाल्यते
तथैव स्वशरीरस्थं चालयेत् पवनं धिया ।।

Yatha lagati hrutkanthe kapalvadhi sasvanam
Vegen purayechchyapi hrutpadmavadhi marutam
Punarvirechayettadvat purayechya punah punah
yatheiva lohakaren bhastra vegen chalyate
tathaiva svashrirastham chalayet pavanam ghiya
—Hathapradipika II: 61–62

Meaning: of *Bhastrika* is bellows of the blacksmith. Like bellows, *puraka* and *rechaka* are done rapidly. Act of exhalation is more forceful and quick, compared to inhalation, which is rather slow and less forceful. *Puraka* and *Rechaka* are performed again and again quickly and with force hence the name *Bhastrika pranayama*.

Technique

There are many techniques of this *pranayama*. Similarity among them lies in the fact that there are two parts of the technique. First part contains forceful and quicker *puraka* and *rechaka* while in second part there are *puraka, kumbhaka* and *rechaka* phases. *Puraka* and *rechaka* are some times done alternately with left and right nostrils. Sometimes left and right nostril are used for even and odd number of inhalations/exhalations. All these techniques are complicated. Therefore, Swami Kuvalayananda has given a technique, which is physiologically safe as well as easy.

Sit in *Padmasana* or in any other meditative posture with straight back and closed eyes. Inhale by expanding the chest and now exhale by contracting the abdomen so that the chest remains expanded and elevated. Every round of *Bhastrika* has got two parts. First part consists of 20–40 strokes of *kapalbhati* and second part contains *puraka, kumbhaka* and *rechaka* phases.

Kapalbhati is done through both the nostrils. Every *rechaka* is done forcefully and rapidly. Therefore a friction sound like 'Ss' is produced with every *rechaka*. *Puraka* is passively done though it is also quick. Immediately after *kapalbhati* part, *puraka* is done through right nostril followed by *kumbhaka* for a proportionate time. All the three *bandhas* viz., *Jalandhara, Uddiyan* and *Moola bandha* are applied. To end *kumbhaka* phase, *rechaka* phase is done through the left nostril, after releasing *bandhas* in the same order, giving double time than *Puraka*. *Gherand Samhita* recommends three rounds, one by one, in one sitting.

Benefits

By doing *Bhastrika pranayama* all the three doshas (*vat, pitta* and *kapha* elements) are maintained in a balanced state. Bodily fire increases. Extra secretion of mucus is stopped. This *pranayama* cleanses all the *nadis* and stimulates sacral part more. Therefore it is useful for *kundalini* awakening. It is an important technique in spiritual course. *Gherand Samhita* says "this *pranayama* does not have any diverse effect on the body, on the contrary one experiences disease free condition and joyous as well as peaceful mental feeling after regular practice" (*Gherand Samhita* V:72).

CAUTION

Puraka and *Rechaka* of the first part should be done rhythmically and equally. In case there is a sense of suffocation at any stage of this *pranayama*, stop the practice and consult the yoga expert/teacher. It is possible that while doing this *pranayama*, the heart rate, bodily temperature and sweating may increase. That is why persons having high blood pressure, insomnia, mental or emotional disturbance should avoid this *pranayama*.

BHRAMARI PRANAYAMA

वेगात् घोषं पूरकं भृंगनादम् ।
भृंगीनादम् रेचकं मन्दमन्दम् ।।
योगीन्द्राणामेवमभ्यास योगात् ।
चित्तेजाता काचिदानन्दलीला ।।

Vegat ghosham purakam bhrunganadam
Bhruginadam rechakam mandamandam
Yogindranam evamabhyas yogat
Chittejata kachidanandalila

—Hathapradipika II:68

While inspiring quickly a humming sound like that of a male bee and while doing *Rechaka* (controlled exhalation) a hum sound like that of a female bee should be produced. Yogis who practice it regularly experience bliss.

TECHNIQUE

Methods like seating posture, time ratios, nature of *kumbhaka*, application of *bandhas* and number of rounds are same as for other *pranayamas* described earlier.

During *puraka* by controlling the pharyngeal muscles and soft palate a vibrational sound is produced. Mouth remains closed. While exhaling for the phase of *rechaka* this sound is produced again but this time it is softer. It is a nasal sound produced due to vibrations of the soft palate. *Rechaka* is as usual prolonged for approximately double time than *Puraka*. It is easier to produce sound in *Rechaka* than in *Puraka*. Many people pronounce 'ma' like that of *Aum*. They close the ears with the respective thumbs and put first fingers gently above the nostrils. This helps them to concentrate on the sound and hence they are able to feel the vibrations of it at the spine or in the forehead and at times even all over the body.

BENEFITS

Mind gets absorbed in this pleasurable and soothing vibratory sound. The practitioner experiences a blissful feeling. It helps integration of internalized awareness and extra-sensory perception on the longer run. Primary effect of this *pranayama* is the tranquilization of mind. It leads the practitioner toward the *Dhyan* (meditation). It reduces instability of mind and calms it down. This *pranayama* is beneficial to those suffering from mental tensions, stress, high blood pressure and cardiac disorders.

CAUTION

Check your capacity to sit in *Padmasana* and to listen to the vibratory sound for a long time with ears shut. Increase the number of rounds gradually. The vibratory sound should not be harsh and too loud.

Four

The Science of Aum

THE GREAT MANTRA—AUM

It is our common observation that whenever we look at ॐ (*Aum*) feeling of devotion and respect is experienced in our mind. Aum is respected by spiritual aspirants all over the world. A few decades back, *Aum* was encircled by mystical notions and myth. But in twentieth century, due to scientific research, its universal and secular nature as well as the therapeutic significance was revealed. *Aum* is undoubtedly a part and parcel of Indian culture. Practically in almost all the languages *Aum* is drawn as a sacred symbol. There are identical type of words in other cultures also viz., Shalom (Hebrew), Salaam (Arabic), Amen (Christian), and Amin (Islam).

Aum is a one-word *mantra* and yet the most powerful *mantra*. It is the essence of all *mantras*. As a rule, every *mantra* begins with *Aum* otherwise it is considered as incomplete. Potency of the *mantras* increases due to *Aum* hence it is regarded as the king of all *mantras*. This is an auspicious *mantra* through which we can experience the spiritual forces or the vibrations or the special kind of sensations in our body. It not only gives material benefits, but the spiritual as well.

It is natural that several questions as to the meaning of *Aum*, its origin, chanting style and frequency, its benefits, etc., would arise in one's mind. Previously, people used to chant *Aum* only during religious worship or ceremony but now anybody can chant *Aum* and obtain the benefits. *Aum* is pronounced and written as *Om*, *Aum* or even as *Omkar*.

INDIAN TRADITION AND AUM

Mandukyopanishad, Kathopanishad, Varahopanishad, Taittariya, Bhagwad Geeta, and Dnyneshwari describe Aum in detail. Patanjali, the composer of Yogasutras says वाचक:प्रणव: (Tasya vachakah pranavah, Patanjali Yogasutra: I:27), meaning Aum is a symbol or emblem of God. It is the representative of the divine consciousness (Ishwar). So whereever there is Aum, there is God. Therefore it is eternal. Aum is surrounded by whatever is auspicious and virtuous. It is a sacred symbol or emblem. Aum welcomes God. Therefore we find Aum written on every temple. By reciting Aum (Omkar) we welcome God and through this medium we can realize the existence of the lord Brahma, the divine creator. Aum is the evidence of the existence of God. Aum carries holy blessings of God. That is why Omkar sadhana is considered as the supreme spiritual practice. Jain (Aum namo arihantaya...) and Bauddha (Aum mani padme hum...) religions also recognize and respect the divine nature of Aum.

Yoga Vashishtha, a great yoga scripture says that we cannot separate mind and the speed of thoughts easily by ordinary methods. Mind and prana (force of life) are deeply connected with and controlled by each other. Different vrittis (tendencies, activities) arise in chitta that stimulate prana and therefore the mental thoughts. So if we control prana, we shall be able to control mind and hence the thought process. This is possible by practicing pranayama as well as Aum chanting. Therefore it is better to practice pranayama first and then chant Aum (Omkar japa). According to Mantra yoga, whosoever listens, sees, chants Aum, will become one with the divine consciousness which is beyond wakeful, dream and sleep states of consciousness. Atharva-Shikhopanishad right in the beginning asks "On which object we should meditate?" and gives the answer, "on Aum". Therefore no yogasadhana will be complete without Aum recitation.

According to Mandukya Upanishad Aum represents past, present and future and also that exists beyond time and space. Aum has no beginning or end. It is beyond the gross subtle and causal bodies because it is an expression by God. *Aum* brings equilibrium in every aspect of our body and destroys our ego, desires and suspicion.

Hatha yoga says "*Pranav* recitation is like *nadanusandhan*" (*Hathapradipika* IV:81–89, 105, 106). It increases concentration of mind and therefore can lead you to *dhyan* and *samadhi*.

During *Yajna* (fire worship) and *Vedaddhyayan* (study by chanting of Vedas), *Aum* is chanted first so that any mistake in the technique will be compensated and there will be no obstacle in *Yajna* or *Vedic* chanting.

FORMATION OF AUM

According to *Sankhya* philosophy *Aakash* (sky) principle was first created and then the first (primordial) vibration (shabda) was produced in the form of *Aum*. Later on the whole universe emerged from the word *Aum* just like different vessels are manufactured from the same earth. That is why *Aum* is called as *Shabdabrahma* (शब्दब्रह्मा). This is the only *mantra*, which is in the form of a pure sound vibration (tone). *Aum* in itself is a sweet and melodious musical tone. One can experience a typical blissful and joyous condition of mind even if one listens to *Aum* chanting, done by others. This condition is known as *Brahmananda* (ब्रह्मानन्द). *Aum* is a response given by Lord Brahma to the invocation by *sadhaka*. Sound vibrations produced due to *Aum* recitation would lead us to Lord Brahma. This effect of *Aum* is due to the vibrations of divine sound (*Nada*). That is why it is also known as *Nadabrahma* (नादब्रह्मा).

Right from the ancient times, there have been different styles of writing *Aum*. During the *Vedic* period it was written in the vertical form (Fig. 35) and later on it was written horizontally as it is written today ॐ. *Aum* contains three and half *matras* (मात्रा) or the potential parts. The crescent with a dot on the top of *Omkar* is the half *matra*. If we remember, the *kundalini shakti* (energy) is also stored in three and half coils. That is why all the *mantras* derive their

Fig. 35

potency from *Aum*. *Aum* is formed out of three alphabets, 'A' 'U' and 'M'. A stands for Lord *Brahma* (creation), 'U' represents Lord *Vishnu* (maintenance) and 'M' stands for Lord *Mahesha* (destruction). It is believed by some that *Aum* and Lord *Ganesha* are same. They look similar.

RELATIONSHIP OF AUM WITH CHAKRAS

'A'(अ) of *Aum* is connected to *Mooladhar* (at the bottom of the spine) and *Swadhishthan* (just below the umbilicus) *chakras*. 'U'(उ) of *Omkar* is related to *Manipur chakra* just above the umbilicus. 'M' (म्) affects *Anahat* (heart), *Vishuddha* (throat) and the *Ajna* (between the eye brows) *chakras* together. That is why the 'M' is deliberately pronounced for longer duration to progress on the spiritual path. As we know, the *chakras* are the wheels of energy, providing us the energy for different bodily and mental functions. *Aum* makes these *chakras* powerful, which in turn keep one energetic and enthusiastic. This indicates that by chanting *Aum*, *prana* gets upward direction or in other words, *kundalini* can be awakened. That is why *Aum* chanting is the superior *mantra sadhana* for the physical, mental and the spiritual benefits.

SCIENTIFIC RESEARCH ON AUM

Many scientific studies have been conducted at different institutions regarding the effect of *Aum* on the body and mind. The results have been published in various scientific journals. It has been observed that when *Aum* is recited ten times in a low pitch, the internalized attention is produced. In simple words the attention turns inward. The number of attention fluctuations is reduced. The concentration is improved and it is well focused. Alpha rhythm is nicely synchronized and blood pressure as well as heart rate is reduced. Galvanic skin resistance is increased. In short, *Aum* recitation done in a lower pitch (voice) and prolonged manner, produces parasympathetic predominance and brings about calmness and peace. Typical sensations are experienced along the spinal cord in the upward direction with

The Science of Aum

blissful condition of mind. When *Aum* is chanted in higher pitch, the heart rate and the muscular activity at the chin as well as the 'cortical arousal' increase. EEG shows reduced alpha rhythm. In short, a sympathetic activity increases indicating a nervous excitation.

When *Aum* is recited in a low pitch the duration of *Aum* decreases but if *Aum* is recited in higher pitch the length of one pronunciation increases by a few seconds. Duration of its recitation also increases if *Aum* is chanted after *Kapalbhati kriya* or *Shavasana*. Depression and anxiety have been seen reduced and a psycho-physiological relaxation increases due to twenty *Aum* recitations done in the morning and evening for a few days. Hypertension is reduced and the sleep pattern improves by *Aum* recitation. The emotional stability, mental peace and the balance increase as the tensions are removed. In case of children the memory and IQ has been found improved after *Aum* recitation. Their perception power also improves. It is postulated that this may happen as the nervous system is influenced by the vibrations and resonance of *Aum*. For these reasons, *Aum* chanting has received a therapeutic importance.

HOW TO RECITE AUM?

Varahopanishad (5.69) says, (*Tailadharamivacchinnam deergha ghanta ninadavat*) तैलधारामिवाच्छिन्नं दीर्घ घन्टा निनादावत्, i.e., it should be chanted very smoothly and continuously like smooth fall of oil (without interruption) like a resonance of a (Church) bell. It should be melodious. Traditionally, *Aum* can be recited in three ways: *Vaikhari*, i.e., loudly, *Upanshu*, i.e., murmuring (as if speaking to oneself) and *Manas*, i.e., mentally, in the mind. Practically, we can recite *Om* in three different ways as follows.

1. O ..... M .....   ओ sssss म् sssss
2. O .... M ...   ओ ssssss म् sss
3. O ... M ....   ओ sss म् sssssss

It is obvious that those who wish to keep balance in physical and mental health as well as the material gains, should adopt the first technique. Those who desire the physical and material wise benefits more, should recite in the second manner and those who are desirous of spiritual benefits more, should resort to third method. This is based on the special association of A (अ), U (उ) and M (म्) with *chakras*.

Sit in *Padmasana* or half *Padmasana* posture or just in 'crossed legs' condition. Keep straight and remain steady and relaxed. Close your eyes and feel the calmness of mind.

Perform three rounds of *Anulom-vilom pranayama*. Now take a deep breath in and say 'O' by parting the lips sufficiently. 'O' should be pronounced in a low voice and pitch. After 2–3 seconds, just by shutting the lips, *'Ma'* is automatically produced, which is nasal (अनुनासिक) in nature. The length of 'O' should be 1/3 and the length of *'Ma'* should be 2/3 of the total time for one *Aum*, in one breath. The voice should be neutral, melodious, sweet and clear. One can even feel its vibrations while chanting. After one recitation do not inhale hurriedly. Wait for a few seconds. Inhale slowly and deeply. Now start next recitation. Recite in this way for minimum ten times at a stretch in one sitting. Count the number of recitations on the right fingers. There is no limit for the maximum number of recitations. Recite in this way with deep faith (श्रद्धा) and devotion (भक्ति). After finishing the recitation (*japa*), sit quietly, visualize 'ॐ' and meditate on it for 5–10 minutes.

BENEFITS OF OMKAR SADHANA

The effect of *Omkar* recitation is very powerful and positive. All the nerves and other channels in the body are cleaned and purified. We experience cheerfulness and get energized. The mind becomes peaceful as its instability is reduced and one can progress successfully in meditation. The practitioner (*sadhaka*) is psycho-physiologically better relaxed and emotionally well balanced after *Omkar* recitation, done in a low pitch manner than in high pitch. The cardiac function is also improved as it helps to remove the blockages in the coronary arteries. The blood pressure is maintained at the normal level.

The state of consciousness becomes conducive for contemplation. The intelligence is sharpened, the memory is improved and the grasping (perception) power is strengthened to perceive and retain various kind of knowledge. Personality becomes magnetically powerful, bright, impressive and yet virtuous (सात्त्विक). One who practices *Omkar japa* regularly and sincerely, always remains happy and contented. One acquires sound mental health and is blessed with joy and tranquility. *Omkar sadhana* bestows us with the prosperity and protection in any situation in life with good fortune on all the fronts.

There is no doubt about the fact that regular *Omkar sadhana* gives extraordinary spiritual enlightenment. Owing to its supremacy, *Omkar* is the bridge, the link between the other forms of *yoga*, precisely *mantra yoga, bhakti yoga, hatha yoga* and *raja yoga*. Daily practice of *Yoga* should include at least 10 chants of *Aum*.

Note

The *Aum* chants should be rhythmic and slow. While chanting *Aum*, irrational pause, frequent change in the pitch, too loud volume, inhalation through the mouth, etc., should be avoided consciously. *Aum* chanting should be with utmost devotion and concentration, and not simply mechanical. The forehead should be wrinkle free. Facial muscles, eyes, eyebrows, and forehead should be loose. One should take into consideration one's capacity of breath, and then chant *Aum* appropriately. Forceful chanting with the attitude of competitive spirit, stubbornness and with unnecessary contraction of the stomach, is strictly prohibited. If chanted properly the effect of *Omkar* would be pleasant and peaceful and will not cause, fatigue, laziness or any sort of breathing problem. After the *Omkar sadhana*, the chanting of the *Gayatri mantra* is recommended for maximum spiritual benefits.

|| ॐ ||

Bibliography

Gherand Samhita, Ed. 1997, Swami Digambarji and Gharote M.L., K.S.M.Y.M. Samiti, Kaivalyadhama, Lonavla 410 403, India.

Hathapradipika, Ed. 1998, Swami Digambarji and Kokje Shashtri, S.M.Y.M. Samiti, Kaivalyadhama, Lonavla 410 403, India.

Patanjali Yogasutra, Ed. 2001, Anand Rishi, Yoga Department, Ghantali Mitra Mandal, Thane, Mumbai 400 603, India.

Physiology Second Ed., 1991, John Bullock, Joseph Boyle Michael B. Wang. Harwal Publishing Company, Media Pennsylvania.

Physiology for Nurses, 1977, D. Taverner, The English language book Society, London.

Principles of Anatomy and Physiology, Fourth Ed. 1984 Tortora and Anagnostakos; Harper and Row Publishers, New York.

Text Book of Medical Physiology, Sixth Ed., 1981 Arthur C. Guyton. W.B. Saunders Company, Philadelphia.

Yoga Mimamsa Journal, (1950–2005), K.S.M.Y.M. Samiti, Kaivalyadhama, Lonavla 410 403, India. All Volumes.

Yoga Therapy, Reprint 1994, Swami Kuvalayananda and Vinekar S.L., Central Health Education Bureau, Ministry of Health and Welfare, Government of India, New Delhi 110 002, India.

APPENDIX

Management of Psychosomatic Disorders Through Yoga

Introduction

Psycho means mind (psyche) and soma means body. A psychosomatic disorder is a disease where mind is involved more. We know that some physical diseases become worse by mental factors such as stress and anxiety. That means a mental state can affect a physical state. Disturbed mind, tense mind affects the physiological functions. Such chronic condition would lead to serious disorder. The term psychosomatic disorder is mainly used to mean... "A physical disease that is thought to be caused, or made worse, by mental factors". A disorder having physical symptoms but originating from mental or emotional causes is psychosomatic disorder. It is a stress disorder whose manifestations are observed in the body. Psychosomatic disorders have definite physical symptoms but are thought to be caused by emotional or psychological factors. Anorexia nervosa is one of the examples of a psychosomatic illness (1).

The term *psychosomatics* first appeared in 1818 in the work of J. C. H. Heinroth, a German psychiatrist, indicating a new approach to medicine. The theory was later formalized in 1945 by British psychologist James L. Halliday. The word has been in use since then among a wide range of practitioners, often with different interests. In the United States it is often referred to as 'psychosomatic medicine'(6).

Which Diseases are Psychosomatic?

That way all the diseases are 'psychosomatic' because both mind and body are involved in them.

- There is a mental aspect in every physical disease. The mental tension is increased when we react to a particular situation in an abnormal way because we lose our balance as we cannot handle the challenging situation. For example, emotional tension is developed when we feel insulted or when we are too much anxious for the results.
- There can be physical changes due to mental illness. For example, with some mental illnesses you may not eat properly or sleep enough which can cause physical problems.

Therefore the disease in which the mental factor is foremost and there is no other apparent reason for the physical symptoms is called psychosomatic disease. For example, a chest pain may be caused by stress, and no physical cause can be found. There are no actual structural changes in Irritable Bowel Syndrome (IBS) patients, and research shows that stress and emotions are significant factors in causing IBS. Rheumatoid arthritis, bronchial asthma, diabetes mellitus, insomnia are few examples of psychosomatic disorders where stress plays cardinal role in pathogenesis (10).

Now a day the psychosomatic disorder is more commonly referred to as psycho-physiologic illness or disorder, where symptoms are caused by mental processes of the sufferer rather than immediate physiological causes. These syndromes are classified as neurotic, stress-related and somatoform disorders by the **World Health Organization** *in the International Statistical Classification of Diseases and Related Health Problems*

Effect of Mind on Physical Health

Although the human body is designed for diverse dynamic activities, if we do not remain conscious to maintain it at the physical, mental, emotional and social levels at an optimum level, it builds up stress subconsciously and accumulates toxins. Our modern sedentary lifestyle, undue feeling of insecurity, competition, anxiety, and lust for comfort and carelessness about health or fitness along with wrong food habits are mainly responsible to build up stress and toxins in our bodies which in turn accelerate the aging process and welcome psychosomatic diseases.

Everybody of us tries to overcome suffering and to enjoy happiness in life. Since all pleasures and comforts are weaving around money, one tries hard to earn maximum money but at the same time he ignores the importance of health. Instead of pleasure and comfort he is struggling with intimidating diseases such as hypertension, insomnia, heart disease, diabetes, asthma, arthritis, spinal disorders where the cause is not the germ or bacteria but the restless and tense mind and stress. While facing the challenges he develops tension and carries it for a long time. Instability of mind, dissatisfaction, dejection, inability to relax and constant tension ultimately gives rise to stress. If the mind remains disturbed, it becomes prone to emotional reactions like, hostility, anxiety and irritability etc. When these reactions overpower one's available resources, one develops stress, the mal perception being underlying cause. When there is intensive stress, one's own (may be faulty) style or tendency to respond to the situation, one's psychological make up and the weakness of particular vital system of the body would contribute for different Psychosomatic disorders to set in.

It is well known that the mind can cause physical symptoms. For example, when we are afraid or anxious (as during examination) the heart rate may increase and symptoms like palpitation, feeling sick, shaking (tremor), sweating, dry mouth, chest pain, headaches, a 'knot in the stomach', fast and shallow breathing may occur. These physical symptoms are due to nerve impulses sent from the brain to various parts of the body, and to the adrenaline gland to release adrenaline into the bloodstream when we are anxious.

However, the exact way by which the mind can cause symptoms is not clear. How the mind can cause actual physical diseases (rashes, blood pressure, etc) is not yet clear. It may have something to do with nerve impulses going to the body which we have not fully understood. There is some evidence that the disturbed CNS loses its control and the defense system is upset, which is seen in various physical diseases.

The suggested mechanism for the development of psychosomatic disease is that the cerebral cortex (via the psyche or mind) supersedes the normal, adaptive, feedback mechanisms by which the pituitary gland regulates the secretion of corticosteroids in response to stress of any sort. For this reason the adrenal cortex is over stimulated, leading to hyperadrenocorticism first and then exhaustion. Stress is such a non specific response by the body to the stressor that can bring about series of neurohumoral, endocrine and metabolic changes with related physiological changes of varying degrees. Adrenal cortex is an integral part of the hypothalamic-pituitary-adrenal (HPA) axis that plays important role in stress disorder (8, 9). The level of Cortisol, a glucocorticoid, secreted by the adrenal cortex, is increased during chronic stress which in turn brings about changes in lipid and glucose metabolism in the body. Increased levels of cortisol build up the blockages in the arteries more rapidly.

Treatment of Psychosomatic Disorders

Each disease requires a particular system of treatment. For physical diseases, medicines or operations are usually the most important. However, we should treat a person as 'a whole' and take into account mental factors which may also be contributing to a disease. Therefore, treatments to reduce stress, anxiety, depression, etc, would help to cure these diseases if they are contributing to the physical disease. Yogic practices are such methods where corrections are brought about in psycho-physiological functions through life style changes and purification of various channels in the body.

Psychosomatic Disorders and Aging

The natural aging process is known to develop some pathological changes. However, chronic stress has a definite influence in the development of psychosomatic disorders, most specifically due to depression or frustration. Major life-events such as loss of parents or beloved relative, the loss of spouse, retirement can

Appendix

cause onset of physical disorders. Some modern diseases are believed to have a psychosomatic component derived from the stresses and strains of everyday living. Lower back pain and high blood pressure are partly related to stresses of everyday life. The body converts psychological distress in to physical symptoms. In modern society, psychosomatic illness has often been attributed to stress, making stress management an important factor in the treatment or avoidance of psychosomatic illness. The aging process is accelerated due to psychosomatic illness.

Yogic approach to Psychosomatic Disorders

According to Patanjali Pancha kleshas are root causes of psychosomatic disorders.

The cardiovascular disorders like Ischemic Heart Disease, Myocardial infarction i.e. acute heart attack, Atherosclerosis etc. are regarded as psychosomatic disorders. Although modern medicines and surgery are available; still success is not 100% in treating these disorders. Uncontrolled emotions like fear, anger, excitement, and behavior as in type 'A' personality, aggressive nature, suppressed desires, holdings on little matters, feeling of being insulted, act as stressors. There are two main causative factors in all the psychosomatic disorders (7).

1. Predisposing factor (Hereditary)
2. Precipitating factor (Stressors)

Stressors act as precipitating factors before the onset of a particular psychosomatic disorder, which is often ignored. It has been observed that many psychosomatic disorders are controlled best with the help of yoga practices because yoga practices work on psycho-physiological principles.

Patanjali advocates *Abhyasa* and *Vairagya* (PYS I:12) to deal with the stressors. The Sadhaka should prepare his mind to continue that practice endlessly until a desired stage is reached. Vairagya i.e. Detachment of mind from external world is also to be practiced. These two techniques of yoga would stabilize and calm down the mind (2).

Normally excessive and chronic stress leads to,
1. Increase in heart rate, palpitation.
2. Disturbance in endocrinal function.
3. Vasoconstriction.
4. Increase in hypertension (BP).
5. Disturbed sleep pattern.

The emotions play a significant role in our life. Positive emotions are constructive while negative emotions (such as conflicts) are destructive in nature. They give rise to disturbed and weak condition of mind (*daurmanasya*). This disturbs the tone of the smooth muscles (3) including those of the blood vessels resulting into decrease in elasticity and hardening of the blood vessels. This further impairs the vital autonomic functions like respiration, circulation and glandular secretion & finally weakens our immune system. Thus, the psychosomatic conditions slowly move from functional impairment and cellular disturbance to the structural alternation (pathological changes). If this situation is not tackled early it leads to permanent organic changes in various parts of the body. The role of interpersonal stress in rheumatoid arthritis (RA) of 20 women who differ in the quality of their relationship with their husbands was studied by Zautra AJ and his colleagues (12). They found that RA aggravated, whenever the disturbance in the interpersonal relationship increased. Women having good marital relationships with their husbands were less affected.

Yoga has an integrated approach which is most effective for the management of psycho-somatic disorders. It works through,

1. Purification of nadis & stimulation of receptors by Shuddhi Kriya.
2. Psychophysiological corrections through Asanas; reconditioning by Pranayama and relaxation through Shavasana and Omkar recitation.
3. Behavioral corrections by attenuating *pancha cleshas* through meditation.

Appendix

Purification of Nadis by removing the obstructing toxins in the body is the first approach of yogic techniques (11). Shuddhi kriyas followed by Anulom vilom pranayama bring about this purification and establish autonomic balance in the body due to smooth muscle stimulation and mental relaxation. Patanjali advices *klesatanukarana* i.e. to reduce *klesha*, as a first preparation on the path of astangayoga (to maintain health) because *kleshas* are not only root cause of pain & sorrow but also the root cause of the unethical acts of man. Therefore the progression on the path of yoga is not much possible unless the klesas are overcome. We can reduce these kleshas by adopting positive life style including regular practice of yoga.

Avidya (ignorance), Asmita (illusion), Raga (attachment), Dvesa (hatred) and Abhinivesa (Strong wish to live, PYS:II/3) are five *kleshas* (troubles, factors or stressors) in our life which can cause trouble in our day to day life. For decreasing these kleshas we should try to control emotions in our daily life. These *Kleshas* constitute particular behavior or habit or mental state of that individual such as aggressive nature, irritability etc. in which there is inbuilt tendency to develop stress. This is the patho-physiology of stress in yogic analysis. By practicing these yoga techniques and life style changes simultaneously the behavioral corrections can be achieved automatically. Therefore, the yogic methods will be very much useful in the management of psychosomatic disorders from prevention, cure and rehabilitation point of view It was found that the insulin dose was reduced from 24 to 14 units within 1.5 months of yogic treatment. Glucose tolerance was increased and medicinal doses reduced in 10 diabetics (5).

The self-destructive behavioral pattern is the result of the stress. By decreasing our needs and demands we can reduce our disappointment and unhappiness. Intimacy, social support and good interpersonal relationship on the other hand will increase our emotional balance which will strengthen our healing process (2). Yoga has tremendous potential to coordinate our scattered feelings, inner peace and relationship with others in a systematic way. While practicing yoga we become more aware of the inner environment. Yoga is not a religion but contains all practical tips that can benefit people of all religions and communities.

Yoga techniques create balance in all the opposing factors and bring about equilibrium, peace and unity in body and mind. Yoga teaches us how much should we respond to a stimuli in what way and then how to relax again. Now the emotions are unable to stir us as before. The emotions would not be able to influence your mind or disrupt harmony in body functions. The energy level is enhanced which can help the process of healing and thus promoting health. Meditation directs this energy for developing strong will power and better creativity. The meditator can observe equanimity in all the aspects e.g. achievements and non-achievement, pain and pleasure, comfort and discomfort etc. and can employ proper visualization to open our heart and feelings for effective healing.

Cultivation of a *satvik* nature i.e. pure, noble, honest and selfless attitude is needed for ideal mental health. Patanjali, the father of Yoga has advocated four important things to be observed. Viz. Friendship *(maitri)*, Compassion *(Karuna)*, Joy *(Mudita)* and Forgiveness *(Upeksha)*. When we are friendly with everybody there cannot be any anger, hatred or jealousy in our attitude which otherwise would lead us to the social isolation, a negative emotion. Compassion and forgiveness are the most powerful tools to develop an ideal positive attitude of love.

Conclusion

We are responsible for our own diseased condition. To achieve more comfort and happiness we adopt wrong life style that is full of *avidya*, based on materialistic demands and desires. We do not follow nature's laws. When we cannot tackle the stress successfully our reaction is on the negative side. This develops chronic dis-stress and threatens our immune system. Instead of supporting our healing process we deteriorate it by crossing all the physical and mental limits. Yoga is a drugless therapy. Regular yoga practices bring peace, stability and satisfaction to us. Relaxation, harmony in all the body-mind functions, positive thinking and attitude culture are the key points in yoga based therapy for all psychosomatic disorders (4). Yoga has also a preventive aspect that can be of great help to every body to promote and maintain health, fitness and happiness through out the life by protecting ourselves against stress and strain.

References

1. ALEXANDER, FRANZ. (1950). *Psychosomatic medicine, its principles and applications.* New York: Norton.
2. ANAND RISHI, 'Patanjal Yoga Sutras', Ed.2001, Yoga Department, Ghantali Mitra mandal, Thane-400 602, (India).
3. BHOLE M. V., "Gastric tone as influenced by mental states and meditation", Yoga Mimamsa], Kaivalyadhama, Lonavla, 1983, Vol. XXII : 1 & 2;54-58
4. DATEY K.K., DESHMUKH S.N. AND DALVI C.P. (1969) "Shavasana -a yogic exercise in the management of hypertension", *Angiology*, 20, 325-333
5. GORE M.M. (1987) "Yogic treatment for diabetes", Yoga Mimamsa vol 26: 3 & 4,135-145
6. KAMIENIECKI, HANNAH. (1994). *Histoire de la psychosomatique.* Paris: Presses Universitaires de France.
7. MARTY, PIERRE, M'UZAN, MICHEL DE, AND DAVID, CHRISTIAN. (1963). *L'Investigation psychosomatique.* Paris: Presses Universitaires de France.
8. MISHRA K.K. ET AL, (2007). 'A clinical study on cortisol and certain metabolities in some chronic psychosomatic disorders', *Ind.J.Clin.Biochem*, 22, 2, 41- 43
9. OLFF M, "Stress, Depression and immunity: the role of defense and coping styles" Psychiatry Res 1999, Jan 18; 85 (I): 7-15 (review)
10. TULPULE T.H. (1977), "Yogic exercises and diabetes mellitus", *J. Diab. Asso.India* Vol 17.

11. SWAMI DIGAMBARJI AND KOKJE SHASHTRI, 'Hathapradipika', Ed.1978, S.M.Y.M.Samiti, Kaivalyadhama, Lonavla-410 403, (India).
12. ZAUTRA AJ, HOFFMANJ M, MATT KS, YOCUM D, POTTER PT, CASTRO WL, ROTH S (1998), ' An examination of individual differences in the relationship between interpersonal Stress and disease activity among women with Rheumatoid arthritis', *Arthritis Care Res*; 11, 4, 271-279

Index

A

Abdominal recti muscles 41
Abhyantara kumbhaka 166
Active posture 94
Active stretching 105
Adrenal glands 74
Agonist muscles 39
Aim and objectives of asanas 102
Aim and objectives of pranayama 168
Alimentary system 11
Anatomy, Definition of 3
Antagonist muscles 39
Anterior lobe of pituitary 72
Anuloma-vilom pranayama 184
Arousal 58, 65
Asana 97
Asanas and exercises 130
Asan-jaya 102, 130
Asthma 28, 30, 35
Atrium or auricle 17
Aum, Science of 209
Autonomic balance 65
Autonomic nervous system 62
Awareness 65, 68
Axon 54

B

Backward bending 82
Bahya kumbhaka 164, 166
Balancing asanas 118
Bandhas 139
Basal ganglia 56
Bhastrika Pranayama 204
Bhramari Pranayama 206
Blood platelets 23
Blood pressure 18
   effect of exercises 19
Bones, types of, 79

C

Calcitonin 73
Cardiac muscle 37, 42
Cartilaginous joints 80
Carotid Sinus 18
Cell 4
Central nervous system 53, 54
Cerebellum 57
Cerebral cortex 55
Cerebrum 55
Cervical vertebrae 82
Chandra nadi 188
Characteristics of asanas 99
Characteristics of pranayama 165
Chemical base 71
Circulatory system 17
Classification of asanas 109
Colon 11
Composition of inspired and expired air 30
Conditioned reflex 62
Connective tissue 6
Consciousness 65, 68

Control of posture 90, 92
Control of respiration 31
Control of blood pressure 18
Corticosterone 74
Corrective asanas 110, 117
Cranial nerves 58
Cretinism 73
Cultural asanas 110, 111, 113, 117, 127

D

Dakshina nauli 150
Deep breathing and pranayama 181
Dendrites 54
Diabetes mellitus 75
Diaphragm 40
Diastolic blood pressure 18
Different time ratios, in pranayama 170
Digestive system 11
Double proportion for rechaka 180
Ductless glands 71
Dynamic aspect, of asanas 99
Dynamic postures 94

E

Efficient posture 89
Endocrine system 71
Epinephrine 75
Epithelial tissue 6
Essential hypertension 20
Estrogen 74
Excitatory impulses 54
Excretory system 85
Expiration 29
External respiration 25
Exteroceptors 66
Extremities 3

F

Fibrinogen 23
Fibrous joints 80
Fight or flight response 64
Flat bones 79
Flexor reflex 62
Forward bending 82
From yoga point of view 14, 24, 35, 50, 69, 76, 83

G

Gastrointestinal tract 11
 influence of nauli 151-152
Glands, endocrine 71
Glottis 26
Gonads 76
Gray matter 54

H

Head 3
Heart 17
Hering Breuer reflex 32
Homeostasis 87
Human body 3
Hypertension 20
Hypothalamus 57
Hypothyroidism 73
Hypertonic condition 45
Hypotonic condition 45

I

Ida nadi 188
Inactive posture 93
Inborn reflex 62
Inhibin 76
Inhibitory impulses 54
Inspiration 27
Insulin 75
Intensity, of sensation 69

Index

Internal respiration 25
Interoreceptors 65
Irregular bones 80
Islets of Langerhans 75
Isolation of recti muscles 149
Isometric contraction 48
Isotonic contraction 48

J

Jalandhara bandha 176
Jiva Bandha 148
Joints, types of 80

K

Kapalabhati 153
Keval kumbhaka 166
Kidneys 85
Kriyas 137
Kumbhaka phase 174
Kyphosis 83, 90

L

Lateral, bending 82
Limbic system 56
Long bones 80
Lordosis 83, 90
Lumbar Vertebrae 82
Lungs 29
Lung volumes and capacities 30

M

Madhavdas vacuum 152
Madhya nauli 151
Mechanism of asanas 103
Mechanism of pranayama 172
Meditative asanas 111, 120, 127
Medulla oblongata 58
Mixed nerves 55, 58
Moola bandha 148
Motor area 56

Motor nerves 58
Movements, types of 82
Mucous membrane 6, 186
Mudras 137
Mueller's maneuver 147
Muscles, types of 37
Muscles tone 43
Muscular fatigue 49, 50
Muscular system 37
Muscular tissue 7

N

Nadi shuddhi pranayama 184
Nasal cycle 36, 186
Nature of sensation 69
Nauli chalan 151
Nauli kriya 149
Nauli madhyama 150
Nervous system 53
Nervous tissue 8
Neural base 53
Neuralgia 54

O

One pointed attention 197
Organs 9
Oxygen debt 49
Oxyhemoglobin 29

P

Passive stretching 108
Parasympathetic nervous system 63, 64
Parathyroid glands 74
Perception 67
Peripheral nervous system 54
Peristalsis 12
Physiology, definition of 3
Pingala nadi 188

Pituitary gland 72
Pleasant pain 109
Posterior lobe of Pituitary 72, 73
Postural pattern 98
Postural reflexes 62, 91, 93
Posture 89
—classification of 93
Prana 163
Pranadharana 69, 101, 116, 124
Pranayama 163
—characteristics of 165
—mechanism of 172
Pratyahar 126
Progesterone 76
Proprioreceptors 65
Pulmonary circulation 21
Puraka phase 172

R

Rechaka phase 177
Rectus abdominus muscles 43
Red blood cells 23
Reflex action 60
Relaxative asanas 111, 120, 122
Relaxin 76
Renal hypertension 20
Respiration 25
   effect of emotion on, 34
   effect of exercise on, 34
Respiratory system 25
Reticular formation 58
Role of Jalandhara bandha 176
Rotation 82

S

Salient features of
   Cultural asanas 117
   Meditative asanas 132
   Relaxative asanas 125

Samadhi 126
Science of Om 209
Scoliosis 83, 90
Sensation 67
Sensory area 56
Sensory nerves 58
Shitali Pranayama 200
Short bones 80
Sitkari Pranayama 198
Skeletal muscles 37
Skeletal system 79
Skin 6, 86
Sleep 65
Smooth muscle 42
Spinal cord 59
Stand-stillness in mind 169
Static aspect, of asanas 99
Static postures 94
Stress 76, 88
Stretch reflex 46, 61
Suprarenal glands 74
Suryabhedan Pranayama 202
Surya nadi 188
Susuhmna nadi 188
Swara yoga 185
Sympathetic nervous system 63
Synovial joints 80
Systems 9

T

Tadagi bandha 142
Tadagi mudra 143
Tendon organ 39, 47
Thalamus 56
Thoracic vertebrae 82
Thyroid gland 73
Time ratios in pranayama 176
Tissues 5
Trataka 159

Index

Tri-ido-thyronin 75
Trunk 3

U

Uddiyana bandha 142
Uddiyana Mudra 142
Ujjayi pranayama 192

V

Valsalva maneuver 150, 151
Vama nauli 151
Vertebrae 82, 83

Vertebral column 81
Visceroreceptors 67
Vital capacity 33
Vocal folds-cords 28

W

White blood cells 23
White matter 54

Y

Yoga danda 187
Yoga point of view 14, 24, 35, 50, 69, 76, 83

AYURVEDA, HEALTH & WELLNESS SERIES

The primary goal of the series is to provide a comprehensive understanding of Ayurveda as a way of life. It will show how Ayurveda's ancient principles of health can help achieve the highest levels of physical, emotional and spiritual well-being. It will provide a profound but practical testament to the healing power of balanced living. It will also bring every feature of Ayurveda back to its true source—the health of the spirit.

The series is aimed at general readers with interest in the art of balanced living. The different volumes in it will be authoritative, informative and interesting.

- **The Ayurvedic Diet:** *The Ancient Way to Health Rejuvenation and Weight Control* –DENNIS THOMPSON
- **Ayurvedic Healing** –DAVID FRAWLEY
- **Neti** –DAVID FRAWLEY
- **Soma in Yoga and Ayurveda** –DAVID FRAWLEY
- **Tibetan Ayurveda** –ROBERT SACHS
- **Vedic Health Care System** –RAM LAL SHAH, BINOD KUMAR JOSHI & GEETA

General Editor
Dr. David Frawley (Vamadeva Shastri)

Editorial Board
Dr. G.C. Jain
Dr. Shekhar Annambhotla, *BAMS, MD-Ayurveda, LMT, RYT*
Dr. Sunil V. Joshi, *MD-Ayurveda*
Dr. Suhas G. Kshirsagar, *BAMS, MD-Ayurveda*

MEDICINE AND SPIRITUALITY SERIES

General Editor

DR. VINOD KUMAR NIGAM, MBBS, MS, FICS (USA), FIAGES, is a Senior Consultant General and Laparoscopic Surgeon at The Apollo Clinic, Max Hospital and a few other leading hospitals in Gurgaon. He is also the inventor of two operative techniques in General Surgery, and has published papers in various national and international journals of repute. He is also the author of three books: *Essentials of Abdominal Wall Hernias, 40 Minutes with God,* and *An Introduction to History of Medicine Through Words of Wisdom.*

Tel.: + 91 11 98100 20467, Email : mukul.mindsport@gmail.com

Editorial Board

DR. JUGAL KISHORE SHARMA, MD, has been a Senior Consultant Internal Medicine (with special interest in Diabetes and Cardiology) with Central Delhi Diabetes Centre & Sharma Cardio Diabetic Clinic, Sir Ganga Ram Hospital, Fortis Jessa Ram Hospital, Delhi Heart & Lung Institute and Kolmet Hospital, New Delhi. He has also been a Consultant Physician with All India Council for Technical Education and National Board of Accreditation, New Delhi. Dr. Sharma has been a Fellow of Indian Association of Clinical Medicine, Indian College of Physicians, Geriatric Society of India and International Medical Sciences Academy.

Tel.: + 91 11 25767475, + 91 11 9810002115
Email : drjugal@yahoo.co.in/drjksharma@gmail.com

DR. AMARENDER SINGH PURI, MD, DM, is the Chief of Gastroenterology service at GB Pant Hospital New Delhi. After obtaining his doctorate in Medicine from Panjab University in 1988, he spent three years at Sanjay Gandhi PGI, Lucknow for his post doctoral degree in Gastroenterology. He has traveled extensively in Europe and USA to present papers in international conferences. He is actively involved in medical research. He has a keen interest in Indian systems of medicine with special reference to the mind-body axis. His other interests include literature, poetry and outdoor travel. Dr. Puri has trained more than 30 post doctoral students during his tenure at the GB Pant Hospital.

Tel.: + 91 11 9718599202
Email : amarender.puri@gmail.com

DR. MARKARAND MADHUKAR GORE, M.Sc. (Physiology), Ph.D., D.Y.Ed. (Yoga), was Asst. Director of Research at the renowned Kaivalyadhama Yoga Institute, Lonavala. He was in the field of scientific research in yoga for 34 years. He is a well-known yoga therapist and a sincere yoga *sadhaka*, blessed by many Gurus. He is an Ayurvedic doctor and a naturopath. He is also a Reiki Grandmaster.
Tel.: + 91 11 9822415033.
Email : mm_gore@yahoo.com

DR. NIKETAN ANAND GAUR, Ph.D., is an internationally renowned Expert & Consultant of Sthapatya Ved-vaastu Shastra. He has a Doctorate in Sthapatya Ved-vaastu Shastra from Maharishi Mahesh Yogi Vedic University, Jabalpur, M.P. (INDIA).
Dr. Gaur has attended and addressed many national and international conferences. He is the author of several books. He has been honoured by many Academic, Cultural and Social Organizations.
Tel.: + 91 11 9811910128, + 91 11 9971314093
Email : niketangaur@yahoo.com;
niketananandgaur@yahoo.co.in

DR. K.S. CHARAK, MS (Surgery), FRCS (UK) was Head of the Department of Surgery, ESI Hospital, Basaidarapur, New Delhi. He was also Honorary Editor of *Vedic Astrology*. He is at present Head, Department of Surgery, Indian Spinal Injuries Centre, New Delhi.